Boomburbs

JAMES A. JOHNSON METRO SERIES

**JAMES A. JOHNSON
METRO SERIES**

The Metropolitan Policy Program at the Brookings Institution is integrating research and practical experience into a policy agenda for cities and metropolitan areas. By bringing fresh analyses and policy ideas to the public debate, the program hopes to inform key decisionmakers and civic leaders in ways that will spur meaningful change in our nation's communities.

As part of this effort, the James A. Johnson Metro Series aims to introduce new perspectives and policy thinking on current issues and attempts to lay the foundation for longer-term policy reforms. The series examines traditional urban issues, such as neighborhood assets and central city competitiveness, as well as larger metropolitan concerns, such as regional growth, development, and employment patterns. The James A. Johnson Metro Series consists of concise studies and collections of essays designed to appeal to a broad audience. While these studies are formally reviewed, some will not be verified like other research publications. As with all publications, the judgments, conclusions, and recommendations presented in the studies are solely those of the authors and should not be attributed to the trustees, officers, or other staff members of the Institution.

Also available in this series:

On growth and development

Edgeless Cities: Exploring the Elusive Metropolis
Robert E. Lang

Growth and Convergence in Metropolitan America
Janet Rothenberg Pack

Growth Management and Affordable Housing
Anthony Downs, editor

Laws of the Landscape: How Policies Shape Cities in Europe and America
Pietro S. Nivola

Reflections on Regionalism
Bruce J. Katz, editor

Sunbelt/Frostbelt: Public Policies and Market Forces in Metropolitan Development
Janet Rothenberg Pack, editor

On transportation

Still Stuck in Traffic: Coping with Peak-Hour Traffic Congestion
Anthony Downs

Taking the High Road: A Metropolitan Agenda for Transportation Reform
Bruce Katz and Robert Puentes, editors

On trends

Redefining Urban and Suburban America: Evidence from Census 2000, vol. 1
Bruce Katz and Robert E. Lang, editors

Redefining Urban and Suburban America: Evidence from Census 2000, vol. 2
Alan Berube, Bruce Katz, and Robert E. Lang, editors

On wealth creation

Building Assets, Building Credit: Creating Wealth in Low-Income Communities
Nicolas P. Retsinas and Eric S. Belsky, editors

The Geography of Opportunity: Race and Housing Choice in Metropolitan America
Xavier de Souza Briggs, editor

Low-Income Homeownership: Examining the Unexamined Goal
Nicolas P. Retsinas and Eric S. Belsky, editors

Savings for the Poor: The Hidden Benefits of Electronic Banking
Michael A. Stegman

On other metro issues

Evaluating Gun Policy: Effects on Crime and Violence
Jens Ludwig and Philip J. Cook, editors

Boomburbs

The Rise of America's Accidental Cities

Robert E. Lang

Jennifer B. LeFurgy

BROOKINGS INSTITUTION PRESS

Washington, D.C.

Library of Congress Cataloging-in-Publication data

Lang, Robert, 1959–
    Boomburbs : the rise of America's accidental cities / Robert E. Lang and Jennifer B. LeFurgy.
        p.   cm.
    Summary: "Addresses the issue of 'boomburbs,' large suburbs of more than 100,000 residents, and examines who lives in them, what drives their development, and how they are governed. Explains why America's suburbs are thriving and how they are shaping the lives of millions of residents"—Provided by publisher.
    Includes bibliographical references and index.
    ISBN-13: 978-0-8157-5114-4 (cloth : alk. paper)
    ISBN-10: 0-8157-5114-1 (cloth : alk. paper)
    1. Suburbs—United States. 2. Suburban life—United States. I. LeFurgy, Jennifer B. II. Title.
    HT352.U6L35 2007
    307.760973—dc22   2007008338

3 5 7 9 8 6 4 2

The paper used in this publication meets minimum requirements of the American National Standard for Information Sciences—Permanence of Paper for Printed Library Materials: ANSI Z39.48-1992.

Typeset in Sabon

Composition by R. Lynn Rivenbark
Macon, Georgia

Printed by R. R. Donnelley
Harrisonburg, Virginia

Contents

Foreword

Statistical work has painted a picture of the American urban frontier. New development is overwhelmingly in the Sunbelt and it is based around the car. The metropolitan areas of Las Vegas, Phoenix, Houston, Dallas, and Atlanta are particular centers for vast amounts of new building, but this building is more likely to be on the edge of the metropolitan area than in the older centers. America's growing exurbs are full of both homes and jobs, as firms followed people to exurbs built around highways. While this statistical portrait is accurate, it is also dry and incomplete. It tells us nothing about the political conditions that made the Sunbelt such a center for new construction. It tells us little about what that new development is like or how the social character is being shaped within the space being built. Robert Lang and Jennifer LeFurgy have turned their strong analytic skills on the fastest growing areas in America: the boomburbs or booming areas that are not urban centers. This volume substantially enriches our understanding of the growth of these areas. I suspect that by understanding these places better, we are coming to better understand the very future of urban America itself.

Lang and LeFurgy's boomburbs are defined by three characteristics: current scale, rate of growth, and not being the centers of their region. Many of these places are as large and important as far more famous older cities. Mesa, Arizona, for example has almost 400,000 people. Arlington, Texas, has more than 300,000 inhabitants. Both of these places are much larger than Pittsburgh, yet while much of America knows something about the city of three rivers, few know anything about Arlington or Mesa. Some of the smaller boomburbs are just amazingly new. Coral Springs, Florida, had less than 1,500 residents in 1970. Today, it has more than 100,000. These are the great growing places of the country. Lang and LeFurgy do a remarkable job of dispelling myths that have occasionally grown up about these new places. While Americans tend to think of suburbs as prosperous white enclaves built to escape inner-city ethnic conflict, the boomburbs are remarkably ethnically heterogeneous. Only 54 percent of their population is white. On average, 29 percent is Hispanic. Some of these places also contain remarkable concentrations of Asian population, such as Daly City, California. Some boomburbs, like Naperville, Illinois, are indeed wealthy. Other boomburbs, like Hialeah, Florida, are substantially poorer than the nation as a whole. The one thing that they all have in common is heavy automobile use. The need to own multiple automobiles does tend to make them less welcoming to the very poor.

The boomburbs also contradict the vision of bedroom suburbs. They are often major employment centers. While the highest human capital industries, such as finance, still tend to locate disproportionately in business centers, I was struck by the remarkable number of corporate headquarters that have located in boomburbs. Exxon/Mobil, for example, has its headquarters in Irving, Texas. Yahoo is in Sunnyvale, California. In 1900 business location was driven by proximity to transport hubs like rail yards and harbors. Today, businesses still locate near hubs, but they are increasingly airports. Several boomburbs, like Naperville and Irving, owe some of their growth to the proximity of a major airport.

But in most cases, the biggest business of the boomburbs is building itself. A city doesn't add 100,000 people without a lot of new construction and all of the boomburbs specialize in growth. Lang and LeFurgy teach us about the two necessary ingredients of high growth places: a vibrant construction sector and progrowth politics. The builders of the boomburbs are generally big operators who put up homes by the hundreds or even thousands. These homes are, like the original Levittown, mass-produced. Unlike Levittown, these mass-produced homes are often quite luxurious. These building assembly lines are turning out Lexuses, not Model Ts. The buildings are also often built on small lots. New Englanders, who are used to the highly zoned areas of the older suburbs, are often struck by the small yards of new homes in desert places such as unincorporated Las Vegas, which seem to be able to deliver infinite quantities of land. Those small lots help keep the price of new construction down, and, clearly, people aren't demanding all that much space.

Many of the builders do more than just create housing. In many cases, developers are creating fully planned communities. Shopping malls increasingly play the role of traditional downtowns. Lang and LeFurgy emphasize correctly that there is plenty of walking in boomburbs, but it takes place in malls that you drive to. The boomburbs are able to deliver some sort of a facsimile of a pedestrian experience, where people mix with each other and experience street life. This experience is, however, planned by developers rather than delivered through the chaotic functioning of the market. While traditional urbanists may find these malls no substitute for the market of the Ponte Vecchio, people do seem to be voting with their feet or at least their tires. It may make more sense to put effort into humanizing the mall than into reinvigorating many older downtowns.

The political regimes in the boomburbs are all progrowth, but in many other ways there is remarkable heterogeneity. In many places, homeowners associations and private developers take over the provision of basic public services. In some areas, county governments are particularly important. The one thing that seems to be missing is old style urban politics, where ethnic divisions create political warfare over government largesse. These cities are more into good management than solving society's wrongs.

We don't know yet what will happen in many of these places. Will they turn into perpetual growth machines or reach some kind of natural limit? We do however know much more about what they look like today because of Lang and LeFurgy's excellent work. It is high time that our knowledge about the growing areas of this country catches up to our understanding of the declining places in America. Lang and LeFurgy's book represents a major step in shedding light on American urban growth.

ED GLAESER
Harvard University

Preface

With a few notable exceptions, it used to be that the suburbs defied examination. If they were studied, it was often with deep disdain bordering on the hysterical. They were the dull, exclusive, Cinnabon-scented "geographies of nowhere." Both of us were former inner-city dwellers and made our livings studying and writing about central cities. After coming to work for the Metropolitan Institute at Virginia Tech, located in Old Town Alexandria, we each moved to Fairfax County, Virginia, and our appreciation and study of the suburbs began in earnest. Suddenly we were the "bridge and tunnel people," identified by our suburban telephone area code as being "so 703" (that is, clueless suburbanites), instead of having the more urbane D.C. area code personality of 202. However, our move from the city gave us something in common with the majority of Americans—we dwelled in the suburbs. Living in and accepting the suburbs broadened our own personal and professional experiences. It also made for a helpful contrast when visiting the boomburbs and experiencing what goes on in other similar places.

Suburbs began to be taken more seriously by researchers such as Delores Hayden, Robert Bruggemann, and John Teaford, who all produced thoughtful studies on the subject between 2003 and 2007. At least two suburban study centers have been founded—one on each coast. In addition, the U.S. census has changed its classification of cities—now suburbs (or newly classified principal cities) appear in the names of Metropolitan

Statistical Areas. We hope here to provide some additional perspective in this burgeoning and important area of metropolitan studies.

This boomburbs study was a multiyear effort that took us to dozens of communities where we engaged hundreds of locals. The list of people to thank is long, starting with our principal sponsors, the Brookings Institution and the Fannie Mae Foundation. Brookings provided both financial support and guidance for the project. We especially thank Robert Puentes, the project coordinator, for a series of thoughtful comments as the book developed. Other people at Brookings providing advice and support include Anthony Downs, Bill Frey Bruce Katz, Amy Liu, and Jennifer Vey. Brookings Institution Press did a great job producing the book, and we thank Diane Hammond for her careful editing, as well as Larry Converse, Janet Walker, and Susan Woollen for their efforts in getting the book to print. We also thank the four anonymous Brookings referees for their very useful comments and critiques.

The Fannie Mae Foundation, which provided major funding, is the place where the boomburb concept originated. Patrick Simmons, a researcher at the Fannie Mae Foundation, coauthored the first boomburb publication in 2001 and ran most of the original data for the project. Pat continued to help with subsequent data analysis, especially boomburb housing conditions. Rebecca Sohmer, formerly with the Fannie Mae Foundation and now at Brookings, coined the term "boomburbs," which is a clever blending of the words "boom" and "suburbs." The label has been a big boost in that it captures perfectly the places we studied. Other people at the Fannie Mae Foundation who have helped with the project are Carol Bell, Jim Carr, and Kris Rengert.

The staff and graduate students at the Metropolitan Institute at Virginia Tech also provided support. Jessica Hanff and Mona Hinds edited the first drafts of the book. Jessica also helped research boomburb histories. Dawn Dhavale ran data for the projects, made some field visits, and generated maps. Kurt Keiser also did some fieldwork and researched the boomburbs politics. Tanya Mejia, a summer intern, analyzed boomburb business conditions. Kristin Haworth did the painstaking work of surveying these outsized suburbs on their buildout plans. Tom Sanchez, a colleague at Virginia Tech, ran the GIS analysis on boomburb office locations, and Karen Danielsen, a doctoral candidate, read the entire first and second drafts and provided numerous comments. The final draft of the book was mostly written in Arizona, and we thank John Hall at Arizona State University for the use of his offices and insights he had regarding development patterns and governance issues in the West.

As this project evolved, presentations on the boomburbs were made at multiple academic forums including talks at Arizona State University, University of Arizona, University of California–Berkeley, University of California–Riverside, University of Pennsylvania, Rutgers University, Hofstra University, and Virginia Tech. We thank the students and faculty at these institutions for their input.

Finally, we want to note the tremendous help that those living in the boomburbs gave to our efforts. Countless boomburb representatives agreed to meet with us and discuss their cities. Many of these people appear as voices in the book, especially the mayors. It is easy to imagine that some of these folks may have been a bit skeptical of our intent, given what inviting targets boomburbs are to suburban critics. Instead, we found an eagerness by locals to tell the story of their communities and a deep civic pride in how their small towns had grown into cities. The boomburbs were fun to visit and get to know. They are inviting places and, we anticipate, will be subjects of much future scholarship.

Boomburbs

Legoland

*A primary LEGO showpiece, Miniland USA is a celebration of
American achievements, a canvas to illustrate the diversification of its
peoples and cultures, past and present.*

—LEGOLAND WEBSITE

The main attraction of Legoland, a theme park just outside of Carlsbad, California, is Miniland USA, which features miniatures of quintessentially American places built from 20 million Legos. Miniland has a replica of Washington, complete with federal museums, monuments, the White House, and the Capitol. It even has a miniature Georgetown and a working model of the Chesapeake & Ohio Canal. Other places in Miniland include the French Quarter of New Orleans, a New England fishing village, and Manhattan. The miniature of California is a hodgepodge of scenes, from an Orange County surfing town to Chinatown in San Francisco.

What's missing from Miniland, however, is the built landscapes so typical of America—the housing subdivision, the retail strip mall, the office park—in short, suburbia. The irony is that Lego building blocks are perfectly suited to make such places, especially the commercial structures. The basic Lego is a small rectangular block. Think of the ease with which the Miniland model makers could depict big-box retail centers or the low-slung, banded-window suburban office building. Just snap a bunch of

Legos together and, presto, instant "edge city."[1] It is not as if the Lego folks could have missed knowing about suburban malls and office buildings: Southern California is chock full of them. Such buildings even lie just outside the gates of Legoland, along Interstate 5 as it approaches San Diego. But apparently suburban sprawl does not count as an "American achievement."

Modern suburbia's absence from Miniland USA reflects a national ambivalence about what we have built in the past half century. We made the suburbs, and we increasingly live in the suburbs, but we still often disregard them as real places. Even though one could describe much of modern suburban commercial development as Lego-like, there was little chance that Miniland would include a replica of nearby Costa Mesa, California, which contains the nation's biggest suburban office complex and one of its largest malls.[2]

Boomburbs: The Booming Suburbs

This book is about the places that rarely inspire theme parks but, interestingly, are home to them, such as Anaheim, California, which is famous for Disneyland. While these booming suburbs may not capture the public imagination, they have consistently been the fastest-growing cities over the past several decades. This growth has not translated into immediate name recognition, except perhaps among demographers, who keep seeing the population growth of these cities exceed that of older cities.

The essence of a boomburb is that people know of them but find them unremarkable and unmemorable. As this book shows, all sorts of high-profile industries and activities occur in boomburbs, but few identify with the city. For example, over a dozen major league sports are centered in boomburbs, but only the Anaheim Mighty Ducks (a hockey team) carries the place name. The fact that the one professional baseball team that had a boomburb identity—the Anaheim Angels—has since become the Los Angeles Angels of Anaheim points to the problem. The city of Anaheim took the trouble to highlight this switch in its entry for Wikipedia.com, an online encyclopedia:

> On January 3, 2005, Angels Baseball, LP, the ownership group for the Anaheim Angels, announced that it would change the name of the club to the Los Angeles Angels of Anaheim. Team spokesmen pointed out that, from its inception, the Angels had been granted territorial rights by Major League Baseball to the counties of Los Angeles, Ven-

tura, Riverside, and San Bernardino in addition to Orange County. New owner Arturo Moreno believed the new name would help him market the team to the entire Southern California region rather than just Orange County. The "of Anaheim" was included in the official name to comply with a provision of the team's lease at Angel Stadium, which requires that "Anaheim be included" in the team's name.

Thus Anaheim, a city with as many residents as Pittsburgh or Cincinnati, is reduced to an addendum on the Angels name—and only then because of a legal technicality.

Scratch most boomburb mayors and you may find that they have a Rodney Dangerfield complex: their cities get no respect. Michael L. Montandon, the mayor of North Las Vegas (one of the nation's fastest-growing boomburbs), tells of an encounter in which the mayor of Salt Lake City dismissed the idea that the two places share common problems, despite the fact that North Las Vegas is both bigger and more ethnically diverse than Salt Lake City.[3]

North Las Vegas is not alone. Few big-city mayors seem to recognize boomburbs as peers, and visa versa. Mayor Keno Hawker of Mesa, Arizona (a boomburb that is now bigger than Atlanta or St. Louis), spent just one year in the U.S. Conference of Mayors before withdrawing his city. His problem (in addition to the stiff dues) was that the other mayors were simply not discussing issues that concerned him.[4] As of 2004 Mesa was the largest city in the nation that does not belong to the U.S. Conference of Mayors.

But boomburbs also have a hard time fitting into the National League of Cities, whose membership is dominated by smaller cities and suburbs. Although most boomburbs do belong to the National League of Cities, their size and growth rates make it difficult for them to share common perspectives and problems with the typical cities in the organization. As one boomburb mayor put it, "How do you relate to cities that are smaller than your city grows in just a year?"

We call boomburbs accidental cities.[5] But they are accidental not because they lack planning, for many are filled with master-planned communities; when one master-planned community runs into another, however, they may not add up to one well-planned city. Too new and different for the U.S. Conference of Mayors and too big and fast growing for the National League of Cities, boomburbs have a hard time fitting into the urban policy discussion. Washington's think tank crowd is simply stumped by them.

It seems that few boomburbs anticipated becoming big cities, or have yet to fully absorb this identity, and thus have accidentally arrived at this status. Part of the confusion may be that in the past the port, the factory, and the rail terminal fueled metropolitan growth. Today booms occur in places with multiple exchanges on new freeways, where subdivisions, shopping strips, and office parks spring up. This is the development zone that Bruce Katz refers to as "the exit-ramp economy."[6] Or as Jane Jacobs would say, boomburbs develop as "micro-destinations" (such as office parks) as opposed to "macro-destinations" (downtowns).[7]

Boomburbs are not traditional cities nor are they bedroom communities for these cities. They are instead a new type of city, a subset of and a new variation of American suburbanization.[8] This book explores the fundamental nature of this new type of city.

The Boomburb Concept

The boomburb concept came from a Fannie Mae Foundation project, undertaken by Robert Lang and Patrick Simmons, to study the 2000 U.S. census to better understand changes in the U.S. city population in the second half of the twentieth century, or since 1950.[9] Lang and Simmons argued that an analysis of five decades of change provides a context for understanding the population shifts of the 1990s.

The year 1950 is an important benchmark for American cities. For many older cities, it was their population high point.[10] Cities swelled as soldiers returning from World War II started families and sought housing in a nation that had built hardly any new residences in twenty years due to war and depression. With the beginning of Levittown and similar tract-style developments in the late 1940s, the 1950 census also marks the start of large-scale suburbanization.[11]

Lang and Simmons were determined to fix two major deficiencies that they saw in most urban population analysis—the lack of historical data and the lumping together of all big cities (comparing, for example, Newark and Las Vegas). By looking at, say, only the hundred biggest cities in the United States in 2000, and using just one decade for comparison (the 1990s), the finding is always the same—Las Vegas blows out Newark. But by developing a peer-city analysis (Newark compared to Cleveland, Las Vegas compared to Phoenix) and by looking at several decades, a more precise reading of urban change is possible.

Lang and Simmons therefore split all major U.S. cities into two categories: boomers and decliners. Boomers were defined as all cities above 100,000 in population as of 2000 that had sustained double-digit population growth since 1950. Decliners included all cities with a 1950 population of 200,000 or more with at least two decades of population loss since 1950.[12]

Looking at the boomers, Lang and Simmons found a surprise—most were not booming cities such as Las Vegas and Phoenix but were instead the suburbs of these big Sunbelt cities. The simple fact is that the fastest-growing U.S. cities with more than 100,000 residents have little identity outside their region. Given this finding, Lang and Simmons decided to focus only on places that are not the central city of their region. So instead of, say, comparing Las Vegas to Phoenix, they compared a Las Vegas suburb, such as Henderson, to a Phoenix suburb, such as Chandler. Thus was born the boomburb concept.[13]

The 2001 boomburb research was covered by such national media as *USA Today*, CNN, and MSNBC. A big reason for such attention, besides the catchy title, was some truly revealing findings. For example, the population of the biggest boomburb—Mesa, Arizona—surpassed that of such traditional big cities as Minneapolis and Miami.[14] Even many smaller boomburbs were now bigger than older and better-known medium-size cities. Tellingly, Peoria, Arizona, was poised to jump ahead of Peoria, Illinois (its namesake)—which it has subsequently done.[15]

The boomburb concept touched a nerve. It tapped into the sense that Americans are building very different places than in the past. There is an extensive literature on the suburbs and even a good deal of work showing that suburbs have evolved past their traditional role as bedroom communities.[16] But the boomburb findings capture the immense scale of this change. The rise of boomburbs has shock value—Mesa bigger than Minneapolis and Miami? It presents the questions, How did this happen and what does it mean?

The idea behind boomburb research was always to explore these places as emerging urban forms and not to judge them. This book seeks to do the same. Boomburbs make an easy target for those who find fault with the way such places are developing.[17] This study does not add to that chorus of criticism. Nor does it apologize for boomburbs. Rather, the book lays out the facts and lets readers render their own verdict. Both detractors and boosters will find plenty of new facts in this book to support their views.

Boomburbs Redux

The starting year in this analysis is 1970, not 1950, as in the original research. This shift added one more boomburb—Palmdale, California—to

Table 1-1. Boomburbs, 2000 Census[a]

Anaheim, California	Gilbert, Arizona	Palmdale, California
Arlington, Texas	Glendale, Arizona	Pembroke Pines, Florida
Aurora, Colorado	Grand Prairie, Texas	Peoria, Arizona
Bellevue, Washington	Henderson, Nevada	Plano, Texas
Carrollton, Texas	Hialeah, Florida	Rancho Cucamonga, California
Chandler, Arizona	Irvine, California	Riverside, California
Chesapeake, Virginia	Irving, Texas	Salem, Oregon
Chula Vista, California	Lakewood, Colorado	San Bernardino, California
Clearwater, Florida	Lancaster, California	Santa Ana, California
Coral Springs, Florida	Mesa, Arizona	Santa Clarita, California
Corona City, California	Mesquite, Texas	Santa Rosa, California
Costa Mesa, California	Moreno Valley, California	Scottsdale, Arizona
Daly City, California	Naperville, Illinois	Simi Valley, California
Escondido, California	North Las Vegas, Nevada	Sunnyvale, California
Fontana, California	Oceanside, California	Tempe, Arizona
Fremont, California	Ontario, California	Thousand Oaks, California
Fullerton City, California	Orange, California	West Valley City, Arizona
Garland, Texas	Oxnard, California	Westminster, Colorado

a. A boomburb is defined as an incorporated suburban city with at least 100,000 in population, as not the core city of their region, and as having double digit population growth in each census since 1970.

the list. Boomburbs are still defined as having more than 100,000 residents, as not the core city in their region, and as having maintained double-digit rates of population growth for each census since the beginning year (now 1970). Boomburbs are incorporated and are located in the nation's fifty largest metropolitan statistical areas as of the 2000 census, areas that range from New York City, with over 20 million residents, to Richmond, Virginia, with just under 1 million people.[18] As of the 2000 census, four boomburbs topped 300,000 in population, eight surpassed 200,000, and forty-two exceeded 100,000. The fifty-four boomburbs account for 52 percent of 1990s' growth in cities with 100,000 to 400,000 residents. (The fifty-four boomburbs are listed alphabetically in table 1-1.)

Boomburbs now contain over a quarter of all residents of small to midsize cities. There may be just a few dozen boomburbs, but they now dominate growth in the category of places that fall just below the nation's biggest cities. Another way to grasp just how big boomburbs have become is by comparing their current populations with those of some better-known traditional cities. Mesa, Arizona, the most populous boomburb at 396,375 residents in 2000, is bigger than such traditional large cities as Minneapolis (population 382,618), Miami (population 362,470), and St. Louis (population 348,189). Arlington, Texas, the third biggest boomburb, with 332,969 people, falls just behind Pittsburgh (with 334,536) and just ahead of Cincinnati (with 331,285). Even such smaller boomburbs as Chandler, Arizona, and Henderson, Nevada (with 176,581 and 175,381 residents, respectively) now surpass older midsize cities such as Knoxville (with 173,890), Providence, Rhode Island (with 173,618), and Worcester, Massachusetts (with 172,648).

By the 2000 census, fifteen of the hundred largest cities in the United States were boomburbs. More significant, from 1990 to 2000, fourteen of the twenty-five fastest-growing cities among these hundred were boomburbs—including five of the top ten. Since the 2000 census, many of the largest boomburbs jumped ahead of their traditional (and much better-known) big-city peers (based on 2002 census estimates). Mesa (with an estimated population of 426,841) edged out Atlanta (estimated at 424,868). Both Arlington, Texas (estimated at 349,944), and Santa Ana, California (estimated at 343,413), passed St. Louis (which lost nearly 10,000 residents by 2002). Anaheim (with an estimated 2002 population of 332,642) is now immediately trailing St. Louis. Aurora, Colorado (286,028), has overtaken St. Paul (284,037). Finally, Peoria, Arizona (123,239), surged ahead of Peoria, Illinois (112,670), which has actually lost residents in recent years.[19]

To put the boomburb rise in perspective, consider that only about a quarter of the U.S. population lives in municipalities that exceed 100,000 people. The fraction of the population living in cities this size or above peaked in 1930. Boomburbs are among the few large cities that are actually booming. Much of the nation's metropolitan population gains have shifted to their edges.[20]

While some boomburbs are well on their way to becoming major cities, at least as defined by population size, it is not surprising that these places fall below the public radar. But it is interesting how little boomburbs register with urban experts, too. For instance, a recent encyclopedia of urban America that covers both cities and "major suburbs" fails to list even one boomburb exceeding 300,000 people; it does, however, have entries for comparably sized (and often even smaller) traditional cities.[21]

This book also tracks, in addition to boomburbs, a category of fast-growing suburban city, the baby boomburb. It meets the same boomburb growth qualifications; however, it ranges in size from 50,000 to 100,000 residents as of the 2000 census. There are eighty-six baby boomburbs in the United States (table 1-2).

Baby boomburbs are important to examine for two reasons. First, many are up-and-coming boomburbs. In fact, several have jumped over the 100,000 mark since 2000.[22] The second reason is that baby boomburbs are numerous. They are especially well represented in the Midwest and the

Table 1-2. U.S. Baby Boomburbs, 2000 Census[a]

Antioch, California	Gresham, Oregon	Pittsburg, California
Apple Valley, California	Hemet, California	Plantation, Florida
Beaverton, Oregon	Hesperia, California	Pleasanton, California
Boca Raton, Florida	Hillsboro, Oregon	Plymouth, Minnesota
Boynton Beach, Florida	Kent, Washington	Renton, Washington
Brooklyn Park, Minnesota	Laguna Niguel, California	Rialto, California
Burnsville, Minnesota	Lauderhill, Florida	Rochester Hills, Michigan
Carlsbad, California	Layton, Utah	Roseville, California
Cary, North Carolina	Lee's Summit, Missouri	Roswell, Georgia
Chino, California	Lewisville, Texas	Round Rock, Texas
Coon Rapids, Minnesota	Livermore, California	San Marcos, California
Cupertino, California	Longmont, Colorado	Sandy, Utah
Davie, Florida	Lynwood, California	Santa Cruz, California
Davis, California	Maple Grove, Minnesota	South Gate, California
Deerfield Beach, Florida	Margate, Florida	St. Charles, Missouri
Delray Beach, Florida	Marietta, Georgia	St. Peters, Missouri
Denton, Texas	Milpitas, California	Sugar Land, Texas
Eagan, Minnesota	Miramar, Florida	Sunrise, Florida
Eden Prairie, Minnesota	Mission Viejo, California	Tamarac, Florida
Edmond, Oklahoma	Missouri, Texas	Thornton, Colorado
Elgin, Illinois	Murfreesboro, Tennessee	Tustin, California
Fairfield, California	Napa, California	Union, California
Federal Way, Washington	Norman, Oklahoma	Vacaville, California
Flower Mound, Texas	North Miami, Florida	Victorville, California
Folsom, California	North Richland Hills, Texas	Vista, California
Frederick, Maryland	Olathe, Kansas	Waukesha, Wisconsin
Gaithersburg, Maryland	Orland Park, Illinois	West Jordan, Utah
Gardena, California	Palatine, Illinois	Yorba Linda, California
Greeley, Colorado	Petaluma, California	

a. A baby boomburb is defined as a suburban city with a population of 50,000 to 100,000 that is not the core city of its region and has had double digit population growth in each census since 1970.

South. They capture the growth in places that boom but lack boomburbs. The change that has swept boomburbs also impacted baby boomburbs. In many instances the latter are at an earlier stage in the process of change than the former. Baby boomburbs came up in many of the discussions the authors had with elected boomburb officials, who often saw these places as potential rivals.

Where Are Boomburbs?

While boomburbs and baby boomburbs are found throughout the nation, they occur mostly in the Southwest in a belt of metropolitan areas stretching from Texas to the Pacific, with almost half in California alone. Even a relatively small Western metropolis such as Las Vegas contains two boomburbs. The Las Vegas region also contains three census-designated places (or unincorporated places) that exceed 100,000 residents and so would qualify as boomburbs were they incorporated.[23]

Two key ingredients are needed to produce boomburbs and baby boomburbs—fast, sustained development in big incorporated places. The West (with eighty-four boomburbs and baby boomburbs) has both. The South (with forty-one boomburbs and baby boomburbs) in general is booming but has mostly smaller incorporated places and even many unincorporated places that capture growth. The Northeast and the Midwest have plenty of large incorporated places but are growing at a much slower rate than the South and the West. Thus, no metropolitan area in the Northeast and Midwest except Chicago has a single boomburb. Even large and rapidly growing Sunbelt metropolitan areas east of the Mississippi, such as Atlanta and Charlotte, often lack boomburbs. Thus, a region can boom and still not have a boomburb.

The one region that could have produced perhaps a dozen boomburbs—metropolitan Washington—has none.[24] Washington's problem is not slow growth, for it is the only real boom region of the megalopolis running from Virginia to Maine.[25] Rather, metropolitan Washington lacks the units of government that would produce boomburbs. Counties are the main unit of governance in suburban Washington, and only incorporated cities qualify as boomburbs. Consider Fairfax County, Virginia, which now has over a million residents and has experienced double-digit growth rates since World War II.[26] Fairfax would likely contain several boomburbs if the county's ministerial districts were separate, incorporated cities.[27]

The Atlanta metropolitan area's rapid growth could also have produced several boomburbs, but the region has only one city above 100,000—Atlanta. By contrast, the Phoenix metropolitan area has eight cities with more than 100,000 people—Phoenix and seven boomburbs (one of which is bigger than Atlanta). This bounty of large cities comes despite the fact that almost a million fewer people live in the Phoenix region than in the Atlanta region. But if boomburbs were counties and not cities, Atlanta and Washington would have plenty of them.[28]

So why does the West have such large incorporated places? There are several reasons. The metropolitan West is home to enormous master-planned communities usually located in a single town. These communities annex unincorporated land as they grow. The land and its new residents are added to municipalities, turning what were once small towns into boomburbs. Also, the public lands in the West that surround big metropolitan areas are often transferred to developers in large blocks.[29] By contrast, Eastern builders of master-planned communities must assemble land from mostly smaller, privately held parcels.[30]

Western water districts also play a role in promoting boomburbs. The West is mostly dry, and places seeking to grow must organize to access water.[31] Big incorporated cities are better positioned to buy water rights, providing an incentive for suburbs to join a large incorporated city.[32] Finally, the revenue system in many Western states relies on municipal-level sales taxes, so the incentive to incorporate land and promote retail development on it has produced what William Fulton calls "sales tax canyons."[33] The only census regions missing both boomburbs and baby boomburbs are the New England and Middle Atlantic states, home to major metropolitan areas such as Boston, Philadelphia, and of course New York. Again, this is not to say that there has been no growth in the Northeast over the past several decades. The New York region in particular has boomed, but much of its development has been in exurban counties. Orange County, New York, and Ocean County, New Jersey (both at least fifty miles from midtown Manhattan), have seen double-digit growth for each census since 1950 and would qualify as boomburbs were they cities.[34] But no incorporated city in either Orange or Ocean Counties is even a baby boomburb.

By contrast, in the Midwest, the Chicago, Detroit, Minneapolis, St. Louis, and Kansas City regions all have many baby boomburbs. Minneapolis alone has seven. Although St. Louis has seen decades of decline, its suburbs of St. Charles and St. Peters have boomed. Baby boomburbs also appear in many of the same metropolitan areas that have boomburbs. Los Angeles and San Francisco have a bunch, as does South Florida. Almost all of the western development edge of Broward County, Florida—which presses against the Everglades—consists of several baby boomburbs.

Boomburb: A Bold New Metropolis or an Updated Satellite City?

When satellite cities in the late nineteenth and early twentieth centuries reached a certain size they became dense urban cores. But as boomburbs grow to be the size of these earlier satellite cities, most remain essentially suburban in character. Just as satellite cities reflected the dominant urban pattern of their time, boomburbs may be the ultimate symbol of the sprawling postwar metropolitan form. Boomburbs typically develop along the interstate freeways that ring large U.S. metropolitan areas. The commercial elements of the new suburban metropolis—office parks, big-box retail stores, and most characteristically, strip malls—gather at highway exit ramps and major intersections. Beyond these lie residential subdivisions dominated by large-lot, single-family homes.

Some may ask whether the boomburb is merely a new kind of satellite city. Business, particularly manufacturing, has been decentralizing for many decades—perhaps even a century. For example, in a 1915 publication titled *Satellite Cities: A Case Study of Industrial Suburbs,* the economist Graham Taylor described an emerging metropolitan pattern in which heavy industry was rapidly shifting to the suburbs in search of more space and lower costs. More than seventy-five years ago, the sociologist Ernest Burgess noted that there was already business growth at Chicago's edge, which he characterized as being "centralized-decentralized" in structure.[35] Early twentieth-century "satellite" and "centralized" suburbs mimicked big cities, although at slightly lower density and scale. Satellites had all of the places that defined a city: a main street shopping area, high-density residential neighborhoods, and by the late nineteenth century, factory districts.[36] In the 1920s it was even typical for larger satellite cities in the New York region, such as Newark, to have a signature art deco office tower, representing an already decentralizing service economy.[37]

Boomburbs, however, do not resemble these older satellites. While boomburbs possess most elements found in cities—such as housing, retailing, entertainment, and offices—they are not typically patterned in a traditional urban form. Boomburbs almost always lack, for example, a dense business core and are thus distinct from traditional cities and satellites—not so much in their function as in their low-density and loosely configured spatial structure. Boomburbs are urban in fact but not in feel.

A distinction must be made between the boomburbs of a traditional city and those of the newer and less traditional Southwestern city. The boomburbs of Phoenix, Dallas, and Las Vegas, for example, are similar to their core city. Glendale, near Phoenix, and Garland, near Dallas, for example, have the density and urban form of their core cities—except for a large downtown. Boomburbs in these metropolitan areas, in other words, are extensions of the auto-dependent city typical of the Sunbelt.

Terms for the Boomburb Phenomenon

Urban scholars have been attempting for the past three decades to characterize the large suburban cities that are referred to here as boomburbs. As William Sharpe and Leonard Wallock note, "In the early 1970s, as concern about the inner-city crisis waned and the decentralization of the metropolis reached new proportions, 'the urbanization of the suburbs' suddenly became a topic of national interest. The ensuing flurry of articles and books introduced neologisms such as 'outer city,' 'satellite sprawl,' 'new city,' 'suburban city,' 'urban fringe,' and 'neo city' to describe this phenomenon."[38] Despite years of effort to label the new suburban form, there remains no single name for it—boomburb being one of many. Instead, as Sharpe and Wallock note, observers use an array of names, suggesting that planners, developers, journalists, and academics do not yet understand it.

Part of the problem is that we are bound by a language that hierarchically ranks living space—urban, suburban, exurban, rural—when the old ladder image no longer applies.[39] But properly naming the new suburban city is an important step in better understanding it. As Pierce Lewis argues, "Language is important. We cannot talk about . . . phenomena unless we possess the vocabulary to describe them, and many observers still cannot agree on what to call this new amorphous form of urban geography."[40]

A boomburb, as defined in this analysis, corresponds to what urban historian Robert Fishman refers to as a technoburb, which he defines as "a hopeless jumble of housing, industry, commerce, and even agricultural uses."[41] In his view, today's sprawling suburban metropolitan areas can no longer be judged by the standards of the old metropolis, in part because the new suburban form "lacks any definable borders, a center or a periphery, or clear distinctions between residential, industrial, and commercial zones."[42] In Jane Jacobs's parlance, boomburbs have far more microdestinations than macrodestinations.[43] Yet while many boomburbs may fit what Robert Lang refers to as edgeless cities, several also are what Joel Garreau calls edge cities, a term for metropolitan focal points outside the urban cores and older satellite suburbs.[44] A list of such terms appears on the next page.[45]

And the names keep coming. Not content with the fast growth implied by the term *boomburb*, Dolores Hayden recently added *zoomburb* to describe even more explosive suburban development.[46]

The terms above capture the dispersal of urban functions, most notably the suburbanization of offices. Thus the terms *suburb* and *suburban* continue to be used. But this process is much more complex than a simple dispersal; the decentralization involves a degree of recentralization, hence the terms *city, urban, center, downtown, core*. The spread-out nature of the phenomenon is reflected in the terms *corridor, regional, spillover, spread, outer, unbound, edge, edgeless, and limitless*. There are also indications that the new forms negate the traditional city, as in *anticity, exopolis*, and *outtown*, and bring together features usually considered opposites, as in *countrified city* and *urban village*. The labels were not conceived in a

anticity	metropolitan-level	sprinkler city
boomburb	core	stealth city
city a la carte	metropolitan suburb	subcenter
concentrated	metrotown	suburban business
decentralization	minicity	center
countrified city	mini-downtown	suburban downtown
disurb	multicentered net	suburban employment
edge city	net of mixed beads	center
edge county	new downtown	suburban freeway
edgeless city	outer city	corridor
exit ramp economy	outtown	suburban growth
exopolis	penturbia	corridor
galactic city	regional city	suburban nucleation
limitless city	regional town center	technoburb
major diversified	rururbia	the new heartland
center	servurb	urban core
megacenter	slurb	urban galaxy
megacounty	spillover city	urban realm
megalopolis unbound	spread city	urban village

political vacuum: derogatory appellations also are used, such as *disurb* and *slurb*.

The Look and Feel of Boomburbs

Boomburbs are much more horizontally built and less pedestrian friendly than most older suburbs. The fifty-four boomburbs collectively—with millions of residents in total—may have fewer urban qualities than those of such older suburbs as Arlington and Alexandria, Virginia, together.

Alexandria is a city of almost 130,000 residents; Arlington is a county of 190,000 people (it is the smallest county in the United States and is often treated in the U.S. census as a city). Together, the population of these two places is slightly smaller than a big boomburb such as Anaheim. Arlington and Alexandria are directly across the Potomac River from Washington and occupy the entire area that was once part of the District but was ceded back to Virginia in the mid-nineteenth century because it was not developing.[47] Compared to the District they are suburbs, but they are urban environments when contrasted to the rest of suburban northern

Virginia. Note also that neither place is known nationally for its big-city qualities. Arlington is famous for its national military cemetery, Alexandria is loved by tourists for its quaint Old Town.

Alexandria's Old Town section is the most pedestrian-friendly area in the two places. Arlington has a much larger office market. Newer parts of Alexandria also have office and high-rise residential buildings. The Washington region's Metrorail system laces through both Arlington and Alexandria (especially the former). Arlington's Metro stops have encouraged mixed-use, high-density development.[48] Alexandria's are beginning to develop in the same way. Both places are fully built, and most new development is within the existing built environment.

Two traditional urban qualities—high-rise buildings and pedestrian-oriented streets—provide a basis for comparing these D.C. suburbs with boomburbs. The number of tall buildings is easy to assess. All buildings worldwide above thirty-five meters tall (about 115 feet) are tracked by Emporis, a real estate consulting firm.[49] Table 1-3 gives the number of high-rise buildings in Arlington and Alexandria and in those boomburbs that have any. Arlington has 152 high-rise buildings, most of them offices, followed by residences and hotels. Alexandria has 52 high-rises. Compare their total of 204 to 160 for all boomburbs combined.

Some boomburbs contain substantial amounts of office space: Scottsdale, Arizona, and Plano, Texas, have dozens of office buildings with millions of square feet of floor space—and mostly upper-end space at that. Yet together these two communities have only four high-rise office buildings. Welcome to the boomburbs, where low-slung office cubes line the freeways.

In recent years there has been a trend in boomburbs toward taller buildings, especially residential towers. Consider Anaheim, which has proposals on the books for six high-rise condominiums, all of which exceed twenty-three floors, with one rising to thirty-five. In fact, Orange County, California, is in a miniboom of high-rises centered mostly in Anaheim, Costa Mesa, Irvine, and Santa Ana.[50] Tempe and Scottsdale, Arizona, are also seeing a burst in this building, with ten condominium towers either approved or under construction. Overall, boomburbs have fifteen residential towers under construction, thirty-three more have been approved, and twenty-three have been proposed.[51]

The other urban quality missing from boomburbs—pedestrian-friendly streets—is harder to measure than building height. Large areas of Alexandria and Arlington were built for pedestrians. These include Old Town, Alexandria, and the areas around the Metro stops along Arlington's Wilson Boulevard corridor at Rosslyn, Clarendon, Virginia Square, and Ballston. Both

Table 1-3. High-Rise Buildings in Two Washington Suburbs and Boomburbs[a]

Suburb/boomburb	Office buildings	Other
Alexandria	8	44
Arlington	78	74
Boomburb	83	77
Anaheim, California	1	8
Arlington, Texas	0	2
Aurora, Colorado	4	0
Bellevue, Washington	11	3
Clearwater, Florida	1	31
Coral Springs	0	1
Costa Mesa, California	9	0
Hialeah, Florida	0	3
Irvine, California	19	3
Irving, Texas	16	6
Lakewood, Colorado	0	2
Mesa, Arizona	1	2
Mesquite, Texas	1	0
North Las Vegas	0	1
Orange, California	7	2
Oxnard, California	2	0
Plano, Texas	3	0
Riverside, California	1	3
Salem, Oregon	0	2
San Bernardino, California	1	1
Santa Ana, California	5	2
Santa Rosa, California	0	1
Scottsdale, Arizona	1	1
Tempe, Arizona	0	2
Westminster, Colorado	0	1

a. Only boomburbs with at least one high-rise building are listed.

places also have densely built pre–World War II subdivisions. Conservatively, perhaps five square miles of Arlington and Alexandria combined is friendly to pedestrians. That may not seem like much, but it may equal or surpass the total of such space in all of the boomburbs in America put together. There are plenty of boomburbs—even big ones—in which pedestrian-oriented areas are only several blocks or even one block. The so-called downtowns of cities such as North Las Vegas and Chandler are quite literally one block. Those boomburbs with several blocks of downtown include Plano, Texas, and Riverside and Orange in California. Tempe has a decent downtown (which is helped by being proximate to Arizona State University), as do Salem, Oregon (the only boomburb state capital—and the biggest outlier in the study), and Bellevue, Washington.

There are also some boomburb new towns on the model of places such as Reston, Virginia. Las Colinas in Irving, Texas, is an example of a well-designed new town, with shopping, residences, and offices mixed together. Further down the pedestrian-friendly scale is a "lifestyle center" such as The Camp in Costa Mesa, which is a shopping area laid out in village form. Victoria Gardens is an ambitious lifestyle center in Rancho Cucamonga, California; it has some high-density housing mixed with retail space and all laid out in an urban grid. Finally, there is Main Street USA at Disneyland in Anaheim, which ironically is a bigger main street than the ones found in perhaps half of all boomburbs.

Boomburbs: Cool, Hip, and Hot

From the perspective of big cities, or even of Arlington, it is easy for some people to feel smug in relation to boomburbs. But attractiveness is an elusive quality. The boomburbs may be horizontally built and virtually 100 percent auto oriented, but some are considered "cool" or even "hot" or at least "hip" by the media. These are the adjectives especially applied to boomburbs in Orange County, California. The Camp in Costa Mesa, in Orange County, for example, is full of twentysomethings trolling for the latest in surfing gear. And nearby Irvine houses the center of auto design, in its Spectrum office complex (because according to a Spectrum developer at the Irvine Corporation, Orange County is a proving ground for "cool" cars).[52]

Even in the remote edges of northeastern Mesa, Arizona, where speculative McMansions are under construction in gated cul de sacs, upscale and trendy shopping and dining are already firmly planted. A major surprise in many of the authors' site tours in the new parts of boomburbs is how much urban artifacts are already present. Not just chain restaurants— although there were plenty—but locally owned, white linen restaurants, many already filled with regulars. Along with restaurants are stores selling high-cost modern furnishings.

Another surprise, and one that contradicts the new urbanist notions on the use of space, is the fact that boomburb mini-malls are alive with street life. New urbanists have been sharply critical of the supposed alienation produced by modern suburban retail centers, in contrast to traditional town centers.[53] But shopping malls have come a long way from the utilitarian days when stores starkly fronted onto parking lots. Sidewalks have widened, and most malls and restaurants in the Sunbelt offer outdoor seating. Chains such as Starbucks often anchor a public space in these places. On site tours to the boomburbs the authors repeatedly observed that social life in mini-malls stands as perhaps the empirical finding most contrary to preconceived ideas of suburban alienation. Some future Jane Jacobs may turn urban planning orthodoxy on its head by describing the intricate social ballet of these spaces and perhaps could argue—as Jacobs did for the city—that boomburbs need to be studied on their own terms.[54]

Money Magazine looked at 271 small to midsize U.S. cities to determine which are the hottest, that is, fast-growing cities where residents can "expect big-time benefits from small-town life."[55] The list includes "towns" with above-average home prices, income, and population growth, arranged by region: East (including the South), Central (the Midwest), and West (from Texas to the Pacific). *Money*, like the boomburb study, uses 100,000 population as the break point between midsize and small towns.

Boomburbs and baby boomburbs dominate *Money*'s hottest towns list. In fact, the hottest town above 100,000 in all three regions is a boomburb. *Money* ranks eight places in the East with more than 100,000 people as hot. Cary, North Carolina (104,210 residents in 2002), tops the list, while Coral Springs, Florida, ranks third, and Chesapeake, Virginia, comes in seventh. Half of the hottest places in the East are in northern Virginia. Alexandria is one, but the other three are not cities at all but rather three ministerial districts in Fairfax County: Dranesville (with 110,480 residents), Hunter Mill (with 115,428), and Sully (with 152,169).

Money lists four places in the Midwest. The top-ranked Naperville, Illinois, and the fourth-place Olathe, Kansas, are boomburbs. But most of the hot towns (thirteen of them) are in the West, as are the highest three: Plano ranks first, Anaheim is second, and Scottsdale is third.[56]

The article is interesting as an example of the way the popular press labels boomburbs. Despite the fact that some of the places *Money* ranks as hot have well over 200,000 residents (or even 300,000 in the case of Anaheim), the magazine refers to them as "towns." Based on the evidence presented here, *Money* has it about half right. Boomburbs may look like towns, but it is hard to argue that living in an Anaheim offers one a "small-town life." That is, of course, unless the person is a permanent resident of Disneyland's Main Street USA.

In 2006 *Money Magazine* published a feature on "America's best small cities," which did include baby boomburbs.[57] The study ranked ninety "cities" of 50,000 to 250,000 residents on criteria similar to *Money*'s hot-city list. Boomburbs and baby boomburbs account for seventeen of the twenty-five best small cities.

Some Surprises

Boomburbs being cool or hip is but one of the surprises that turned up in the research for this book (of which being hot was not a surprise). Another opinion of boomburbs—that they are rich, elitist, white, and exclusive—is also wrong for the most part. Here are our findings:

—Several boomburbs have some of the highest percentages of foreign-born populations in the United States, often exceeding that of central cities. Boomburbs with diverse populations have been labeled "new Brooklyns."

—Housing in some new Brooklyns is among the most crowded in the United States, with two or more people to a room.

—Boomburbs have less affordable housing than much of the nation—only about half of boomburb residents can afford to buy houses in their community, as opposed to a U.S. average of nearly 59 percent. Because of this, homeownership in boomburbs tends to be lower than the national average.

—Boomburbs are much more like one another than like a comparably sized traditional city. Multiple demographic forces sustain growth, with often high levels of both immigration and migration.

—Many boomburbs have a right side and a wrong side of the tracks—or, more accurately, of the freeway. For example, Interstate 15 literally divides North Las Vegas's affluent and distressed halves.

—The Southwestern boomburbs are a land of big skies and small lots, ironically, for a place with such open spaces.

—Boomburbs can be so big that parts of the city may be declining while other parts are still developing. For instance, the central parts of Chandler, Arizona, badly need redevelopment, although developers are building new housing in open desert that the city has annexed.

—Most boomburbs are newer than the rest of the nation, with housing eight years newer than the U.S. average (1979 versus 1971). Yet seven boomburbs have housing older than the national average.

—Many, if not most, boomburbs are approaching their buildout point. The year each runs out of land—and its peak population when it does—is usually easily predicted. By 2020 more than half of present-day boomburbs will be built out.

—Just about every boomburb mayor interviewed would like to have light-rail transportation in his or her city, reflecting a shift in projection of growth from out to up: light rail would promote real estate development in the downtown. Light-rail projects are under way in Tempe and Mesa, Arizona, Lakewood, Colorado, and Mesquite, Texas.

—Only three boomburbs contain edge cities (or large clusters of suburban offices and shopping malls). But boomburbs collectively do contain plenty of office space in edgeless cities (scattered developments that never coalesce into edge cities).

—A dozen boomburbs and eighteen baby boomburbs have more jobs than households, and about two-thirds of both city types nearly have a jobs-to-housing balance.

—Boomburb leaders often worry about the next round of boomburbs that are gaining on their city—and maybe at the expense of their city.

—Almost all boomburb mayorships are part-time (often nonpaying) jobs. Given the size of these places, it is hard to believe that more of these positions are not full time.

—Boomburbs have devised a number of strategies to adapt governments intended for small towns to the realities of big cities. In many cases, private solutions relieve the burden on both public finance and management.

—Most boomburbs have been growing rapidly since 1940, so their boom started with World War II and did not wait for the postwar era.

—Several dozen new boomburbs could form by the mid-twenty-first century. Interestingly, some of these places are as yet unoccupied and unnamed but are part of big proposed projects, such as Superstition Vistas east of Phoenix.[58]

Why Study Boomburbs?

Boomburbs and baby boomburbs are critical cities to examine on their own terms. For one thing, they contain one in nine U.S. suburban dwellers. Since 1990 over half of all growth in cities of 100,000–400,000 residents has been in these cities: boomburbs now account for a quarter of all people who live in this size city. When the bank robber Willie Sutton was asked, Why do you rob banks? his famous answer was, Because that's where the money is. For similar reasons we study boomburbs and baby boomburbs: because that is where the people are. . . . In addition, a study of boomburbs reveals how large-scale communities are being built and points to how America is growing.

The key finding is not entirely surprising: U.S. cities developed since 1950 have been built around automobiles. But what fills this auto-dependent space is often unexpected. For example, America's new face of poverty is surprisingly often seen in boomburb neighborhoods of small single-family homes, neighborhoods that once represented the American dream. In addition, these cities constitute a new census type. In the Census Bureau's redefinition of metropolitan America, it reformulated its municipal classification from the old central-city concept to the new principal-city concept.[59] Interestingly, dozens of boomburbs and baby boomburbs, once termed *noncentral cities* (that is, suburbs), are now termed *principal cities* and have a metropolitan statistical area identification.[60]

The Census Bureau, in loosening its concept of what constitutes a city in the metropolitan context, recognizes that boomburbs have a principal role in their regions, and some metropolitan statistical areas may incorporate their names (such as the Phoenix, Mesa, Scottsdale metropolitan statistical area). Redefining many suburbs as cities added almost 13 million people to the principal-city share of metropolitan area population.[61] Were it not for the new category, central cities would be seen as losing a significant share of metropolitan growth.

A study of boomburbs and baby boomburbs also sheds light on other fast-developing parts of the country, such as fast-growing counties containing mostly unincorporated land. Further, the patterns of growth found in boomburbs often apply to big suburban counties around large cities like Atlanta, Nashville, and Washington.[62] The major exception to this observation concerns governance: boomburbs and baby boomburbs are incorporated and thus are managed differently from unincorporated developments, and understanding this contrast can help shape development patterns. For example, commercial development in large suburban counties may occur across a wide area, with the tax benefits being shared equally. By contrast, boomburbs—as separate incorporated places—often compete against one another for land uses that generate high sales taxes. This theme is explored throughout the book and forms a major focus in the business and governance chapters.

In an even broader sense, studying boomburbs provides insight into metropolitan change writ large. There is a tradition in the sociological literature to do a depth analysis on one type of city or even of individual neighborhood to catch sight of the larger theoretical currents. Consider such classic works as *Middletown* and *Levittown* and more contemporary studies such as *Streetwise* and the *Celebration Chronicles*.[63] In *Levittown*, the new town is treated as both an exemplar and a metaphor for all U.S. post–World War II suburbia. This work does suffer somewhat from a limitation due to face validity (a problem with all case analysis), but it succeeds in fleshing out some basic truths about life in tract-style subdivisions. In *Celebration Chronicles*, the approach is to treat the town of Celebration as representative of the most modern manifestation of suburbia and to test (and find wanting) the "new urbanist" claim that an "architecture of engagement" enhances social interaction.[64]

By offering an in-depth, objective, nonpolarizing view of large suburban cities, this book can be important not only to policymakers but also to developers, city officials, and of course all who find themselves living in a boomburb. It may be no accident that boomburbs boomed, but the size these places reached and the speed at which they became complicated urban environments have an accidental quality. Boomburbs were often planned, but few planned to become cities (and some even remain in denial). Even boomburbs that have stopped growing face the consequences of their earlier growth. As this book shows, they are the proving grounds for a twenty-first-century suburban cosmopolitanism.

2

From Settlements to Super Suburbs

One word describes Glendale from the 1950s to the present: growth.

GLENDALE, ARIZONA, WEBSITE

So where did boomburbs come from? Although most boomburbs have become cities over the past few decades, many began as minor settlements in the late nineteenth and early twentieth centuries (as shown by such sources as census data, municipal web pages, the online encyclopedia wikipedia [www.wikipedia.org], historical societies, old guide books, photographs, and maps). If they existed at all before the mid-twentieth century, boomburbs were tiny specks on the map.

By contrast, the nation's original satellite cities were well established by the start of the twentieth century, but none of them qualifies as a boomburb. For example, Newark, New Jersey, Alexandria, Virginia, and Long Beach, California, are big enough to be boomburbs, but they have grown too slowly in recent years to qualify. Even most late-starting industrial satellites, such as Gary, Indiana (built by the U.S. Steel Corporation beginning in 1906), are by now fading and losing population.

A couple of traditional satellite cities almost made the baby boomburb list (that is, having populations between 50,000 and 100,000). Passaic, New Jersey, in the New York metropolitan area, had double-digit growth in both the 1980s and 1990s, but it lost people in the 1970s. As discussed below in more detail, Passaic's recent boom is due to the surge in immigration that swept some traditional cities in the past two decades and sustained growth that otherwise might have slowed down or even declined. The other traditional satellite city that nearly made the boomburb list is Boulder, Colorado, home to the University of Colorado. Boulder boomed in the 1970s and 1990s but had below double-digit growth in the 1980s. (The 1980s were an especially hard time for the Denver area, as its energy sector suffered.)

The four big boomburbs that exceeded 300,000 people in the year 2000—Mesa, Arizona, Santa Ana and Anaheim, California, and Arlington, Texas—were small towns in the early twentieth century. In 1910 Santa Ana and Anaheim had 3,000 and 8,000 people, respectively. In 1930 both Arlington and Mesa had well below 4,000 residents. By 1930 Santa Ana reached 30,000 and Anaheim stood at 11,000 people.

By 1950 a few boomburbs had grown into little cities, but only one had passed 50,000 residents (the benchmark for a baby boomburb). The biggest boomburb in 1950 was San Bernardino, California, with 63,058 people. Two other California cities followed: Riverside (with 46,764 residents) and Santa Ana (with 45,533). The only other city with more than 40,000 residents in 1950 was Salem, Oregon (population 43,140).

What unites these early developing boomburbs is that they are all government centers. San Bernardino, Riverside, and Santa Ana are county seats and, more important, centers of what was becoming the vast polycentric metropolis of greater Los Angeles.[1] Salem is Oregon's state capital. Among all boomburbs, Salem is easily the most traditional city and also the only boomburb that was a city in the nineteenth century. Although a population of 60,000, or even 40,000, is not small, in the case of bigger boomburbs, such populations were just a hint of what was to come.

Panoramic Maps

Besides population figures, there are other—more descriptive—ways of understanding how significant a place is at various points in time. Around the beginning of the twentieth century cities often commissioned "panoramic maps," which were part of booster efforts to show how significant the cities were—or were to become.[2] These maps often depicted platted streets with no buildings along them, an indication of speculators' hopes.

The U.S. Library of Congress maintains a collection of panoramic maps, which has been scanned into an online database under the title "American Memory Historical Collections for the National Digital Library." The maps are listed by location, allowing a search by city name. Boomburbs and baby boomburbs are so new that very few appear on these maps. Only 8 of the 140 boomburbs and baby boomburbs have panoramic maps in the online collection: three boomburbs (Santa Rosa, California, Naperville, Illinois, and Salem, Oregon) and five baby boomburbs (Greeley, Colorado, Elgin, Illinois, St. Charles, Missouri, Edmond, Oklahoma, and Waukesha, Wisconsin).

No boomburbs above 200,000 population have panoramic maps in the collection. Those that do have maps tend to be Eastern or in old metropolitan areas. Not one place in Los Angeles, Phoenix, or Dallas—all regions with multiple boomburbs—is in the panoramic map collection.

However, John Reps of Cornell University has gathered a collection of early panoramic maps for "frontier cities," and his collection does include several big boomburbs.[3] Most of his maps depict cities at their very origin: whole sections of a town may be platted, complete with improved streets, but they were in fact not yet there. These maps were often shown to prospective lot buyers who had yet to see the town they were purchasing land in and needed assurance that it was an established place. Three boomburbs missing from the American Memory online catalogue are found in the Reps collection: Mesa, Arizona, Anaheim, California, and San Bernardino, California. Panoramic maps of Salem, Oregon, are in both collections.

The 1882 "Plan of Mesa" shows a one-square-mile grid of sixteen blocks with wide streets.[4] Mesa was originally a Mormon settlement (and still supports a large Mormon temple), platted according to a standard church-mandated plan. A temple was begun in the late nineteenth century but was not completed until 1927. So it was well into the third decade of the twentieth century that Mesa became an official "Temple city."[5] Anaheim is shown in 1877 as a village of a few square blocks, with the towering San Gabriel Mountains off in the distance (today the mountains are nearly impossible to see due to smog).[6] San Bernardino in 1886 appears similar to the Anaheim view—big mountains, small town. The Reps collection also includes a panorama of Salem in 1876, and it is indeed already a substantial place.[7] It could easily swallow several late-nineteenth-century Anaheims and San Bernardinos. At this stage, Mesa was but a dream.

In sum, the American Memory and the Reps map collections indicate that most boomburbs were at best a glimmer in a nineteenth-century speculator's eyes. But anyone who speculated on the land shown in the panoramic boomburb maps and held his or her property even to the mid-twentieth century made a fortune.

Works Progress Administration State Guides

Another good resource for determining the early significance of cities is the Works Progress Administration's (WPA) famous late-1930s' state Guide Books.[8] The WPA, as part of its "writers' project," employed out-of-work authors to develop comprehensive guides to all (then) forty-eight states and several major cities, such as New York and Washington. The WPA Guides are a remarkable resource. They survey every state's history and current conditions in several key areas such as agriculture, industry, people, education, and urban life. Under a section titled "The Urban Scene," the Guide Books provide histories of each state's principal cities. Only Salem, of the 140 boomburbs and baby boomburbs, has a city history in the Guides.

This is not to say that the WPA Guides skip boomburbs altogether. Each Guide Book also includes a section on auto tours that traverse the state using its main (pre-interstate) highways. Boomburbs often show up as wayside stops and points of interest on these tours. But the coverage is hit or miss. If a boomburb was on an early major highway, chances are good that it has a line or a paragraph in a WPA Guide Book. But recall that the Guides were written two decades before the federal interstate highways were started. Therefore many places that were to boom with the advent of the interstates and their beltways are not included. The WPA Guides catch America at the eve of World War II. The country had just been through the boom of the 1920s and the Great Depression of the 1930s.

Thirty-three boomburbs merit a mention in the WPA series. Many entries run just a single line. Most do not even hint at the dramatic change that was soon to come in these places. For example, the entry for Sunnyvale, in the very heart of today's Silicon Valley, describes the city in 1939 as "a quiet rancher's trade center."[9]

An example of a WPA Guide entry for a midsize city is that for Garland, Texas, a boomburb east of Dallas: "Many of the residents of suburban Garland commute to offices in Dallas. Almost razed by a tornado in 1927, this town today has beautiful residences, a modern business area and a large hat factory."[10] This description is one of the few mentions in a WPA Guide that comes close to describing a contemporary boomburb. To this day Garland is a suburb of Dallas, has lots of commuters, and still makes Stetson hats—same old Garland, just 132 times bigger than it was in the 1930s.

The WPA Guides also contain a few major entries for boomburbs. Below is the longest description of any boomburb (other than the ten pages on Salem) in the whole WPA Guide Series. It is for Tempe, a boomburb just east of Phoenix:

> Tempe is on the south bank of the Salt River at the foot of Tempe Butte. Tall cottonwood, tamarisk, eucalyptus, and palm trees border its broad paved streets, and its modern brick business buildings are interspersed with low flat-roofed adobes. It was so named by an early settler and English expatriate, Darrell Dupa, because of its likeness in contour to the Vale of Tempe between Mounts Olympus and Ossa in Thessaly. It is on the Salt River in the midst of a general crop-growing, dairying, and stock-raising region and is the headquarters for the Farm Security Administration's experimental project, Casa Grande Farms. In 1872 Tempe was a trading post called Hayden's Ferry, for Charles Trumbull Hayden, who in 1849 had brought an ox-cart load of goods to Santa Fe and had remained there as a merchant till 1858 when he moved to Tucson. During these years Hayden's trading expeditions had taken him as far south as Sonora where he had many Indian fights. In 1872 he moved to this site, built a ferry and a flour mill, and opened a store that became the trading center for all the southern Salt River valley. His son, Carl Hayden, is (1939) a United States Senator.[11]

The thirty-three boomburb entries in the WPA Guides do have some common themes. Most of them refer to agriculture—as in *they grow such and such a crop or fruit in this town.* If industry is mentioned it is usually a rurally based one, such as grain processing. Many of today's bigger boomburbs also seemed to be trading centers for agricultural products back in the WPA era. Although by definition boomburbs are part of the nation's biggest metropolitan areas, the WPA Guides refer to only two boomburbs as suburbs in the 1930s. One is Garland (as cited above) and the other is Aurora, a suburb east of Denver. This odd finding may be a quirk of the writers, or it could indicate that many places now swept up into the twenty-first-century metropolis were once isolated farming villages. Both factors probably explain the lack of references made to boomburbs as suburbs.

The WPA Guides show how much the urban geography of Sunbelt America has shifted in the past sixty-plus years. For example, the Arizona Guide contains no mention of the big boomburb of Scottsdale, but Bisbee (now a kind of tourist ghost town) gets a full seven-page write-up complete with maps. Similarly, the now almost empty city of Goldfield (2000 population, 190) gets several pages in the Nevada WPA Guide, while the boomburbs of Henderson and North Las Vegas are not mentioned. In 1940 the

Southwest's old mining towns easily trumped the one-time farming outposts that are today's boomburbs.

The bottom-line finding from the historical documents—both the panoramic map collections and the WPA Guides—is that despite some impressive origin dates in the late nineteenth century, boomburbs are essentially new places. The majority of their buildings, industry, and people have been added in the post–World War II era—and in many cases even more recently. Boomburbs, which by 2000 would have a total population surpassing the entire Chicago region, were mostly scattered little cow towns in the first decades of the twentieth century.

Websites and Wikipedia

The most comprehensive history available on boomburbs comes from city websites and wikipedia, an online encyclopedia.[12] All fifty-four boomburbs had a city website as of May 2006.[13] Histories appear on thirty of the sites and range from a few perfunctory sentences to lengthy and detailed entries. These histories provide an additional context for examining boomburb origins. They indicate what boomburbs think about their past. Website histories also offer an interesting extension of those found in the WPA Guides. Recall the WPA pre–World War II depiction of a sleepy Sunnyvale, California. The passage below is taken from Sunnyvale's web history and notes the impact of the war.

> Without a doubt, World War II is the single most important event that changed history in Sunnyvale, the San Francisco Bay Area and all of California. Some people date the beginning of the defense era in Sunnyvale with the arrival of Lockheed Missiles & Space Company in 1956. But defense industry roots were planted much earlier because Sunnyvale has a long history of actively recruiting industry by offering land and labor.[14]

The website and wikipedia histories share several common themes. As might be expected, rapid population growth is the biggest topic. In fact, more of the websites mention fast growth (thirty-six) than have full city histories. The forces that sparked this growth are also major themes. The most frequently cited causes for growth are highways, defense industries, water, and annexation. One even lists air conditioning as a factor.

Highways apparently loom large in the Denver area, with both Aurora and Westminster website histories referring to them. Aurora's website says that "the 1970s were prosperous for Aurora with the city benefiting from new highway construction." Westminster's notes that "with a population of 1,686 in 1950, Westminster was still a quiet rural town northwest of Denver. That all changed when the Colorado State Highway Department began construction of the Denver-Boulder Turnpike, a toll-road that operated between the City of Boulder and the Valley Highway (I-25)."[15]

Or consider this entry from wikipedia.org on the role that transportation played in promoting economic development in Olathe, Kansas: "After the construction of the transcontinental railroad, the trails to the west lost importance, and Olathe faded back into obscurity and remained a small, sleepy prairie town until the 1950s. With the construction of the Interstate Highway system and, more directly, I-35, Olathe was directly linked to nearby Kansas City and began an economic boom that accelerated in the 1980s and continues today."

The military turned the San Diego region from an American outpost near Mexico into a strategic metropolis on the Pacific, populating its boomburbs in the process.

The Oceanside website has this to say:

World War II saw Oceanside grow from a sleepy little town to a modern city. With the construction of the nation's largest Marine Corps Base, Camp Pendleton, on her border, the demand for housing and municipal services exceeded supply. The best illustration of the tremendous growth of the city is found in the census figures. The population of Oceanside jumped from the 1940 figure of 4,652 to 12,888 in 1950. In 1952 a special census showed the city's population exceeding 18,000 as the Marine Base grew with the Korean War and more service-connected families moved into the area.[16]

According to Chula Vista's website,

World War II ushered in changes that would affect the city of Chula Vista forever. The principal reason was the relocation of Rohr Aircraft Corporation to Chula Vista in early 1941, just months before the attack on Pearl Harbor. Rohr employed 9,000 workers in the area at the height of its wartime production. With the demand for housing, the land never returned to being orchard groves again. The population of Chula Vista tripled from 5,000 residents in 1940 to more than 16,000 in 1950. After the war, many of the factory workers and thousands of servicemen stayed in the area resulting in the huge growth in population.[17]

The same kind of military-driven growth narratives appear in wikipedia. org. For example, consider the case of Clearwater, Florida:

> During World War II, Clearwater became a major training base for U.S. troops destined for Europe and the Pacific. Virtually every hotel in the area, including the historic Belleview Biltmore and Fort Harrison Hotel, became luxury barracks for new recruits. Vehicle traffic regularly stopped for companies of soldiers marching through downtown, and nighttime blackouts to confuse potential enemy bombers were common. The remote and isolated Dan's Island, now Sand Key, was used as a target for U.S. Army Air Corps fighter-bombers for strafing and bombing practice.

Of Fontana, California, wikipedia.org says, "Fontana was radically transformed during World War II by the construction of a steel mill belonging to the Henry J. Kaiser Company." A similar remark is made for the baby boomburb of Renton, Washington: "The town's population boomed during World War II when Boeing built a factory in Renton to produce the B-29 Superfortress. The factory has continued to operate since then, and still produces 737 aircraft. In 2001, 40% of all commercial aircraft were assembled in Renton. Boeing remains the largest employer in Renton."

As one would guess, water fed boomburb growth in the Southwest. This is especially true in the Central Valley of Arizona, where the Phoenix region, like the mythical bird, rose from the ashes of a lost Native American civilization—the Hohokam. The trick Phoenix used was rebuilding the ancient canal system left by the Hohokam. In Mesa, the Mormons got the water flowing early. Its website notes that "water entered the canals in April of 1878."[18] Two early twentieth-century major dam projects greatly enhanced the supply of water to Phoenix—Roosevelt Dam to the northeast and Hoover Dam (originally Boulder Dam) to the northwest. Both of these dams, and the lakes they formed, are often cited in metro Phoenix boomburb website histories. In fact, so many boomburbs around Phoenix mention water and canals one might think the place were Venice, Italy.

As their regions developed, boomburbs gobbled up unincorporated land wherever they could. Gilbert, Arizona, for example, aggressively expanded well beyond its original borders: "Gilbert began to take its current shape during the 1970s when the Town Council approved a strip annexation that encompassed 53 square miles of county land. Although the population was only 1,971 in 1970 the Council realized that Gilbert would eventually grow and develop much like the neighboring communities of Tempe, Mesa, and Chandler."[19] For Gilbert the plan apparently worked, because this boomburb is now the fastest-growing U.S. city above 100,000 residents so far in this decade.

Scottsdale, Arizona's, website notes the role that air conditioning played in its growth and gets a plug in at the same time for its high quality of life.

> The small community attracted rattlesnakes and artists for its first few decades of life until the air conditioning revolution of the fifties. Suddenly, nearby Phoenix exploded with retirees and real estate salesmen and swallowed Scottsdale into the urban agglomeration along with several other formerly independent towns. Scottsdale managed to rise above the riff-raff, however, and emerged as one of the West's most desirable communities beginning in 1956, when *Life* magazine rated it amongst the country's best addresses.[20]

The websites also share some funny and telling stories about the road from small towns to big suburbs. Consider the passage below about how Chandler, Arizona, reoriented its town center to accommodate cars.

> By the late 1930s, Chandler was experiencing some problems spurred by growth and technology. Drivers of the new faster cars sometimes didn't realize that Arizona Avenue then ended at the town plaza. Cars often jumped the curb and drove right into the park. And the large diesel trucks that made deliveries to businesses around the park had trouble navigating the narrow roads around the plaza. In 1940, the state proposed to align Route 87 down Arizona Avenue. Residents were not happy to see their beautiful park divided in half for a highway, but the town's original design was no longer safe or practical.[21]

Chandler was not the type of place to let sentimentality over a town square stand in the way of progress. To this day, Arizona Avenue splits Chandler's little downtown in half and breaks up just about the only pedestrian-friendly area in the boomburb.

Another amusing tale is of the time the whole town of Henderson, Nevada, was put on the auction block, to be sold as military surplus after World War II. "Henderson was actually 'born in America's defense' ten years prior to its incorporation during World War II with the building of the Basic Magnesium Plant. . . . In 1947 the United States War Asset Administration actually offered Henderson for sale as war surplus property. . . . With the help of local industry, the City of Henderson, Nevada, was officially incorporated on April 16, 1953."[22] The reason Henderson was not mentioned in the 1930s Nevada WPA Guide is that it was a product of the federal government during the war and thus did not yet exist. What was once army surplus is now the second largest city in Nevada, an appropriate status for a city in a state whose motto is "Battle Born."

Coral Springs, Florida, apparently began as a large World's Fair exhibit. The city of the future was conceived of as the home of the future: "In 1966, Westinghouse Electric Corporation acquired Coral Ridge Properties (the master planned community that eventually became Coral Springs) so that they could use the new City as an 'urban laboratory' to evaluate new products, such as a home utility center, home sewage disposal systems, an infrared heating system, full electric kitchens, and central air-conditioning and heating systems."[23]

Commenting on the master-planned community of Green Valley, in Henderson, Nevada, David Guterson observes that cities used to make products but that now the city itself is the product.[24] It certainly seems that way in Coral Springs: it was quite literally a product of corporate America. In the 1960s General Electric showcased its new consumer goods in its Carousel of Progress at Disneyland in Anaheim; Westinghouse had the whole town of Coral Springs with which to experiment. It sounds like something out of a *Twilight Zone* episode, the one where a couple wakes up to find themselves in a modern subdivision with no people. Another odd thing: Why test home heating systems in south Florida?

Finally, one boomburb admits that its whole existence was due to a desire not to pay taxes into Los Angeles County:

> The City of Santa Clarita was formed by incorporation on December 15, 1987. The achievement of a new city was a 20-plus-year process that actually began with the goal of creating a new county. Although the proposal for a new city was met with resistance, the popular vote brought Los Angeles a new city by a landslide vote. The ability to keep local tax dollars local was a huge reason why the City incorporated and continues to be a big reason for this City's success.[25]

Santa Clarita, one of the nation's newest boomburbs, was looking to keep a big taxpayer—Six Flags Magic Mountain theme park. The city's history can best be summed up by the title from a 1996 John Carpenter film, *Escape from LA*.

Boomburbs: Inventions of the Modern Era

Just as the great industrial cities were built on their era's cutting-edge technologies—structural steel, elevators, streetcars—so boomburbs got a boost from a new wave of invention. They are an outgrowth of major innovations such as air conditioning, big dams, low-down-payment mortgages, tract-style houses, and limited-access freeways. Places can exist without these innovations—indeed, many of them do—but they are not boomburbs. They are villages or, at best, small cities.

Boomburbs also got a big lift from the federal government. This came in the form of direct investment (defense plants and army bases), infrastructure (dams and interstates), and subsidies (federally subsidized home mortgages and state road bonds). Excellent histories of suburban development have been written by authors such as Kenneth Jackson, Robert Fishman, and Dolores Hayden that document the important role played by the federal government in fostering rapid growth.[26] As the nation's biggest suburbs, boomburbs were especially affected by the federal government's role.

In 1999 the Fannie Mae Foundation commissioned a survey of urban historians on the key influences that shaped the American metropolis in the second half of the twentieth century.[27] The survey asked respondents to rank a set of twenty-five influences by the impact they had in shaping metropolitan development. The result is the list below of the top ten of these influences ranked by order of impact:

—The 1956 Interstate Highway Act
—Federal Housing Administration (FHA) mortgages
—The deindustrialization of central cities
—Urban renewal
—Levittown (the mass-produced suburban tract house)
—Racial segregation and job discrimination
—Enclosed shopping malls
—Sunbelt-style sprawl
—Air conditioning
—Urban riots of the 1960s

Five of these influences supported boomburb growth: interstates, air conditioning, tract-style homes, enclosed shopping malls, and FHA mortgages. Sprawl is what boomburbs became (which in turn served as an influence on suburban development in the rest of the United States): boomburbs were cited as the poster child for Sunbelt-style sprawl by the historians who conducted this survey.

Boomburb Population Growth, 1930 to 2000

This section looks at boomburb and baby boomburb population changes, showing their rise from small towns to big suburbs. The population analysis is broken into three main growth periods: 1930 to 1950, 1950 to 1970, and 1970 to 2000.

Depression and War: The Growth of Boomburbs, 1930 to 1950

During the Depression and the war years of the 1930s and 1940s, most boomburbs were either small or did not exist. However, enough data are available from the era to track population gains in many of these places. For many boomburbs this period was a warmup act for the real growth surge that was to follow in the postwar years. But in other places the rapid expansion that would become even more visible in the postwar years had already begun in earnest.

Table 2-1 shows population growth from 1930 to 1950 for thirty-one of the fifty-four boomburbs.[28] The cities collectively shared strong growth, considering that the United States during the 1930s registered its slowest growth rate since the census began collecting population data in 1790. The median (or midpoint) in growth for the group was 132.6 percent, more than doubling in size in just two decades. Nearly all of these gains came in the 1940s, especially in those places that played a major role in the World War II effort. Most of the 1930–50 growth occurred in the latter decade. All but a few of the older boomburbs have seen double-digit growth for six straight decades.

There were four "big" boomburbs in 1930: San Bernardino, Santa Ana, Riverside, and Salem. As noted earlier, all four were government centers. These four government-dominated cities remained the biggest boomburbs of 1950, but by 2000 only Santa Ana, the seat of Orange County's government, remained among the four biggest boomburbs (behind Mesa, Arizona).

The five fastest-growing boomburbs during the war and Depression years are found in five different metropolitan areas—Dallas, Miami, Denver, Los Angeles, and Phoenix. The next five are all in the West. Their website histories seem to show one overriding theme explaining this rapid expansion: the war. The histories often note specifically that most of their growth came post-1940 rather than in the Depression years of the 1930s.

Consider Grand Prairie, Texas, the fastest-growing boomburb in table 2-1: it had over an eightfold increase in just the 1940s (the 1930 population figure was unavailable). The Texas State Historical Association's history of the city attributes the boom to one major aviation facility located there in 1940.

> The area just east of Grand Prairie was chosen as the site for a federally operated defense plant, North American Aviation, Incorporated.

Table 2-1. Boomburb Growth, 1930–50, by Percent Change

Boomburb[a]	Metropolitan area	Population, 1930	Population, 1950	Population change	Percent change
Grand Prairie	Dallas	1,595[b]	14,594	12,999	815.0
Hialeah	Miami	2,610	19,676	17,066	653.9
Aurora	Denver	2,295	11,421	9,126	397.6
Thousand Oaks	Los Angeles	251	1,243	992	395.2
Mesa	Phoenix	3,741	16,790	13,049	348.8
Chula Vista	San Diego	3,896	15,927	12,031	308.8
Oceanside	San Diego	3,508	12,881	9,373	267.2
Oxnard	Los Angeles	6,285	21,567	15,282	243.2
Sunnyvale	San Francisco	3,094	9,829	6,735	217.7
Tempe	Phoenix	2,495	7,684	5,189	208.0
Chandler	Phoenix	1,378	3,799	2,421	175.7
Mesquite	Dallas	729	1,696	967	132.6
Lancaster	Los Angeles	1,550	3,594	2,044	131.9
Glendale	Phoenix	3,665	8,179	4,514	123.2
Arlington	Dallas	3,661	7,692	4,031	110.1
Clearwater	Tampa	7607	15,581	7,974	104.8
Daly City	San Francisco	7,838	15,191	7,353	93.8
Escondido	San Diego	3,421	6,544	3,123	91.3
Ontario	Los Angeles	12,583	22,872	10,289	81.8
San Bernardino	Los Angeles	36,486	63,058	26,572	72.8
Santa Rosa	San Francisco	10,636	17,902	7,266	68.3
Salem	Portland	26,266	43,140	16,874	64.2
Riverside	Los Angeles	29,696	46,764	17,068	57.5
Santa Ana	Los Angeles	30,322	45,533	15,211	50.2
Naperville	Chicago	5,118	7,013	1,895	37.0
Anaheim	Los Angeles	10,995	14,556	3,561	32.4
Fullerton	Los Angeles	10,860	13,958	3,098	28.5
Corona	Los Angeles	8,101	10,223	2,122	26.2
Orange	Los Angeles	8,066	10,027	1,961	24.3
Plano	Dallas	1,554	1,696	142	9.1
Garland	Dallas	1,584	1,610	26	1.6
Total or median		175,286	492,240	316,954	132.6

Source: WPA Guides; U.S. census; city websites; city technical reports.
a. Boomburbs not listed either do not have 1930 data or were not included in the 1950 census.
b. The figure is for 1940. The city had a 1925 population of 1,263.

By 1941 the plant had 5,000 employees. This led to a severe housing shortage in Grand Prairie and the formation of the Grand Prairie Housing Authority. The city rushed to provide services and expanded utilities, built new schools, increased fire protection, and implemented city mail service. At its peak production the airplane plant employed 38,500 workers.[29]

As web histories for Chula Vista and Oceanside note (see passages above), World War II brought rapid growth to their cities as well in the form of military bases and defense plants. The same was true for Oxnard, north of Los Angeles, and Sunnyvale, in the Bay Area. The other fast-growing boomburbs in table 2-1 had diverse reasons for their big gains. Mesa expanded—literally—in this period by annexing several towns around it, starting in 1931. Hialeah benefited from spillover growth from Miami, as Aurora benefited from spillover from Denver. The small town of Thousand Oaks, California, had nowhere else to go but up (or more likely out). The "city" had just 251 residents in 1930 and was, as the California WPA Guide describes, "a gathering of tourist accommodations around the Goebel Lion Farm (admission 25¢), which supplies many animals used by movie studios. In the afternoon between 3:30 and 5:00 the trainer sometimes obliges spectators by putting his head into a lion's mouth."[30] Although Thousand Oaks nearly quadrupled during the 1930s and 1940s, it still gained less than a thousand people. That is still solid growth when the chief economic development engine is a circus act.

On the flip side of the growth spectrum were the Dallas-area boomburbs of Plano and Garland. These are the only two cities that failed to achieve double-digit growth from 1930 to 1950, and thus their boom clearly begins in the postwar years. The fact that the top and bottom gainers were in the same metropolitan area indicates how fickle development can be. Plano and Garland lacked war industries and had yet to fully flourish as suburbs. It also did not help Garland that it had to spend the 1930s (a time of limited credit supply) rebuilding after the devastating tornado of 1927. Grand Prairie may have been in the same situation as Plano and Garland were if not for its selection as the site of a big defense plant. Or it may have grown strongly, if not spectacularly, such as Mesquite and Arlington.

The thirty-one boomburbs for which there were data available in 1930 had, together, just over 175,000 people. That same year, one good-sized traditional city, such as Akron, Ohio (with over 250,000 people), or Jersey City (with over 300,000 residents), easily beat the bunch. By 1950 these same boomburbs had nearly a half million people and had gained over 300,000 of them in just the previous two decades. This was impressive population growth, but the thirty-one boomburbs in table 2-1 still had less total population in 1950 than Cincinnati, Ohio, with just over a half million residents. But that was soon to dramatically change.

Highways and Housing: Growth of Boomburbs, 1950 to 1970

As noted above, the stars seemed to line up for rapid boomburb growth by 1950. During the next two decades, the thirty-seven boomburbs for which there are 1950 data would collectively more than quintuple in population—adding almost 2 million more residents. The 1970s also mark the first time that any of the boomburbs show up on the list of the hundred biggest U.S. cities. In 1970 Anaheim ranked eighty-second, Santa Ana hit eighty-seventh, and Riverside reached the ninety-seventh spot. Table 2-2 shows that seven boomburbs exceeded a 1,000 percent growth rate from 1950 to 1970. Another ten cities expanded by more than 500 percent. The really big gains were in Texas, California, Arizona, and Nevada.

The 1950s and 1960s were boom times in the Dallas region. Only one of the region's seven boomburbs failed to at least quintuple in population. Growth in the Dallas boomburbs of Irving, Mesquite, and Arlington took off. Both Irving and Mesquite registered over a 3,000 percent increase in population. Arlington followed with an almost 2,800 percent gain. The three boomburbs jumped from villages to decent-sized cities in just twenty years. By 1970 any one of the three boomburbs was big enough to anchor its own metropolitan area. Irving had practically overtaken the slower growing San Bernardino, one of the original four big boomburbs. The city was ready to make its next big move to steal the Cowboys football franchise from Dallas.

Scottsdale, Arizona, similarly leapt from a small town to midsize city in just two decades. This boomburb was once an artists' colony made famous for being home to the great architect Frank Lloyd Wright. Like the elderly snowbirds that would soon fill Scottsdale, Wright came to the city late in life to escape the harsh Midwest winters. Wright liked the weather so much that he built a Western version of his beloved Wisconsin Taliesin studios in Scottsdale during the 1930s. In locating his complex in a remote corner of the town at the foot the McDowell Mountains, Wright is reputed to have said "find your ideal country location, and then go ten miles further on out."[31]

Wright's intent was to put as many miles as he could between his studios and the city so that he could maintain his solitude. He died in 1959, having lived about halfway through Scottsdale's transformation into a booming, upscale suburb of Phoenix. Wright could not have liked what he saw in his final years, but at least he did not live long enough to see what was to come. Today, affluent, master-planned communities (complete with fancy golf courses) sweep around Wright's Taliesin West on three sides. The main arterial road running through all of this new (and very un-Wright-like development) is Frank Lloyd Wright Boulevard. It turns out that ten miles might not be enough distance "further on out" to find solitude when you live in what will soon become a boomburb. As the inventor of the Broadacre City concept, Wright should have known better. Broadacre City was a model for an auto-dependent and spread-out, twentieth-century metropolis, which Wright introduced in 1932 in his book *The Disappearing City*.

Table 2-2. Boomburb Growth, 1950–70, by Percent Change

Boomburb[a]	Metropolitan area	Population, 1950	Population, 1970	Population change	Percent change
Irving	Dallas	2,621	97,280	94,659	3,611.6
Scottsdale	Phoenix	2,032	67,839	65,807	3,238.5
Mesquite	Dallas	1,696	55,209	53,513	3,155.2
Thousand Oaks	Los Angeles	1,243	35,935	34,692	2,791.0
Arlington	Dallas	7,692	91,473	83,781	1,089.2
Westminster	Denver	1,686	19,359	17,673	1,048.2
Anaheim	Los Angeles	14,556	166,701	152,145	1,045.2
Sunnyvale	San Francisco	9,829	95,200	85,371	868.6
North Las Vegas	Las Vegas	3,875	36,216	32,341	834.6
Lancaster	Los Angeles	3,594	32,570	28,976	806.2
Carrollton	Dallas	1,610	13,870	12,260	761.5
Plano	Dallas	2,126	17,872	15,746	740.6
Tempe	Phoenix	7,684	62,876	55,192	718.3
Orange	Los Angeles	10,027	77,292	67,265	670.8
Garland	Dallas	10,571	81,324	70,753	669.3
Aurora	Denver	11,421	74,868	63,447	555.5
Fullerton	Los Angeles	13,958	85,919	71,961	515.6
Escondido	San Diego	6,544	36,792	30,248	462.2
Hialeah	Miami	19,676	102,136	82,460	419.1
Fremont	San Francisco	22,000	100,875	78,875	358.5
Glendale	Phoenix	8,179	36,305	28,126	343.9
Daly City	San Francisco	15,191	67,246	52,055	342.7
Chula Vista	San Diego	15,927	67,777	51,850	325.5
Mesa	Phoenix	16,790	62,929	46,139	274.8
Chandler	Phoenix	3,799	13,747	9,948	261.9
Grand Prairie	Dallas	14,594	50,907	36,313	248.8
Santa Ana	Los Angeles	45,533	156,601	111,068	243.9
Naperville	Chicago	7,013	23,850	16,837	240.1
Clearwater	Tampa	15,581	51,624	36,043	231.3
Oxnard	Los Angeles	21,567	69,783	48,216	223.6
Oceanside	San Diego	12,881	40,491	27,610	214.3
Riverside	Los Angeles	46,764	140,089	93,325	199.6
Ontario	Los Angeles	22,872	64,105	41,233	180.3
Santa Rosa	San Francisco	17,902	49,873	31,971	178.6
Corona	Los Angeles	10,223	27,506	17,283	169.1
San Bernardino	Los Angeles	63,058	104,394	41,336	65.6
Salem	Portland	43,140	68,249	25,109	58.2
Total or median		535,455	2,447,082	1,911,627	419

Source: U.S. census.

a. This table contains only the thirty-eight boomburbs that had data for 1950.

Five years later Wright moved to what would become Scottsdale. The city is now Broadacre incarnate. In an ironic twist of history, Wright's own Broadacre City swallowed his beloved Taliesin West.

While Irving, Scottsdale, and Mesquite all expanded the fastest from 1950 to 1970, the city to add the most people was Anaheim. The city picked up 152,145 new citizens in just two decades, jumping from 14,556 inhabitants in 1950 to 166,701 by 1970. Only one other boomburb, neighboring Santa

Ana, gained more than 100,000 new residents. In 1970, six boomburbs (of an eventual fifty-four by 2000) had populations exceeding 100,000. Three of the six could be found just in Southern California.

Anaheim, like Scottsdale, is another case of a city whose prospects were tied to an American visionary. But where Wright sought solitude, Walt Disney hoped to attract a crowd. Even though Disney put his now-famous theme park, Disneyland, in the then small town of Anaheim, he, like Wright, was soon hemmed in by development. Surrounding the park, just several years after it opened in 1955, was strip development that would make Las Vegas proud.[32] When people reached the top of the Matterhorn rollercoaster, they saw not the Alps but rather a sea of subdivisions. Disney grew so frustrated by the honky-tonk commercialism around his Disneyland in Anaheim that he decided to start from scratch on a new theme park on forty-seven square miles of land (about the size of San Francisco) in central Florida. He, like Wright, had underestimated the growth potential of boomburbs.

Rise of the New Sunbelt: Growth of Boomburbs, 1970 to 2000

By the 1970s people were picking up on the fact that vast, new, sprawling cities were on the rise in the southern rim of the nation and that these places were now rivaling the traditional urban centers of the Northeast and Midwest.[33] One of the first issues was the shift in political power toward these still upstart places. As the author Michael Lind notes, "In the 1970s, Kevin Phillips, Kirkpatrick Sale, and other observers of American politics predicted the rise of 'the Sun Belt' (Phillips coined the term). The region included California and the Southwest as well as states on the periphery of the South such as Texas and Florida. Indeed, in the early 1970s such a shift appeared to be well under way."[34] At this stage in the Sunbelt's development, the focus remained on New York versus Los Angeles, or Chicago versus Dallas—the old Eastern establishment of Boston versus the "Oil Club" of Houston, their downtown versus our downtown.

But as the Sunbelt grew, its original centers began to age. Just as Northeastern and Midwestern cities had their local rivals in the suburbs, so did Sunbelt cities. At first it was barely noticeable—in part, because the centers and edges of these regions seemed alike (and remain more alike than other parts of the country). Yet in the past two to three decades, as boomburbs became political players in their regions, differences became more apparent. Boomburbs became the older Sunbelt's new Sunbelt. The center of Dallas or Denver looks different from that of Plano or Peoria. The "new urbanists," with their love of walkable places and mixed uses, find many parts of these cities, such as LoDo (short for Lower Downtown) in Denver and

Deep Ellum in Dallas, to be wonderful places. Even the older Encanto-Palmcroft section of sprawling Phoenix, built mostly in the 1920s, would bring a smile to a new urbanist. But most boomburbs feature very few of these types of neighborhood. In fact, most of what they have to offer would almost certainly make a new urbanist frown.

Boomburbs finally emerged as major places in the last three decades of the twentieth century. By 2000 fifteen boomburbs had a place on the list of the hundred cities with the most population; they ranged from Mesa in the forty-second spot to Irving, which squeaked onto the list in the hundredth place. In the 1950s New Yorkers found it difficult to accept losing their beloved baseball teams the Giants (to San Francisco) and Dodgers (to Los Angeles) to what they saw as outposts on the Pacific. But by the 1970s Washington was losing its baseball team to the boomburb of Arlington, Texas. That had to hurt.

As table 2-3 shows, boomburbs gained nearly 6 million residents from 1970 to 2000, adding almost the equivalent of a good-sized state such as Indiana (fourteenth-ranked in population) in just thirty years. Conversely, the thirty-six decliner cities tracked by Robert Lang and Patrick Simmons—places ranging from New York to Worcester, Massachusetts—lost about 3.5 million residents in just the 1970s, or the rough equivalent of a state such as Connecticut.[35]

Seven Boomburbs shot up more than 1,000 percent in the last three decades. Three of these were in the Phoenix region. Gilbert and Peoria grew over 5,000 percent and 2,000 percent, respectively. But the highest flyer was Coral Springs, Florida; Westinghouse's one-time consumer testing lab logged a remarkable 7,795 percent growth rate. The place jumped from 1,489 people in 1970 to 117,549 by 2000.

The midpoint for growth from 1970 to 2000 (or three decades) actually lagged the period 1950 to 1970 (or just two decades). Two reasons appear to explain this difference. Very fast growth was more evenly distributed among boomburbs in the 1950s and 1960s as these places were just starting to take off. The other reason for the difference concerns compounding. It is easy to grow over 1,000 percent when places start out with just a few thousand people. Notice in table 2-1 that all five of the fastest-growing cities had fewer than 10,000 people to start. Five places picked up at least 100,000 new citizens by 2000. These late bloomers began to catch up with many older and more established boomburbs by adding a comparable number of people.

In terms of actual people gained from 1970 to 2000, exactly half of boomburbs (twenty-seven) gained at least 100,000 new residents. Three

Table 2-3. Boomburb Growth, 1970–2000, by Percent Change

Boomburb[a]	Metropolitan area	Population, 1970	Population, 2000	Population change	Percent change
Coral Springs	Miami	1,489	117,549	116,060	7,794.5
Gilbert	Phoenix	1,971	109,697	107,726	5,465.6
Peoria	Phoenix	4,730	108,364	103,634	2,191.0
Rancho Cucamonga	Los Angeles	5,796	127,743	121,947	2,104.0
Palmdale	Los Angeles	8,511	116,670	108,159	1,270.8
Chandler	Phoenix	13,747	176,581	162,834	1,184.5
Plano	Dallas	17,872	222,030	204,158	1,142.3
Henderson	Las Vegas	16,395	175,381	158,986	969.7
Irvine	Los Angeles	14,231	143,072	128,841	905.4
Pembroke Pines	Miami	15,589	137,427	121,838	781.6
Carrollton	Dallas	13,870	109,576	95,706	690.0
Moreno Valley	Los Angeles	18,871	142,381	123,510	654.5
Mesa	Phoenix	62,929	396,375	333,446	529.9
Fontana	Los Angeles	20,568	128,929	108,361	526.8
Glendale	Phoenix	36,305	218,812	182,507	502.7
Naperville	Chicago	23,850	128,358	104,508	438.2
Westminster	Denver	19,359	100,940	81,581	421.4
Corona	Los Angeles	27,506	124,966	97,460	354.3
Oceanside	San Diego	40,491	161,029	120,538	297.7
Aurora	Denver	74,868	276,393	201,525	269.2
Lancaster	Los Angeles	32,570	118,718	86,148	264.5
Arlington	Dallas	91,473	332,969	241,496	264.0
Escondido	San Diego	36,792	133,559	96,767	263.0
Thousand Oaks	Los Angeles	35,935	117,005	81,070	225.6
North Las Vegas	Las Vegas	36,216	115,488	79,272	218.9
Scottsdale	Phoenix	67,839	202,705	134,866	198.8
Santa Rosa	San Francisco	49,873	147,595	97,722	195.9
Garland	Dallas	81,324	215,768	134,444	165.3

(continued)

cities, Plano and Arlington, Texas, and Aurora, Colorado, added over 200,000 people, while Mesa picked up a whopping 333,446 inhabitants. That is the equivalent to adding a Cincinnati or Pittsburgh to Mesa's population.

The Best Decades for Growth, 1970 to 2000

While all boomburbs have been growing at double-digit rates for at least three straight decades (and for all those with 1950 starting dates, five decades), growth rates of individual cities change from one decade to the next. Table 2-4 shows decade (1970s, 1980s, or 1990s) that each of the fifty-four boomburbs had their highest population growth. Twelve places had their strongest growth in the 1970s, twenty-five in the 1980s, and seventeen in the 1990s.

All three Denver-area boomburbs saw their strongest growth in the 1970s. But only one each of the seven Phoenix and Dallas boomburbs had

Table 2-3. Boomburb Growth, 1970–2000, by Percent Change *(continued)*

Boomburb[a]	Metropolitan area	Population, 1970	Population, 2000	Population change	Percent change
Chula Vista	San Diego	67,777	173,556	105,779	156.1
Tempe	Phoenix	62,876	158,625	95,749	152.3
Grand Prairie	Dallas	50,907	127,427	76,520	150.3
Ontario	Los Angeles	64,105	158,007	93,902	146.5
Oxnard	Los Angeles	69,783	170,358	100,575	144.1
Mesquite	Dallas	55,209	124,523	69,314	125.5
Chesapeake	Norfolk	89,580	199,184	109,604	122.4
Hialeah	Miami	102,136	226,419	124,283	121.7
Santa Ana	Los Angeles	156,601	337,977	181,376	115.8
Clearwater	Tampa	51,624	108,787	57,163	110.7
Fremont	San Francisco	100,875	203,413	102,538	101.6
Salem	Portland	68,249	136,924	68,675	100.6
Irving	Dallas	97,280	191,615	94,335	97.0
Anaheim	Los Angeles	166,701	328,014	161,313	96.8
Simi Valley	Los Angeles	56,676	111,351	54,675	96.5
Riverside	Los Angeles	140,089	255,166	115,077	82.1
Bellevue	Seattle	61,331	109,569	48,238	78.7
San Bernardino	Los Angeles	104,394	185,401	81,007	77.6
Orange	Los Angeles	77,292	128,821	51,529	66.7
Lakewood	Denver	92,716	144,126	51,410	55.4
Daly City	San Francisco	67,246	103,621	36,375	54.1
West Valley City	Salt Lake City	72,378[a]	108,896	36,518	50.5
Costa Mesa	Los Angeles	72,729	108,724	35,995	49.5
Fullerton	Los Angeles	85,919	126,003	40,084	46.7
Sunnyvale	San Francisco	95,200	131,760	36,560	38.4
Santa Clarita	Los Angeles	110,642[a]	151,088	40,446	36.6
Total or median		3,111,285	8,915,435	5,804,150	181

Source: U.S. census.

a. 1990 data.

their best decade in the 1970s. Additionally, only three of nineteen boomburbs in the Los Angeles metropolitan area added their most new people over that decade.

The 1980s were a big growth era for Dallas's boomburbs. Five of the region's seven boomburbs picked up their most new residents ever. All three San Diego boomburbs did the same in the 1980s. Los Angeles saw a dozen of its boomburbs reach their peak population gains during the decade. The 1980s may turn out to be the strongest period of growth ever in California. The California economy performed remarkably well over the decade, barely even slowing down for an early 1980s' national recession.

The 1990s were another story. Much of Southern California was stuck in a 1990s' recession for at least half the decade. Home prices peaked in the region in 1991 and in many cases did not recover these highs until very late in the 1990s. The Bay Area saw stronger economic growth, reaching a climax in the dot.com boom at decade's end.

Table 2-4. Boomburbs, 1970–2000, Decade of Most Growth in Population

1970s	*1980s*	*1990s*
Aurora, Colorado	Arlington, Texas	Anaheim, California
Clearwater, Florida	Carrollton, Texas	Bellevue, Washington
Fullerton, California	Chula Vista, California	Chandler, Arizona
Garland, Texas	Coral Springs, Florida	Chesapeake, Virginia
Glendale, Arizona	Costa Mesa, California	Corona, California
Hialeah, Florida	Daly City, California	Gilbert, Arizona
Lakewood, Colorado	Escondido, California	Henderson, Nevada
Oxnard, California	Fontana, California	North Las Vegas, Nevada
Rancho Cucamonga,	Fremont, California	Pembroke Pines, Florida
California	Grand Prairie, Texas	Peoria, Arizona
Tempe, Arizona	Irvine, California	Plano, Texas
Thousand Oaks, California	Irving, Texas	Salem, Oregon
Westminster, Colorado	Lancaster, California	Santa Clarita, California
	Mesa, Arizona	Santa Rosa, California
	Mesquite, Texas	Scottsdale, Arizona
	Moreno Valley, California	Sunnyvale, California
	Naperville, Illinois	West Valley City, Utah
	Oceanside, California	
	Ontario, California	
	Orange, California	
	Palmdale, California	
	Riverside, California	
	San Bernardino, California	
	Santa Ana, California	
	Simi Valley, California	

Source: U.S. census.

The Phoenix and Las Vegas metropolitan areas have been gathering momentum for the past fifty years and are now the fastest growing among U.S. metropolitan areas of over a million population. This growth is reflected in the gains made by boomburbs in both places during the past decade. Both Las Vegas and four Phoenix boomburbs picked up their most new residents ever in the 1990s. The technology boom that started in San Francisco and lifted two of its boomburbs to their biggest population gains during the 1990s also helped the Portland metropolitan area. Salem had its best decade for adding new residents in the 1990s after seeing its growth slowing down for decades.

Boomburbs by Metropolitan Area

Los Angeles, with nineteen, has the highest number of boomburbs and biggest cumulative boomburb population for 2000 (table 2-5). But metropolitan Los Angeles (with over 16 million people) is so large that its boomburbs account for just less than one in five residents. Yet at over 3 million residents, the boomburb total approaches the city of Los Angeles in population, which has about 3.7 million people. More important, boomburbs

Table 2-5. Metropolitan Areas, by Boomburb Population as Percent of Total Population

Metropolitan area	Number of boomburbs	Boomburb population	Metro area population	Boomburb populations as percent of metro area population
Phoenix	7	1,371,159	3,251,876	42.2
Dallas	7	1,323,908	5,221,801	25.4
Denver	3	521,459	2,582,506	20.2
Los Angeles	19	3,080,394	16,373,645	18.8
Las Vegas	2	290,869	1,563,282	18.6
San Diego	3	468,144	2,813,833	16.6
Norfolk	1	199,184	1,569,541	12.7
Miami	3	481,395	3,876,380	12.4
San Francisco	4	586,389	7,039,362	8.3
Salt Lake City	1	108,896	1,333,914	8.2
Portland	1	136,924	2,265,223	6.0
Tampa	1	108,787	2,395,977	4.5
Seattle	1	109,569	3,554,760	3.1
Chicago	1	128,358	9,157,540	1.4
Total or average	54	8,915,435	62,999,640	14.2

Source: U.S. census.

keep adding a substantial number of new residents to greater Los Angeles, while the city itself has mostly leveled off in terms of growth.

At 42.2 percent in 2000, Phoenix has by far the highest percentage of its metropolitan population living in boomburbs. Phoenix, with seven (tied with Dallas), follows Los Angeles in number of boomburbs. The region also contains the second highest number of residents living in boomburbs. The Phoenix area has 1.37 million people living in boomburbs, which slightly exceeds the number of people living in the city of Phoenix. Again, as in Los Angeles, the seven Phoenix boomburbs (which in 1950 were more like the Seven Dwarfs) account for much of the region's new growth.

Dallas, Denver, Las Vegas, and San Diego also have large proportions of boomburb residents. Boomburbs in these places exceed the central cities of Dallas and Denver. Boomburbs around San Diego are also greatly outstripping the city in terms of growth. In Las Vegas, boomburbs gained people even faster than their central city—and in Las Vegas that is no small feat.

"Almost" Boomburbs

A bunch of cities did not quite meet the qualifications to be an official boomburb, but these places are worth considering because they illustrate how fleeting growth can be: some of these cities have been growing at a double-digit growth rate for the past two, but not three, censuses. If they maintain another decade of growth at this rate, these cities will shift from almost boomburbs to the real deal.

The "almost" city that was the very closest to becoming a boomburb is Aurora, in suburban Chicago. Aurora was made famous in the popular culture in the 1980s and 1990s as home to Wayne Campbell in the film *Wayne's World*. The movie depicts Aurora as an aggressively suburban place and home to people who seem to have a rather extended adolescence. Apparently the fame came too late to help Aurora in the 1970s, because the city grew at just under 10 percent (9.28 percent, to be precise), thereby not qualifying as a boomburb by a hair. The cutoff had to be made somewhere, but Aurora is unofficially a boomburb.

Other places with below 10 percent growth rates that subsequently boomed since 1980 include three more Los Angeles suburbs and one more San Francisco suburb: Downey, Garden Grove, Pomona, and Haywood (in the Bay Area). The first two places likely had slow 1970s growth because they were then older, declining suburbs. But the landmark 1965 Immigration Act would soon transform these places. Downey, in a belt of eastern Los Angeles County's industrial towns, and Garden Grove, in increasingly dense and diverse northern Orange County, became home to numerous immigrants and their children in two decades (a situation also shared by Haywood). Pomona, at Los Angeles County's border with Inland Empire County San Bernardino, grew moderately in the 1970s, with over 6 percent growth, but could not match such nearby boomburbs as Rancho Cucamonga and Ontario.

Other places missed being boomburbs because their growth either slowed in the 1990s or they went through a boom-bust-boom cycle. Two suburbs that were likely caught in the energy downturn and the savings and loan crisis of the 1980s were Arvada, Colorado (in suburban Denver), and Pasadena, Texas (in suburban Houston). Both these places dipped below 10 percent growth in the 1980s. Three other Denver boomburbs hung on to double-digit growth, but as shown above, not one of these places had their best decade in the 1980s.

Ventura, California, had strong growth in the 1970s and 1980s (and in the 1940s, 1950s, and 1960s), but the city apparently has had enough and is now saying no to more development. In the early 1990s the city enacted restrictions that simply shut down new housing construction.[36] The effect was to drop Ventura's population gains from 27 percent in the 1970s, and 25 percent in the 1980s, to 9 percent by the 1990s. The city just missed being a boomburb, which would probably be interpreted as something of a victory by Ventura residents.

Finally, one city grew below 10 percent in both the 1970s and 1980s and then skyrocketed in the 1990s—Vancouver, Washington, in suburban Portland. The city exploded by over 200 percent in the 1990s, jumping from 46,380 residents in 1990 to 143,560 people by 2000. This growth is so strong that it might even qualify the place as one of Dolores Hayden's zoomburbs.[37] Vancouver is worth mentioning because its development is caught up in the debate over growth management in the Portland metropolitan area.

The Portland, Oregon, region is famous for its urban growth boundary, designed to prevent low-density development in the area's metropolitan fringe. There is an extensive literature on how Portland's growth management works.[38] But because Vancouver, Washington, is directly across the Columbia River from Portland, Oregon (which is to say, in another state), the city was not included in the region's urban growth boundary and was thus free to boom—and boom it did. Carl Abbott refers to Vancouver as a release valve on the Portland region because it absorbed much of the area's demand for large-lot subdivision, which the Portland urban growth boundary prevented.[39] But Washington has enacted state land use regulation similar to Oregon's, so the Vancouver release valve is now closed. The city is unlikely to see 1990s-era growth rates for a long time, if ever again.

Baby Boomburb Population Growth, 1970 to 2000

The Sugarland Express is a 1974 film with the actress Goldie Hawn as the heroine who breaks her husband out of prison so that the two can regain custody of their child, who is in foster care.[40] The couple race to the town of Sugar Land through lonely Texas back roads toward a place that sounded so remote in the film that it was closer to Mexico than the Houston metropolitan area. At the 1970 census, sleepy little Sugar Land had just over 3,000 people. But this city boomed in the past thirty years—and particularly the last ten—by gaining 60,000 residents. Houston's Southwest Freeway, lined with malls and offices, now runs right through the town. Now when attention is focused on Sugar Land, it is depicted as the rock-solid Republican home of the former House majority leader Tom Delay and a symbol of GOP political strength in the fast-growing exurbs.[41]

As table 2-6 shows, a place can go from village to city in just thirty years—especially if the village lies in the path of a sprawling metropolis. And a small town does not necessarily have to be in the Sunbelt to undergo an urban transformation. At the top of the baby boomburb list for fast growth sits St. Peters, Missouri. This city jumped from just 486 residents in 1970 to 51,381 by 2000, or a gain of well over 10,000 percent. This boom

Table 2-6. Baby Boomburb Growth, 1970–2000, by Percent Change

Baby boomburb	Metropolitan area	Population 1970	Population 2000	Population change	Percent change	Best decade
St. Peters	St. Louis	486	51,381	50,895	10,472.2	1980
Flower Mound	Dallas	1,685	50,702	49,017	2,909.0	1990
Round Rock	Austin	2,811	61,136	58,325	2,074.9	1990
Sugar Land	Houston	3,318	63,328	60,010	1,808.6	1990
West Jordan	Salt Lake City	4,221	68,336	64,115	1,519.0	1990
Roswell	Atlanta	5,430	79,334	73,904	1,361.0	1990
San Marcos	San Diego	3,896	54,977	51,081	1,311.1	1980
Sandy	Salt Lake City	6,438	88,418	81,980	1,273.4	1970
Hesperia	Los Angeles	4,592	62,582	57,990	1,262.8	1980
Laguna Niguel	Los Angeles	4,644	61,891	57,247	1,232.7	1980
Davie	Miami	5,859	75,720	69,861	1,192.4	1990
Missouri	Houston	4,136	52,913	48,777	1,179.3	1970
Cary	Raleigh	7,686	94,536	86,850	1,130.0	1990
Sunrise	Miami	7,403	85,779	78,376	1,058.7	1970
Tamarac	Miami	5,193	55,588	50,395	970.4	1970
Gresham	Portland	10,030	90,205	80,175	799.4	1980
Folsom	Sacramento	5,810	51,884	46,074	793.0	1990
Lewisville	Dallas	9,264	77,737	68,473	739.1	1990
Apple Valley	Los Angeles	6,702	54,239	47,537	709.3	1980
Maple Grove	Minneapolis	6,275	50,365	44,090	702.6	1980
Orland Park	Chicago	6,391	51,077	44,686	699.2	1970
Eden Prairie	Minneapolis	6,938	54,901	47,963	691.3	1980
Mission Viejo	Los Angeles	11,933	93,102	81,169	680.2	1970
Lauderhill	Miami	8,465	57,585	49,120	580.3	1970
Gaithersburg	Washington	8,344	52,613	44,269	530.5	1970
Thornton	Denver	13,326	82,384	69,058	518.2	1970
Eagan	Minneapolis	10,398	63,557	53,159	511.2	1980
Margate	Miami	8,867	53,909	45,042	508.0	1970
Victorville	Los Angeles	10,845	64,029	53,184	490.4	1980
Carlsbad	San Diego	14,944	78,247	63,303	423.6	1980
Olathe	Kansas City	17,917	92,962	75,045	418.8	1990
Yorba Linda	Los Angeles	11,856	58,918	47,062	396.9	1980
Hemet	Los Angeles	12,252	58,812	46,560	380.0	1990
Hillsboro	Portland	14,675	70,186	55,511	378.3	1990
Union	San Francisco	14,724	66,869	52,145	354.1	1970
Kent	Seattle	17,711	79,524	61,813	349.0	1990
Roseville	Sacramento	18,221	79,921	61,700	338.6	1990
Lee's Summit	Kansas City	16,230	70,700	54,470	335.6	1990
Layton	Salt Lake City	13,603	58,474	44,871	329.9	1980
Edmond	Oklahoma City	16,633	68,315	51,682	310.7	1970
Beaverton	Portland	18,577	76,129	57,552	309.8	1990
Vacaville	San Francisco	21,690	88,625	66,935	308.6	1980
Deerfield Beach	Miami	16,662	64,583	47,921	287.6	1970
Plymouth	Minneapolis	18,077	65,894	47,817	264.5	1980
Vista	San Diego	24,688	89,857	65,169	264.0	1980

(continued)

Table 2-6. Baby Boomburb Growth, 1970–2000, by Percent Change *(continued)*

Baby boomburb	Metropolitan area	Population 1970	Population 2000	Population change	Percent change	Best decade
Plantation	Miami	23,523	82,934	59,411	252.6	1970
Pleasanton	San Francisco	18,328	63,654	45,326	247.3	1970
North Richland Hills	Dallas	16,514	55,635	39,121	236.9	1980
Boynton Beach	West Palm Beach	18,115	60,389	42,274	233.4	1970
Chino	Los Angeles	20,411	67,168	46,757	229.1	1970
Rialto	Los Angeles	28,370	91,873	63,503	223.8	1980
Antioch	San Francisco	28,060	90,532	62,472	222.6	1990
Longmont	Denver	23,209	71,093	47,884	206.3	1970
Tustin	Los Angeles	22,190	67,504	45,314	204.2	1980
Miramar	Miami	23,997	72,739	48,742	203.1	1990
Burnsville	Minneapolis	19,940	60,220	40,280	202.0	1980
Delray Beach	West Palm Beach	19,915	60,020	40,105	201.4	1980
Cupertino	San Francisco	17,895	50,546	32,651	182.5	1970
Pittsburg	San Francisco	21,423	56,769	35,346	165.0	1980
Boca Raton	West Palm Beach	28,506	74,764	46,258	162.3	1970
Murfreesboro	Nashville	26,360	68,816	42,456	161.1	1990
Brooklyn Park	Minneapolis	26,230	67,388	41,158	156.9	1970
Davis	Sacramento	23,488	60,308	36,820	156.8	1990
Palatine Village	Chicago	26,050	65,479	39,429	151.4	1990
Milpitas	San Francisco	26,561	62,698	36,137	136.1	1980
Frederick	Washington	23,641	52,767	29,126	123.2	1990
Petaluma	San Francisco	24,870	54,548	29,678	119.3	1990
Fairfield	San Francisco	44,146	96,178	52,032	117.9	1980
Marietta	Atlanta	27,216	58,748	31,532	115.9	1990
Denton	Dallas	39,874	80,537	40,663	102.0	1980
Coon Rapids	Minneapolis	30,505	61,607	31,102	102.0	1980
Napa	San Francisco	36,103	72,585	36,482	101.0	1980
Greeley	Denver	38,902	76,930	38,028	97.8	1990
Livermore	San Francisco	37,703	73,345	35,642	94.5	1990
Renton	Seattle	25,878	50,052	24,174	93.4	1980
St. Charles	St. Louis	31,834	60,321	28,487	89.5	1980
Norman	Oklahoma City	52,117	95,694	43,577	83.6	1970
North Miami	Miami	34,767	59,880	25,113	72.2	1990
Santa Cruz	San Francisco	32,076	54,593	22,517	70.2	1970
Elgin	Chicago	55,691	94,487	38,796	69.7	1990
South Gate	Los Angeles	56,909	96,375	39,466	69.3	1980
Waukesha	Milwaukee	39,695	64,825	25,130	63.3	1970
Lynwood	Los Angeles	43,354	69,845	26,491	61.1	1980
Gardena	Los Angeles	41,021	57,746	16,725	40.8	1990
Rochester Hills	Detroit	a	68,825			1990
Federal Way	Seattle	b	83,259			1990
Total/median		1,635,233	5,905,900	47,677	298.1	

a. Incorporated 1984.

b. Incorporated 1990.

happened in the St. Louis area, a region not known for fast growth. While the metropolitan area as a whole may not grow, exurbs like St. Peters can rapidly develop as the people in the center move to the edge. William Fulton refers to metropolitan areas that experience this type of shift as "thinning," because they lose population density in the process.[42] St. Louis is one such region, as are others with boomburbs, such as Kansas City and Milwaukee, and to a lesser extent Minneapolis and Chicago.

Behind St. Peters in growth are thirteen baby boomburbs that grew over 1,000 percent. These are scattered throughout the United States but are generally found in fast-gaining metropolitan areas, with three of the top five growers in Texas alone. The overall growth rate was faster in baby boomburbs than in boomburbs, with almost a quadrupling from 1970 to 2000 for baby boomburbs, compared to a near tripling among boomburbs. Had some baby boomburbs eked out just a bit more growth they would have made the cutoff as boomburbs.

But many baby boomburbs are just getting started, and for the most part these places gained residents faster in the 1990s than boomburbs did. Of eighty-six baby boomburbs, thirty-one (or 36 percent) added most of their new people in the last decade of the twentieth century. That figure is much higher than the number and percentage of boomburbs that had their best decade in the 1990s. Many of the fast-growing 1990s' baby boomburbs have the size and the momentum to become full-fledged boomburbs by 2010. Most of them define the very edges of urbanized growth in their regions. As a group baby boomburbs had over 1.6 million residents in 1970. By 2000 their population was approaching 6 million. They added over 4 million people in just thirty years, or an equivalent of a state such as South Carolina.

The Boomburbs Keep Booming, 2000 to 2002

Finally, it is worth exploring how boomburbs are doing in the first years of the twenty-first century. Census estimates show that most boomburbs continue to boom (table 2-7).[43] In fact, boomburbs are the fastest-growing U.S. "cities" of over 100,000 people. The nine top growth cities over the period April 1, 2000, to July 1, 2002, were boomburbs.[44] Additionally, boomburbs made up six of the top ten fastest-growing cities from July 1, 2001, to July 1, 2002, including four of the top five of these cities.[45] The five fastest-growing boomburbs (and the five fastest-growing U.S. cities above 100,000 population from 2000 to 2002) are in the Phoenix and Las Vegas metropolitan areas. The next five quick growers are in Southern

California—four in the Los Angeles region and one in the San Diego metropolitan area.

Gilbert, Arizona (the fastest-gaining boomburb), grew by nearly a quarter (23 percent) in just over two years.[46] At that pace, Gilbert could easily more than double its population in a decade. The next eight boomburbs following Gilbert all grew by more than 10 percent over the same period. Henderson, Nevada (south of Las Vegas), added 30,722 new residents from 2000 to 2002, leading all boomburbs in number of new people. Henderson was followed by Mesa, Arizona, with a gain of 30,466 people during the period. Almost a third (sixteen) of boomburbs gained over 10,000 residents each.

As a group, boomburbs jumped from 8,915,435 to 9,397,793 in population, or a gain of nearly a half million residents in just over two years. To put that in perspective, consider that that is about how many people lived in all boomburbs in 1950. Together, boomburbs now have a population larger than the Chicago metropolitan area (with 9,286,207 people as of July 1, 2002), the nation's third largest metropolitan area behind New York and Los Angeles.[47]

Boomburbs Still Gaining on Traditional Cities

Boomburbs significantly outpaced their traditional urban peers in population growth from 2000 to 2002. Nonboomburb cities from 100,000 to 400,000 in population (the size range for boomburbs) had a 1.1 percent median and a 1.5 percent average growth rate for the period. By contrast, boomburbs had a 4.5 percent median and 5.6 percent average growth rate between 2000 and 2002. In addition, 55 of the 158 nonboomburbs (or 34.8 percent) lost population, while only 4 of the 53 boomburbs (or 7.5 percent) contracted.

In total, cities between 100,000 and 400,000 gained 891,058 people from 2000 to 2002. The 54 boomburbs accounted for 482,358 of the growth, while the 157 nonboomburbs added 408,700 new residents. Thus despite representing only a quarter of U.S. cities between 100,000 and 400,000 (and a quarter of the current population), boomburbs contributed more than half (54 percent) of all the population growth for cities in this range.

As noted in chapter 1, boomburbs captured over half of the city growth in their size range during the 1990s. They gained about 2.1 million new residents in the 1990s.[48] That figure works out to a gain of just over 200,000 a year. Based on the performance of the first two years of the current decade, boomburbs as a group are well on pace to match or better their population growth of the 1990s.

Table 2-7. Boomburb Growth, 2000–02, by Percent Change[a]

Boomburb	Metropolitan area	Population 2000	Population 2002	Population change	Percent change
Gilbert	Phoenix	109,697	135,005	25,308	23.07
North Las Vegas	Las Vegas	115,488	135,902	20,414	17.68
Henderson	Las Vegas	175,381	206,153	30,772	17.55
Chandler	Phoenix	176,581	202,016	25,435	14.40
Peoria	Phoenix	108,364	123,239	14,875	13.73
Irvine	Los Angeles	143,072	162,122	19,050	13.31
Rancho Cucamonga	Los Angeles	127,743	143,711	15,968	12.50
Chula Vista	San Diego	173,556	193,919	20,363	11.73
Fontana	Los Angeles	128,929	143,607	14,678	11.38
Corona City	Los Angeles	124,966	138,326	13,360	10.69
Mesa	Phoenix	396,375	426,841	30,466	7.69
Riverside	Los Angeles	255,166	274,226	19,060	7.47
Plano	Dallas	222,030	238,091	16,061	7.23
Coral Springs	Miami	117,549	125,674	8,125	6.91
Pembroke Pines	Miami	137,427	146,637	9,210	6.70
Palmdale	Los Angeles	116,670	124,346	7,676	6.58
Scottsdale	Phoenix	202,705	215,779	13,074	6.45
Santa Clarita	Los Angeles	151,088	160,554	9,466	6.27
Grand Prairie	Dallas	127,427	135,303	7,876	6.18
Moreno Valley	Los Angeles	142,381	150,773	8,392	5.89
Naperville	Chicago	128,358	135,389	7,031	5.48
Glendale	Phoenix	218,812	230,564	11,752	5.37
Arlington	Dallas	332,969	349,944	16,975	5.10
Carrollton	Dallas	109,576	115,107	5,531	5.05
Lancaster	Los Angeles	118,718	124,592	5,874	4.95
Thousand Oaks	Los Angeles	117,005	122,700	5,695	4.87
Simi Valley	Los Angeles	111,351	116,562	5,211	4.68
Oxnard	Los Angeles	170,358	177,984	7,626	4.48

(continued)

Some Built-Out Boomburbs Stall

While most boomburbs are on pace to grow at double-digit rates this current decade, some are slowing down or even declining. One reason for having stalled-out population growth is that some boomburbs are simply built out. As shown in chapter 1, most boomburbs are horizontal cities that grow out rather than up. Boomburbs such as Tempe, Arizona (with a 0.6 percent growth rate from 2000 to 2002), have nowhere to go but up. The city had its biggest decade of growth in the 1970s.

Such boomburbs are at a crossroads: to keep growing they must change their land use patterns to accommodate higher-density development, but their original competitive advantage has been their greenfield, or open-space, development opportunities. The infill market remains untested in

Table 2-7. Boomburb Growth, 2000–02, by Percent Change[a] *(continued)*

Boomburb	Metropolitan area	Population		Population change	Percent change
		2000	*2002*		
Ontario	Los Angeles	158,007	165,064	7,057	4.47
Santa Rosa	San Francisco	147,595	153,489	5,894	3.99
Chesapeake	Norfolk	199,184	206,665	7,481	3.76
Aurora	Denver	276,393	286,028	9,635	3.49
Mesquite	Dallas	124,523	128,776	4,253	3.42
San Bernardino	Los Angeles	185,401	191,631	6,230	3.36
Bellevue	Seattle	109,569	112,894	3,325	3.03
Oceanside	San Diego	161,029	165,880	4,851	3.01
Salem	Portland	136,924	140,977	4,053	2.96
Westminster	Denver	100,940	103,599	2,659	2.63
Irving	Dallas	191,615	196,119	4,504	2.35
Fullerton City	Los Angeles	126,003	128,842	2,839	2.25
West Valley City	Salt Lake City	108,896	111,254	2,358	2.17
Orange	Los Angeles	128,821	131,606	2,785	2.16
Garland	Dallas	215,768	219,646	3,878	1.80
Escondido	San Diego	133,559	135,908	2,349	1.76
Fremont	San Francisco	203,413	206,856	3,443	1.69
Santa Ana	Los Angeles	337,977	343,413	5,436	1.61
Anaheim	Los Angeles	328,014	332,642	4,628	1.41
Costa Mesa	Los Angeles	108,724	110,126	1,402	1.29
Hialeah	Miami	226,419	228,149	1,730	0.76
Tempe	Phoenix	158,625	159,508	883	0.56
Lakewood	Denver	144,126	143,754	–372	–0.26
Clearwater	Tampa	108,787	108,313	–474	–0.44
Sunnyvale	San Francisco	131,760	129,687	–2,073	–1.57
Daly City	San Francisco	103,621	101,901	–1,720	–1.66
Total/median		8,915,435	9,397,793	482,358	5.62

a. Data for 2000 are dated April 1; data for 2002 are dated July 1.

most boomburbs. Many now have the scale and the economic assets that technically make them central places, but their mostly centerless form does not offer the type of dense urban environment that attracts citiphile consumers of infill housing.[49] The future of built-out boomburbs may depend on the success of urban design movements, such as the new urbanism, to introduce more traditional citylike development into the suburbs (a topic that is taken up in detail later in the book).

The "New Brooklyns" Slow Down

The term "new Brooklyns" applies to boomburbs that are now, or are rapidly becoming, immigrant-dominated communities, like the old Brooklyn (the full definition of what constitutes a new Brooklyn is presented in the next chapter). This particular type of boomburb may also be losing steam.

New Brooklyns such as Hialeah in Florida and Santa Ana and Anaheim in California have foreign-born populations that either match or exceed that of Brooklyn, N.Y. (which has a 38 percent foreign-born population). Other examples of new Brooklyns include Pembroke Pines, Florida, Irving, Texas, and Aurora, Colorado, all of which have a foreign-born population that greatly exceeds the national average of 11 percent.

New Brooklyns tend to be old, dense, and built-out suburbs, which dampens their population growth. As Rick Hampson observes, "Although the New Brooklyns were once new settlements on the suburban frontier, they're getting old. Their housing, accordingly, is more attractive to immigrants looking for bargains and is less attractive to longtime [mostly native-born] Americans, who can afford to move up."[50] Some new Brooklyns can continue to gain population (if not quite boom) provided that their foreign-born population maintains a high rate of natural increase. These places have also seen a turnover, as young immigrant families replace older empty-nest couples, which also adds to population growth. In time, the foreign-born population will age and assimilate, which should slow down the new Brooklyns even further. Chapter 3 covers the demographic nature of the new Brooklyns in detail.

National Economic Boom in 1990s Turns Bust

Another reason some boomburbs are slowing down and even declining is due to the recent recession (2001–03) in the national and regional economies. The 2000 census gathered data at the peak of the last economic expansion, when employment and equity markets were at their previous highs. Many cities fared well in the 1990s leading up to the 2000 census. Even older industrial cities experienced their best decade for population gains since the 1940s.[51]

The latest census estimates hint at a reversal in the gains of the 1990s. Traditional cities that were growing in the 1990s, such as Chicago and San Francisco, experienced population loss from 2000 to 2002.[52] Boomburbs in places such as the Bay Area, which has been hard hit by a technology recession, are not immune to economic downturns. For example, Sunnyvale, California, as noted earlier—the heart of the Silicon Valley—has lost 1.6 percent of its population since 2000. The fastest-declining boomburb is Daly City (with a 1.7 percent loss), just south of San Francisco. Sunnyvale and Daly City also happen to be new Brooklyns, which combined with the Bay Area's economic problems turned them from 1990s' boomburbs into this decade's bustburbs.

The Future of Boomburbs

For now, most boomburbs seem to be humming right along. But many will experience relative decline in perhaps the not too distant future. One problem could be that the West (where most boomburbs are found) is running out of water. Almost all of the West's current water sources—from Denver to Southern California—have been overallocated.[53] Unless more water is diverted from agriculture or new supplies are tapped, the West will face a crisis that could significantly dampen the growth rates of its boomburbs.

Even assuming that the problem of water supply for new growth is resolved, the current group of boomburbs will ultimately experience much slower population gains. The fact is that no place can (or should) boom forever. Today's boomburbs are tomorrow's mature cities. But a whole new batch of boomburbs and baby boomburbs is already emerging. Look at the Central Valley of Arizona; as Tempe stalls and Mesa slows down, places such as Goodyear and Buckeye are just getting started. The future of boomburbs is discussed more fully in the final chapter of the book.

Finally, the economic drivers of urban growth are ever shifting. As noted, many boomburbs and baby boomburbs got a big lift initially from World War II and were sustained by cold war defense industries. Defense helped ratchet up boomburb growth just as suburbanization swept the metropolis. The general patterns that tilted U.S. growth to the suburbs in the post–World War II years as highlighted above—new highways, cheap mortgages—helped further develop boomburbs.

Recent boomburb expansion is due in part to a continued urban shift to the Sunbelt. Most boomburbs and baby boomburbs possess two qualities in particular that the urban economist Edward Glaeser argues drive growth: sun and sprawl.[54] Glaeser developed the idea that growth derives from a combination of sun, sprawl, and skills (or human capital). The Glaeser "three S" concept provides an alternative to Richard Florida's "three Ts," or talent, tolerance, and technology.[55] As a *New York Times Magazine* article on Glaeser's work notes:

Glaeser likes to point out the close correlation between a city's average January temperature and its urban growth; he also notes that cars per capita in 1990 is among the best indicators of how well a city has fared over the past 15 years. The more cars, the better—a conclusion that seems perfectly logical to Glaeser. Car-based cities enable residents to buy cheaper, bigger houses. And commuters in car-based cities tend to get to work faster than commuters in cities that rely on public transit.[56]

Boomburbs, as mostly warm, auto-friendly environments, fit this description. As a result, boomburbs and baby boomburbs should continue to grow until these drivers lose their steam and a new development model emerges.

Who Lives in the Boomburbs?

3

As much of the research based on the 2000 census reveals, the 1990s witnessed a radical departure from standard demographic trends. Hispanics passed African Americans as the nation's largest racial or ethnic group, while the Asian American population strengthened its presence by more than 50 percent.[1] The proportion of foreign-born persons reached 11.1 percent, the highest level since 1930. This surge of immigration is changing how communities plan and develop, especially since slightly more than half of all of immigrants who arrived in metropolitan areas in the 1990s chose to live outside central cities.

The country's median age is 35.3 years—the oldest it has ever been. Aging baby boomers are becoming empty nesters and fueling the development of "active adult" communities. Suburbs now contain more nonfamily households (largely young singles and elderly people living alone) than married couples with children.[2] In 2000 less than 25 percent of all households nationwide were nuclear families. This is a significant change from 1970, when the figure stood at around 40 percent. The nuclear family is a shrinking phenomenon, as acceptance of nontraditional approaches to marriage, divorce, childbearing, and cohabitation grows.

Overall, the share of racial and ethnic minorities living in the suburbs increased substantially in the 1990s—moving from less than one-fifth to more than one-quarter of all suburbanites. This trend is most evident in metropolitan areas that had a strong immigrant base. A study by the demographer William Frey finds that the growth of racial and ethnic groups fueled the 1990s population growth.[3] According to this study, in the largest 102 metropolitan areas, more than half of the Asian population and nearly half of the Hispanic population lived in the suburbs. Blacks showed the greatest increase in suburban living—in 1990 less than 33 percent of blacks lived in the suburbs studied; in 2000, almost 40 percent did.

During the past ten years suburban growth outpaced city growth irrespective of whether a city's population was falling, staying stable, or rising.[4] Minorities have driven most of this growth, and this is reflected in the boomburbs. Most but not all are ethnically and racially diverse. The majority of boomburbs have Hispanic populations above the national average, and Hispanics make up over half the population in six boomburbs and five baby boomburbs. Over three-quarters of boomburbs have Asian populations above the national average, and 85 percent of boomburbs had foreign-born populations above the national average of 11 percent.

Not only are boomburbs ethnically diverse, they also contain different strata of income. While most boomburbs are affluent, few are exclusive. Boomburb percentages, compared to the top fifty metropolitan areas, rank higher in categories such as race, foreign-born population, and median income (table 3-1). However, the percentages of families in poverty, postgraduate education, home ownership, and white non-Hispanic populations are lower. This chapter examines the demographics within boomburbs (using primarily census data); discusses their ethnic, educational, and economic diversities; and identifies two subcategories that emerge from the data: "new Brooklyns" and "cosmoburbs."

Race and Immigration

Some boomburbs defy the suburban stereotype put forth over the last four decades by cultural critics. They have grown not because of white flight but because of immigration, influxes of retirees, and business expansion. These suburbs have developed their own economies and diverse populations. Figures 3-1 and 3-2 illustrate the decrease in non-Hispanic white populations in boomburbs and baby boomburbs since 1980. Although baby boomburbs started off and remain more white, Hispanic inmigration has grown as a greater share of their population over the last twenty years.

Boomburbs are surprisingly diverse in their Hispanic and Asian populations. For example, forty-five of the fifty-four boomburbs have Hispanic populations larger than the national percentage, which is about 12 percent. Five boomburbs are over 50 percent Hispanic. Hialeah, Florida, with

90 percent Hispanic population, tops the list; the other nine of the top ten are in California:

—Hialeah, Florida: 90 percent Hispanic
—Santa Ana, California: 76 percent Hispanic
—Oxnard, California: 66 percent Hispanic
—Ontario, California: 60 percent Hispanic
—Fontana, California: 58 percent Hispanic
—Chula Vista, California: 50 percent Hispanic
—San Bernardino, California: 48 percent Hispanic
—Anaheim, California: 47 percent Hispanic
—Escondido, California: 39 percent Hispanic
—Moreno Valley, California: 38 percent Hispanic

Similarly, forty-two of the fifty-four boomburbs have a higher percentage of Asians than the U.S. percentage of 4 percent. The ten boomburbs with the highest percentages of Asians are

—Daly City, California: 50 percent Asian
—Fremont, California: 37 percent Asian
—Sunnyvale, California: 32 percent Asian
—Irvine, California: 30 percent Asian
—Bellevue, Washington: 17 percent Asian
—Fullerton, California: 16 percent Asian
—Anaheim, California: 12 percent Asian
—Carrollton, Texas: 11 percent Asian
—Chula Vista, California: 11 percent Asian
—Plano, Texas: 11 percent Asian

Three of these boomburbs—Daly City, Fremont, and Sunnyvale—are outside of San Francisco.

As of 2000, blacks were 12.3 percent of the U.S. population. The biggest gains were in Florida's baby boomburbs of Lauderhill, Miramar, and North Miami. Ten boomburbs lost black population during the 1990s (Irvine, Oceanside, Fremont, Thousand Oaks, Simi Valley, Oxnard, Sunnyvale, Daly City, Santa Ana, Hialeah), but the remaining forty-four boomburbs increased their black population. The black population of Gilbert, Arizona, rose from only forty-one persons in 1980 to well over 2,000 in the year 2000. The following list shows those boomburbs with black percentages of their population that exceeded the national average at the 2000 census:

—Chesapeake, Virginia: 28.3 percent black
—Moreno Valley, California: 19.3 percent black
—North Las Vegas, Nevada: 18.6 percent black

Table 3-1. Boomburbs Compared to the Top Fifty Most Populous Metropolitan Areas, Various Demographic Measures

Percent, except where noted

	Hispanic (any race)	Asian	Foreign-born	English as a second language	No schooling	Families in poverty	Having a BA or more	Home-owners	Household median income ($)	White
Boomburbs										
Weighted average	28.7	7.6	22.4	33.4	2.2	7.9	26.3	62.4	51,709	67.6
Median	20.8	5.0	19.9	28.0	1.4	6.7	24.3	64.2	49,713	69.1
Top 50 U.S. metropolitan areas										
Weighted average	15.7	5.1	15.7	23.3	1.6	8.4	28.3	62.6	48,042	70.0
Median	6.4	2.3	8.9	12.9	1.0	7.6	26.5	66.0	45,997	75.3
Total	12.5	3.6	11.1	17.9	1.4	9.2	24.4	66.2	41,994	75.1

Source: U.S. Census, 2000.

Figure 3-1. Racial and Ethnic Composition of Boomburbs, 1980, 1990, 2000

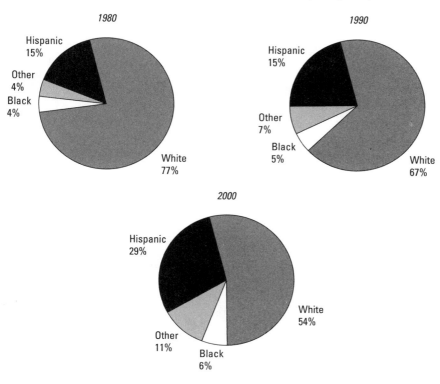

—San Bernardino, California: 16.0 percent black
—Lancaster, California: 15.6 percent black
—Palmdale, California: 14.1 percent black
—Arlington, Texas: 13.5 percent black
—Grand Prairie, Texas: 13.3 percent black
—Mesquite, Texas: 13.2 percent black
—Aurora, Colorado: 12.7 percent black
Boomburbs also contain a high percentage of foreign-born residents. Although only 11 percent of the U.S. population is foreign-born, a typical boomburb is 21 percent foreign-born. Forty-six of the fifty-four boomburbs have foreign-born populations higher than the national average. Further, there is a high correlation between share of Hispanic population and share of foreign-born population.[5] Nine of the ten boomburbs with the highest percentages of foreign-born residents are in California:

Figure 3-2. Racial and Ethnic Composition of Baby Boomburbs, 1980, 1990, 2000

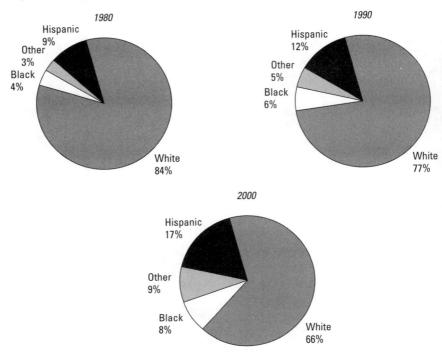

—Hialeah, Florida: 72 percent foreign-born
—Santa Ana, California: 53 percent foreign-born
—Daly City, California: 52 percent foreign-born
—Sunnyvale, California: 39 percent foreign-born
—Anaheim, California: 38 percent foreign-born
—Fremont, California: 37 percent foreign-born
—Oxnard, California: 37 percent foreign-born
—Irvine, California: 32 percent foreign-born
—Ontario, California: 31 percent foreign-born
—Costa Mesa, California: 29 percent foreign-born

In 1990 Santa Ana and Anaheim in northern Orange County, California, had 50.9 and 28.4 percent foreign-born populations, respectively. Both
those figures increased significantly by 2000. Boomburbs in Southern California and south Florida also contain a large share of foreign-born population; these areas are both considered "Hispanic heartlands."[6] Hialeah, a
suburb of northwest Miami, had a 36.8 percent foreign-born population in

Table 3-2. Ten New Brooklyns, by Various Demographic Measures, 2000

Percent

New Brooklyn	Foreign-born	English as a second language	No schooling	Renting	Families in poverty
Hialeah, Florida	72.1	92.6	4.4	49.3	16.0
Santa Ana, California	53.3	79.6	10.2	50.7	16.1
Daly City, California	52.4	66.4	2.7	40.2	4.2
Anaheim, California	37.9	54.8	4.2	50.0	10.4
Oxnard, California	36.9	62.1	6.7	42.7	11.4
Ontario, California	31.1	53.0	4.6	42.4	12.2
Chula Vista, California	28.7	52.6	2.0	42.6	8.6
Escondido, California	25.5	38.1	3.6	46.8	9.3
Irving, Texas	26.5	38.3	2.3	62.8	8.0
North Las Vegas, Nevada	25.1	37.2	3.5	30.0	11.8

Source: U.S. census.

1980; this increased to 72.1 percent by 2000. South Gate, California, a baby boomburb, went from 10.7 percent in 1980 to 49.3 percent in 2000.[7]

New Brooklyns

Certain boomburbs with large foreign-born, working-class populations can be classified as "new Brooklyns." Much like Brooklyn, New York, of a century ago, working immigrant families who speak English as their second language densely populate these cities. Although they have relatively large populations, as in the old Brooklyn, they play a secondary role in their region. Manhattan was home to the cosmopolitan tastemakers, while Brooklyn was Manhattan's bedroom community, where immigrants lived in tightly clustered neighborhoods and strived for middle-class existences.[8]

New Brooklyn boomburbs are characterized by a significant percentage of working-class, foreign-born citizens who speak another language besides English at home (table 3-2). They also contain populations claiming to have had no schooling at all, a higher than the national average of renters, and a relatively high population of families in poverty. Median household incomes are either slightly above or close to the national median. Baby boomburbs that meet similar criteria are Lynwood, California; South Gate, California; North Miami, Florida; and Rialto, California.

New Brooklyn suburbs are more ethnically diverse than their core cities, meaning they have a higher percentage of Hispanics and Asians than their core cities (table 3-3).

New Brooklyns tend to have larger than average family sizes. Most new Brooklyns rank above the national average family size of 3.1 members.

Table 3-3. Hispanic and Asian Population, Core Cities and New Brooklyns, 2000
Percent

Core city and New Brooklyn	Hispanic	Asian
Las Vegas	23.6	4.8
North Las Vegas	31.6	3.1
Miami	65.8	0.7
Hialeah	90.3	0.4
Los Angeles	46.6	10.0
Anaheim	46.8	11.9
Ontario	59.9	3.7
Oxnard	66.2	7.2
Santa Ana	76.0	8.7
San Francisco	14.1	30.8
Daly City	22.3	50.3
Dallas	35.6	2.7
Irving	31.2	8.2
San Diego	25.4	13.7
Chula Vista	49.6	10.6
Escondido	38.7	4.4

Source: U.S. Census.

Santa Ana has the highest (4.6), followed by Oxnard (3.9) and Ontario (3.6). The highest baby boomburbs are Lynwood (4.9), South Gate, California (4.2) and Chino, California (3.9). According to the 2000 census, three new Brooklyns—Santa Ana, Oxnard, and Hialeah—are among the top ten boomburbs with the highest incidence of crowded units. The incidence of overcrowding is now at record levels in California.[9]

Inside a New Brooklyn: Anaheim

On July 15, 1955, Walt Disney opened the gates to Disneyland and forever changed the course of history in Anaheim. Anaheim was now home to a great economic development engine, called "the happiest place on earth." Several years earlier, Disney had driven south away from the Los Angeles smog on the freshly paved asphalt of the Santa Ana Freeway. Once in Orange County, he found the skies clear and bright and the land so pastoral that it reminded him of his home town in Missouri. Disney saw that this was the place to realize his dream of building a park where children could play on miles of parkland and parents could escape their adult pressures. He also realized that he would have plenty of customers that would flood out from the postwar subdivisions rising out of the ground in and around Los Angeles.

Anaheim, however, was not Disney's first choice. A consulting firm recommended Long Beach, a coastal community to the north. However, Disney rejected this location on the assumption that people would enter the park in their swimsuits and this would undermine the fantasy environment he was trying to create. The success of the park would depend on people being able to leave the outside world completely behind. He was met with NIMBY resistance in Palos Verde and Canoga Park. Anaheim, by contrast, was open to the idea on the condition that Disney would not create a tawdry carnival atmosphere. Anaheim mayor Charles Pearson specifically requested that Disneyland not be a "peanut-shell-littered" honky-tonk. Disney vowed to ban peanuts and gum, and the park was opened in a year and a half. Only seven weeks later, the one-millionth guest passed through the turnstiles.

The defense and aerospace industries had already brought jobs and housing to Anaheim. Disneyland became its tipping point: Anaheim's population went from 14,556 in 1950 to 104,184 in 1960. However, Disney's insistence on shutting out the "real" world resulted in the park being cut off from its associated tourism industries and also from its host city. Disneyland exists as an isolated pod surrounded by highways and off-ramp hotels and conference centers. Anaheim's main street is in disrepair, while a hodge-podge of tourist development has sprung up, especially along Harbor Boulevard. Ironically, Harbor Boulevard hosts the blinking-light, honky-tonk strip that the city originally wanted to avoid.[10]

Anaheim's downtown continued to decline with the advent of shopping malls and the movement to bigger and newer houses on the outskirts of town. Tourist-related venues such as the Anaheim Stadium and Anaheim Arena (now known as Arrowhead Pond) were built. As an indication of Anaheim's growing diversity, the first performance in the arena was by 1970s era crooner Barry Manilow in 1993; it now features acts such as Paquita la del Barrio, a feminist Latina singer.

Anaheim is really two cities. Upscale Anaheim Hills to the east, where minimum lot size for new single-family homes is 5,000 square feet; 5,500 houses have been built there since 1990. The other part is central Anaheim, or the flatlands, which contains the original World War II tract housing, where most of the immigrants reside. Only 285 apartments and about 700 new homes have been built in the flatlands since 1990. The population of Anaheim has grown by 61,608 since 1990: roughly 45,000 in the flatlands and 16,000 in the hills. The growth in the central section pushed Anaheim's density to 6,702 people per square mile. The number of children in Anaheim grew by 8,892 since 1990, but the schools have room for only half that number.[11] Anaheim has become exactly what Disney wanted to avoid: a sprawling yet congested city.

The roots of Anaheim's segregation lie in its history, which aligns itself with the settlement patterns of Orange County. Founded in the nineteenth century as a wine-growing colony, it claims to be the oldest city in California of non-Spanish origin (although the German settlers bought the land from Spaniards). Many settled Southern California as hobby farmers who valued their rural lifestyle. California's political structure was mostly decentralized and depoliticized, and therefore many Californians came to distrust big government and political machines.[12] In the mid-1920s Klu Klux Klan members were elected to the town council, and the town was still tagged "Klanaheim" long after these council members were ousted. Part of the reason the Klan was able to take root in Anaheim was that the population was misled by the powers that be into believing that foreigners would upset the town's moral order. In reality, the financial interests of a few were served by such political intimidation, which the Klan provided.[13]

During this period, Los Angeles and its environs had become a haven for old-line Protestants who wanted nothing to do with big urban cities. During the Depression residents fought to hold onto their jobs and resented immigrant labor. Orange County in particular was built out as a big, quietly appealing suburb during the post–World War II boom, as people sought to escape cities and their congestion. The 1965 race riots fed the worst fears of Orange County suburbanites, and exclusive planned communities quickly grew. Orange County would become known as a bastion of conservatism, and groups such as the rabidly xenophobic John Birch Society made it their home.

Meanwhile, Anaheim's burgeoning tourism industry drew foreign workers to clean and construct the venues. As service industry jobs grew, numbers of immigrants increased, fanning the resentment of local cultural conservatives. During the 1980s and 1990s, city voters supported the state initiative to make English the official language and to deny children of illegal immigrants access to schools. The school board even suggested billing the Mexican and U.S. governments for the cost of educating undocumented children. Conservative firebrand and polemicist Robert "B-1 Bob" Dornan served as Anaheim's congressional representative from 1985 to 1996, as Anaheim held on to its belief that it was still a traditional, idyllic suburb, protected from the multiculturalism of Los Angeles by the "Orange curtain."

However, Anaheim changed, both by necessity and by choice. Its Hispanic citizens are fueling a backlash put in motion by anti-immigration movements such as the 1994 Proposition 187, which sought to deny state and local government benefits to undocumented aliens. Dornan was unseated in 1996 by the Democratic Latina Loretta Sanchez, and the city council now has two Hispanic members. In addition, the Mexican American Arturo Moreno bought the Los Angeles Angels of Anaheim in 2003, becoming the first Hispanic owner of a national league baseball team. So much like the old Brooklyn Dodgers fans, immigrants living in Anaheim and surrounding towns cheer on their Anaheim Angels.[14] And Disneyland is their Coney Island.

Anaheim is about half Latino, a tenth Asian, and a third Anglo. Its people speak more than sixty languages, and (as one study concludes) the city has more integrated and diverse neighborhoods than Los Angeles.[15] The median housing age in 2007 is thirty-six years (median year built is 1971), and Anaheim households rank as among the worst for overcrowding. The city's average household size (a little more than three people) is 29 percent higher than the national average, and the percentage of children under eighteen years is a third higher. People are poor but generally hard working, as shown by the fact that although 75 percent of students at Anaheim High School are eligible for school lunch aid, only 6 percent of the school's families are on welfare.[16]

As Anaheim's neighboring community and fellow new Brooklyn, Santa Ana has also experienced friction between the "natives" and the Latino community. Immigrants have flooded into Santa Ana seeking jobs and low-cost housing. Consequently, the schools became overcrowded, causing the mostly Hispanic school board to request additional school construction in 2002. However, the ideal site for a new school was in one of the city's remaining majority white neighborhoods, Floral Park. Floral Park residents, with the support of the then mostly white city council, vigorously opposed a new school being built in their neighborhood, prompting a bitter debate. Council members proposed tearing down apartment buildings elsewhere in the city to make room for schools, but Latinos objected, saying it would unfairly displace immigrant families.

Santa Ana and Anaheim are urban in their nature—dense, diverse, and plagued with the type of problems (school funding and racial tension) that inner cities face. These boomburbs even have traditional city functions. Anaheim has a world-class convention center, tourist attractions, and major performance venues. Santa Ana is the county seat and has one of the few historic main streets in Orange County. Santa Ana even maintains an "artists village" and recently opened live-and-work units in its historic district. The developer of the units claims that they are the first such loft projects in Orange County.

Table 3-4. Eight Cosmoburbs, by Various Demographic Measures, 2000

Percent (unless indicated otherwise)

Cosmoburbs	Foreign-born	English as a second language	Having a BA or more	Home-ownership	Median income ($)
Fremont, California	37.1	47.0	43.2	64.5	76,579
Irvine, California	32.1	39.7	58.4	60.0	72,057
Sunnyvale, California	39.4	45.8	50.8	47.6	74,409
Thousand Oaks, California	15.6	19.1	42.2	75.4	76,815
Naperville, Illinois	11.7	15.2	60.6	79.1	88,771
Plano, Texas	17.1	22.1	53.3	68.8	78,722
Carrollton, Texas	20.0	29.1	37.0	65.7	62,406
Bellevue, Washington	25.3	26.9	54.1	61.5	62,338

Source: U.S. Census.

Cosmoburbs

Another boomburb category, like new Brooklyn, is characterized by a high percentage of foreign-born residents and those speaking English as a second language. However, these cities tend to have a significant population with college and postgraduate educations, high rates of home ownership, and relatively high median incomes. Jobs in cosmoburbs tend to center on technology or white-collar professions, and the percentage of PhDs is higher than the national average. Eight Fortune 500 companies and eleven Fortune 1000 companies are located in cosmoburbs. There is often a relationship between fast growth rates and a high percentage of resident "human capital"—that is, the percentage of the population over twenty-five years old and holding a college degree.[17]

Cosmoburbs have lower than average family sizes. The national average family size is 3.1 members, while the average cosmoburb family has 2.7 members. Their populations are marked by relatively high concentrations of whites and Asians. Table 3-4 lists eight cosmoburb cities (baby cosmoburbs include Davis and Cupertino, California; Cary, North Carolina; and Gaithersburg, Maryland).

Marketing experts have caught on to demographic shifts and have changed the labels they use to identify population clusters that retailers, advertisers, and government agencies want to reach. Claritas, a marketing research firm, finds that many Hispanics do not fit the "Hispanic mix" or "Latino America" categories any longer and have since moved on to the "white picket fences" category, which is mostly white. Claritas has a similar category for the cosmoburb—"brite lites, li'l city"—marked by upwardly mobile couples who live in suburban comfort and have access to upscale amenities such as coffee shops and boutiques.[18]

Cosmoburbs face different and perhaps fewer obstacles than new Brooklyns face. High homeownership rates and high incomes are characteristics that cities desire. However, their real challenge is to maintain their quality of life and stay competitive with other jurisdictions that may offer better tax breaks or a better selection of housing and jobs. Cosmoburbs may experience incidents of cultural and ethnic unease. A recent *Wall Street Journal* article describes a new form of white flight in the baby cosmoburb of Cupertino. White families are transferring their children out of schools that have become predominantly Asian, saying that their children feel culturally alienated and that there is too much academic competitiveness.[19]

Inside a Cosmoburb: Naperville

Naperville, Illinois, lies thirty miles due east of Chicago, just off of U.S. Interstate 88. German and Scotch immigrants settled the area in the 1830s; with the advent of the railroad it became a primary station stop on the way to and from Chicago. It was known for its breweries and furniture making; its quarries helped rebuild Chicago after the fire of 1871. Nothing much happened for the next seventy years. Then Enrico Fermi, at the University of Chicago, created the first nuclear chain reaction.

Like many boomburbs, Naperville was a relatively small and sleepy town until World War II, when the military-industrial complex created much of the surge in the population. Naperville's beginning as a boomburb started not with a military base or munitions factory but with the outgrowth of Fermi's experiments: the Atomic Energy Commission's Argonne National Lab. The lab was built on 3,600 wooded acres near Naperville in 1947. Its presence attracted highly educated researchers and scientists to Naperville, and with them came growth and prosperity. The lab now employs over 1,000 scientists and engineers, of whom 750 have doctoral degrees.

Naperville's good fortune continued in 1954, when plans for a major toll road into Chicago were announced. The East-West toll road (also known as I-88 and now a high-tech corridor) linked with the new Eisenhower Expressway, leading to Chicago. Not only could one take the train directly from Naperville to Chicago, one could drive directly into the Loop. Soon developers such as Harold Moser were selling single-family homes faster than they could build them.[20] Naperville grew from 7,000 residents in 1950 to 128,000 in 2000, becoming Illinois' fourth largest city.

Much of Naperville's highly educated workforce is foreign-born. Since 1970, its foreign-born population has grown from 3 percent to 12 percent of the population; its percentage of Asians has increased more than that of blacks, whites, or Hispanics. Its "knowledge economy"—boosted by the presence of not only the Argonne Lab but also such high-tech research firms as Lucent Technologies (formerly Bell Labs) and BP/Amoco—accounts for this. Naperville's mayors traditionally come from the business community and use their connections to woo and maintain corporate presences. The building blocks of Naperville in the early boom years were not residential subdivisions but jobs. Residents describe Naperville as a "technoburb" because of the abundance of high-tech jobs. A technoburb, as defined by the historian Robert Fishman, has residents who "look to their immediate surroundings rather than to the city for their jobs and other needs, and its industries find not only the employees they need but also the specialized services."[21] The abundance of jobs and housing in and around Naperville means residents' needs are, to some degree, self-contained. This, combined with Naperville's early foray into high-tech economic development, resulted in Naperville never developing a blue-collar enclave. Its white-collar population throughout its history has been accompanied by expensive single-family homes and a lack of apartments or below-market housing.[22]

Despite its rapid growth, Naperville still retains its small town charm. Its streets are clean, the landscaping green, old building are preserved, and new buildings fit in. Its prosperity is evident as one drives through its tree-lined neighborhoods or visits cafés and restaurants. The city is regularly listed in *Money Magazine* as one of the best places to live. It has also been named one of the best places to retire and one of the best places to raise children. The city's promotional literature boasts of its excellent public schools and extraordinary public library. Naperville is what Walt Disney dreamed of when he went to Anaheim.

Naperville officials attribute its desirability to a commitment to planning and regulation. There is some sprawl on its outskirts, but visual blight is kept to a minimum: business signs are small, and there is abundant landscaping. There are only a few bars (or "taverns," as the mayor calls them), and they must serve food in order to keep away the barfly crowd. However, Naperville's growth rate peaked in the 1980s, and it cannot grow outward as it has in the past. City planners estimate they have about ten years until they have reached the buildout limit. The decline in available subdivision parcels has triggered an interest in moving closer to downtown. These older neighborhoods in Naperville are thus experiencing the controversial practice of teardowns—replacing an old, small house with a large, new one. National press accounts and the National Trust for Historic Preservation have brought attention to the flamboyant superhouses being squeezed between more modest homes.[23] Neighbors argue that the bulk and style of the new houses directly impact their quality of life, while developers argue that any restrictions will hamper redevelopment efforts. The city does not discourage teardowns, but in 2005, after some debate, it mandated height restrictions on new housing of forty feet and footprint restrictions of 35 percent of the lot.

Naperville's history of attracting knowledge-based industries and associated talent has enabled its prosperity and fueled its growth. Its lack of working-class neighborhoods and blue-collar or service sector jobs distinguishes it from Anaheim. Naperville's unemployment rate in 2000 was 2.2 percent, while Anaheim's was 14.1 percent. Both cities attract foreign-born populations, but their employment base, along with housing options and cultural influences, determines which populations seek them out.

Education and Income

Compared to national averages, most boomburbs have well-educated and prosperous populations: 60 percent of boomburbs rank above the national average in bachelor's degrees and 53 percent are above the national average in master's degrees. Of all the boomburbs, Irvine, California, has the highest percentage of persons with doctoral degrees (4 percent) and professional degrees (4.7 percent). This is most likely due to the high concentration of research and development businesses and the presence of a University of California campus. Other boomburbs containing large universities and populations with an above-average number of doctoral degrees include Tempe, Arizona, and Riverside and Fullerton, California.

According to the 2000 census, the national median income was $41,994 and the median boomburb income was $49,713. Naperville, the only Midwestern boomburb, ranks the highest, at $88,771; Hialeah, Florida, ranks the lowest, at $29,492. Naperville's economy has greatly developed since the 1980s, and the city is now a major office and corporate center. Hialeah, on the other hand, is a major immigrant gateway and has a manufacturing-based economy.[24] The following boomburbs had the ten highest and lowest median incomes in 2000:[25]

The top ten are
—Naperville, Illinois: $88,771
—Plano, Texas: $78,722
—Thousand Oaks, California: $76,815
—Fremont, California: $76,579
—Sunnyvale, California: $74,409

—Irvine, California: $72,057
—Simi Valley, California: $70,370
—Gilbert, Arizona: $68,032
—Santa Clarita, California: $66,717
The bottom ten are
—Mesa, Arizona: $42,817
—Escondido, California: $42,567
—Ontario, California: $42,452
—Tempe, Arizona: $42,361
—Lancaster, California: $41,127
—Salem, Oregon: $38,881
—Clearwater, Florida: $36,494
—San Bernardino, California: $31,140
—Hialeah, Florida: $29,492

Households

Boomburbs tend to have smaller households (2.9 members) than the national average (3.1 members). Santa Ana, California, has the largest average (4.6); Clearwater, Florida, the lowest (2.2). Boomburbs also have fewer married families with children under eighteen years. Two-thirds of boomburbs have fewer married families with children than the national average of 32.8 percent. This is in line with the national trend of family and household sizes, which shrunk between 1970 and 2000. Fontana, California, has the highest share of married couples with children (43.1 percent), while Clearwater, Florida, has the lowest (13.3 percent). Boomburbs have fewer singles living alone: an average of 20.2 percent of households, lower than the national average of 25.8 percent. Clearwater has both the highest percentage of single households (35.4 percent) and of women living alone (20.7 percent).[26]

Age

Younger people tend to populate the boomburbs. Only ten boomburbs have median ages above the national median of 35.3 years: Clearwater, Florida, has the oldest median (41.8 years), while Fontana, California, has the youngest (26.2 years). Santa Ana, California (26.5 years), and West Valley City, Utah (26.8 years), were the next youngest. Interestingly, they rank well below university towns such as Tempe, Arizona (28.8 years), Riverside, California (29.8 years), and Irvine, California (33.1 years). Due to boomburbs' relatively young populations, it follows that they do not have large percentages of people sixty-five years and older. Clearwater is the exception, with one in five people being aged sixty-five years and older. Florida, a state with many boomburbs, has the highest percentage of people sixty-five years and older (17.6 percent). Other boomburb states have much fewer people of that age group, even the retiree haven of Arizona (13 percent).

Suburbs with large populations aged sixty-five years and older are located in the Rust Belt and New England. These suburbs were settled mostly by today's older generations when they were young adults. As the job base of these suburbs eroded, they lost younger workers but gained older residents.[27]

Transportation and Commuting

Only six boomburbs and seven baby boomburbs rank above the national average (4.7 percent) of people using public transportation on their journeys to work. Most of those boomburbs rely on rail systems. Daly City, California, for example, is just outside of San Francisco on a Bay Area Rapid Transit line, so it is not surprising that 17.8 percent of its residents use public transit to commute to work. Daly City is followed by Gaithersburg, Maryland (12.9 percent), and North Miami, Florida (10.6 percent). About 7 percent of the residents of Bellevue, Washington, use public transportation (mainly buses) for commuting. Several other boomburbs are located along rail lines, but this does not seem to affect the percentage using public transportation for commuting. For example, Metrolink commuter trains serve Irvine, California, but only 0.1 percent of the population uses it to travel to work. Several boomburbs outside of Dallas (Plano, Irving, Garland) have added light-rail lines since 2000, and this may significantly increase their percentages of public transit use.

Public transportation use and growth rates were in opposition during the 1990s.[28] Cities with substantial public transportation systems lost population during the 1990s: those with more than 10 percent of their population using public transit had low growth rates. Conversely, the average growth rate for those cities in which less than 3 percent of commuters used public transportation was almost 17 percent. Boomburbs follow this trend: the average growth rate during the 1990s was about 41 percent; only a little over 2 percent used public transit.

Boomburbs are truly "driving cities." Not only is public transit use low, but also average travel time to work is high. The national average is about twenty-three minutes. Only seven boomburbs have shorter commuting times, and these are just barely less than the national average. Tempe, at about twenty minutes, has the lowest. Eight of the ten longest commutes are in Southern California boomburbs; residents of Palmdale, for example, spend an average of forty-three minutes getting to work.

Boomburb households tend to own more than one automobile. Nationally, 17 percent of households have three or more vehicles. Only four boomburbs have less than the national average, and in 44 percent of boomburbs, over one-quarter of households have three or more vehicles.

National Politics

Growth brings problems, but it also brings power. Boomburbs are changing and increasing their states' political representation. After the 2000 census results were released California, Colorado, Nevada, North Carolina, Georgia, Texas, Arizona, and Florida were awarded additional seats in the U.S. House of Representatives, and each state has at least one boomburb. New York and Pennsylvania lost two seats, while Connecticut, Illinois, Michigan, Mississippi, Indiana, Ohio, and Wisconsin each lost one seat, with Illinois being the only state having a boomburb (Naperville).

The results of the 2004 election were surprising to many, including demographers and political analysts. Very few predicted that the nation's exurban areas would come out so heavily in favor of Bush. Democratic strategists courted large cities and areas that had been the party's mainstays in previous elections. Meanwhile, and to their advantage, Republican strategists reached out to the rapidly growing exurbs. They predicted that those moving to burgeoning areas would most likely be politically unaffiliated and more easily encouraged to register as Republicans and vote for Bush.[29]

Boomburbs exist in large-scale mature counties that are typically not on their region's edge. They are not exurban, nor are they necessarily urban; therefore they do not fall into traditionally Republican or Democrat territories. Unfortunately, city-level data for elections are not readily available; therefore individual boomburb election results cannot be known. However, a study of the 2004 election results from county-level data reveals that Bush won the faster-growing boomburb counties (Collin County, Texas; Maricopa County, Arizona; and Riverside County, California).[30] These places have a long history of voting Republican, although Bush's victory margins were some of the narrowest in these counties' presidential election histories. Counties containing boomburbs with slow or negative growth rates (such as King County, Washington, and Sonoma County, California) tended to vote for Kerry.

There is also evidence that as counties age, they become more politically liberal. Fairfax County, Virginia, in suburban Washington, voted majority Democratic for the first time in a presidential election. This could be in part due to Fairfax County becoming more diverse and populous and having a larger share of multifamily housing than it did thirty years ago. The tensions between the old way of life and the new are becoming apparent. A local representative, Republican Tom Davis, opposes a proposed high-density, transit-oriented, mixed-used development in his district (made up of mostly single-family homes and single-use subdivisions), claiming increased traffic congestion. However, Davis may fear that Democrats will move into the new development and vote him out of office. He lost a precinct in 2004 to a Democrat for the first time in his eleven years in his seat. It just so happens that that precinct is home to two new high-density residential projects.[31]

Representative Loretta Sanchez spoke of this tension as her district in Orange County, California, shifted from primarily Anglo to Hispanic and Asian. Sanchez famously defeated Bob Dornan in 1996. Dornan's cocksureness and bluster no longer rang true to his voters, while Sanchez's steady campaigning and broad-based appeal have made her popular in her district. However, according to Sanchez, much of the "old guard" still remains in power in places such as Anaheim and Santa Ana. Minorities are elected to local offices, but whites tend to hold key positions of authority. Some school boards, she claims, are out of step with challenges such as language barriers, uneducated parents, and lower-income families. They are operating on the old model: two-parent, white-collar families where the mother does not work—the suburbia of 1950. "It simply isn't that way anymore," she said.[32]

Boomburbs built their appeal on quality-of-life issues—job growth, pleasing climates, an abundance of single-family homes. As metropolitan areas expand into their exurban areas, many boomburbs and their counties find themselves now in older parts of their metropolitan area. They increasingly face issues that ruin the suburban idyll: traffic congestion, increasing demand for social services, aging housing stock, and competition from newer, farther-out suburbs. As the demographics and densities of boomburbs shift, so might their politics.

Conclusion

Boomburbs are the new face of the American suburb. No longer can suburbs be dismissed, as many cultural critics did during the 1960s and 1970s, as predominately monolithic, white, middle-class bedroom communities. Immigration, large-scale master-planned communities, retirees, and knowledge-based employment have caused population explosions in places that either were sleepy towns fifty years ago or were nonexisent.

Boomburbs are the result of the 1990s' radical departure from historical trends. They are more racially and ethnically diverse and contain fewer traditional families than other secondary cities. In the coming decade, boomburbs may or may not continue to boom, but they will provide valuable lessons in dealing with the problems and advantages that come with rapid growth. As immigration and suburban expansion continue, their stories will be of interest to the next generation of boomburbs.

The Business of Boomburbs 4

The only way you could tell you were leaving one community and entering another was when the franchises started repeating and you spotted another 7-Eleven, another Wendy's, another Costco, another Home Depot.

TOM WOLFE

Tom Wolfe's line from *A Man in Full* is like catnip to critics of suburbia.[1] The suburbs are repetitious. They look like a cheap animator's drawing of a commercial landscape by reusing cartoon frames rather than drawing new ones. It is like watching Fred Flintstone drive around Bedrock and seeing the same buildings pop up behind him again and again.

Wolfe's fictional story centers on an Atlanta developer. But had he based his book in, say, Dallas, his famous line about the sameness of suburbia might read, "The way that you know you have entered a boomburb such as Arlington, Texas, is that the franchises start repeating themselves—*and you are still in the same community.*"

In many ways the boomburbs are like smaller suburbs, only more so. They have more of everything: more people, more freeways, and, yes, more businesses, including multiple locations for the same franchises. There is not *a* 7-Eleven in Arlington, Texas; rather, there are *eighteen* 7-Elevens. But the real question is, Are boomburbs more than the sum of their parts, or are they simply eighteen suburbs that have spread into each other? The answer is, a little of both.

This chapter covers the business of boomburbs, exploring such topics as economic development strategies, job concentration, and business types. The chapter also reports on where the boomburb white-collar economy is located by looking at office markets. There is a special focus on the Dallas and Phoenix regions, which offer a very progrowth climate for business and maintain big office economies. Insights, observations, and data taken from case analysis of the Dallas and Phoenix boomburbs are threaded throughout the chapter, but the business development in all regions is also covered to varying degrees below.[2]

Types of Businesses

Boomburbs are typically not bedroom communities. Many contain diverse industry, including the headquarters of some nationally recognized firms. Boomburbs are also home to many high-technology businesses; some of these were spun off from the defense contracting that started many boomburbs booming in the first place. Other boomburbs are major tourist destinations, chock full of professional sports stadiums and theme parks.

In general, commerce abounds in the boomburbs: Bellevue, Washington, is headquarters to Expedia and Eddie Bauer; Chandler, Arizona, is home to large Intel and Motorola plants; Google could soon locate a major facility in Scottsdale, Arizona; Clearwater, Florida, is home to the original Hooters; Tempe, Arizona, is headquarters to U.S. Airways; and Federal Way, Washington, is home to Weyerhaeuser, the largest private owner of softwood timberland in the world.

Even baby boomburbs attract plenty of industry. Although the nation's biggest exporter, aircraft maker Boeing, is now headquartered in Chicago, the company still has its largest plant in the baby boomburb of Renton, Washington. The Lockheed Martin facility in Marietta, Georgia, another baby boomburb, makes the military's most advanced fighter jets. The SAS Institute, one of the world's leading providers of statistical software—and often rated among the best U.S. companies to work for—is headquartered in the baby boomburb of Cary, North Carolina. The city, which also contains numerous biotechnology firms, is adjacent to the high-tech research triangle formed by Raleigh, Durham, and Chapel Hill. Gaithersburg, Maryland, also supports a biotech industry due to its proximity to the National Institutes of Health in Rockville.[3]

Silicon Valley includes the boomburbs of Sunnyvale (headquarters for Yahoo and Advanced Micro Devices) and Fremont. It also includes two baby boomburbs, both featuring headquarters, research and development, and manufacturing facilities for dozens of software, computer, and biotech firms. Bay Area baby boomburbs are also home to numerous tech firms.

The Saw Grass Mills Mall in Sunrise, Florida, claims to be the world's most popular retail outlet, with 26 million visitors a year. After shopping, people can go next door to the Office Depot Center and watch professional hockey's Florida Panthers play. The arena is named for another large baby boomburb business, Office Depot, which is headquartered in nearby Delray Beach. Megamalls owned by The Mills corporation are found in three other boomburbs: Tempe (Arizona Mills), Lakewood (Colorado Mills), and Ontario, California (Ontario Mills). Baby boomburbs are also home to famous sporting goods makers. Callaway Golf Company is based in Carlsbad, California; Nike is based in Beaverton, Oregon.

The two leading headquarter cities for Fortune 1000 companies in 2005 were both in the Dallas region. Irving had Exxon Mobil, Kimberly-Clark, Advance PCS, Michaels Stores, Zale, Pioneer Natural Resources, and FelCor Lodging. Plano was home to JC Penney, Electronic Data Systems, Triad Hospitals, Rent-A-Center, and Perot Systems.

Major educational institutions are also in boomburbs and baby boomburbs, including four of the eight branches of the University of California: Davis, Irvine, Riverside, and Santa Cruz. Fullerton is home to the largest branch in the California State University system. Arizona State University, the biggest university in the United States, is in Tempe. And the main campus of the University of Oklahoma is in the baby boomburb of Norman.

Boomburbs and baby boomburbs feature some of the nation's best-attended theme parks. The San Diego area alone has three: San Diego Wild Animal Park in Escondido, Knott's Soak City in Chula Vista, and Legoland in Carlsbad. There are also three parks in surrounding Los Angeles boomburbs: Disneyland in Anaheim, Castle Park in Riverside, and Six Flags over Southern California in Santa Clarita. The original Six Flags park is in Arlington, Texas.

All of this commerce and industry seems to serve boomburbs well. As a group, these cities had a median unemployment rate of 4.7 percent in 2003, when the national figure stood at 6.0 percent.[4] In many ways, boomburbs are the economic engines of their regions. Arlington, Texas, for example, has had a big General Motors plant in operation since 1950 and has been selected to manufacture the GMC Yukon and Chevrolet Tahoe gas-electric hybrid. GM currently employs 3,000 workers at its Arlington facility and is the city's single biggest private employer. Going forward, Arlington would like to attract more high-tech business. It has a large and growing branch of the University of Texas that is expanding research in fields such as nanotechnology.

High technology is an especially important dimension to boomburb businesses. Some of these businesses are spinoffs from the military industry. But in addition both boomburb start-up technology businesses and boomburb corporate divisions have played key roles in development technology. Consider computing: Cupertino, California, is home to Apple; Round Rock, Texas, is home to Dell. Also note that the original IBM personal computer (PC) was developed in a baby boomburb: in 1981 Boca Raton became home to the IBM division that designed its first PC. Boomburb high tech is widely distributed around the country. It is not just in places such as Sunnyvale, in the heart of Silicon Valley, but can be found from the Silicon forest (Beaverton, Oregon) to the Silicon prairies (Round Rock, Texas, and Eden Prairie, Minnesota). The new technology also includes biotechnology (Gaithersburg, Maryland), telecommunications (Lakewood, Colorado), broadband communications (Eden Prairie, Minnesota), avionics (Renton, Washington), and information technology (Bellevue, Washington).

The Jobs-to-People Ratio

One gauge of overall Boomburb business development is number of jobs compared to number of residents. This is expressed as a ratio, jobs per 1,000 residents. For example, if a city has 1,000 jobs for every 1,000 residents the ratio is 1.0. Any city—boomburb or otherwise—that has more jobs than people is clearly a business center. Even cities with a 0.5 ratio in job to residents are commuter destinations.

The average job ratio in the boomburbs is 0.4, while baby boomburbs average 386 jobs per 1,000 residents. The ratios indicate that both boomburbs and baby boomburbs, while not always job centers, are significant employment bases. Given household size, the number of jobs in these places is typically in balance with the number of households. In the early twentieth century utopian writers and urban reformers, such as Ebenezer Howard, advocated for "garden cities" that could relieve the congestion of old city cores.[5] The hope was that these "new towns" would develop self-sustaining local industry and would thus be more than simple bedroom communities. While boomburbs clearly lack the garden city form, they often function in a way that Howard predicted—as economically semi-autonomous places that remain embedded in a larger metropolis.

Not surprisingly, the two boomburbs with the tallest office buildings—Irvine, California, and Irving, Texas—have the highest ratio of jobs to people. Irvine's ratio is 1.2, and Irving's is 1.0. No other boomburbs have more jobs than residents. However, ten of them do have a jobs ratio that exceeds 0.5. Two of these are Orange County neighbors of Irvine: Costa Mesa, home to the upscale South Coast Plaza Mall, and Santa Ana, home of the John Wayne Airport. Costa Mesa has 709 jobs for every 1,000 residents, or a 0.71 ratio, while Orange has a 0.68 ratio. Dallas boomburbs near Irving are also job rich: Plano, home to several Fortune 1000 headquarters, has a 0.55 job ratio; Carrollton has a 0.63 job ratio. Two Phoenix boomburbs—Tempe and Scottsdale—are major employment centers: Tempe, home to Arizona State University and Arizona Mills shopping mall, has 893 jobs for every 1,000 residents; Scottsdale, which lies in Phoenix's favored quarter and contains several upscale shopping and office districts, has a job ratio of 0.62.

Western boomburbs also have high employment concentrations. Sunnyvale, in the heart of the Bay Area's Silicon Valley, has a ratio of 0.59. Seattle's major suburb Bellevue has 811 jobs for every 1,000 residents. Ontario, California, where there is a major airport and Ontario Mills mall, has a job ratio of 0.58. And Thousand Oaks, California, just west of Los Angeles, has just over half as many jobs as people, with a 0.52 ratio. Interestingly, no boomburb east of Texas has a job ratio above 0.5, indicating that boomburbs in the East may be more like overgrown bedroom suburbs than like new cities. By contrast, many Western boomburbs often match their core city in terms of employment concentration.

Eighteen baby boomburbs also have a jobs ratio above 0.5. This means more than one in five baby boomburbs is employment rich, which matches the proportion of boomburbs with high job concentrations. Like boomburbs, most of these places are in the West, with the notable exception of those around Minneapolis. Four of these exceed 500 jobs per 1,000 residents. Another place with baby boomburb job concentrations is the Bay Area, which is home to the high-tech and mostly suburban Silicon Valley.

There are also boomburbs and baby boomburbs with few jobs. Moreno Valley, California, in the Inland Empire, has just 109 jobs for every 1,000 residents, the lowest job ratio of any boomburb. Moreno Valley has a history of being an affordable alternative to coastal Los Angeles and Orange Counties. It is one of the largest and fastest-growing bedroom communities in the nation. The baby boomburb with the lowest concentration of jobs is Missouri City, Texas, just south of Houston.

The Business Landscape

The boomburb urban form presents a complicated commercial geography. The boomburb has obviously evolved well past its bedroom era to now possess some of the most high-profile and productive businesses in the nation. Yet touring a typical boomburb could lead one to recall the famous line from Gertrude Stein regarding Oakland, California, where she grew up: "There is no there there."[6] The first word of advice for anyone looking to see a boomburb business district is to forget about downtown and head out for the highways. You may not find much of a "there" in a traditional sense, but boomburb freeways often anchor some of their region's biggest economic engines and recreational attractions.

Highways, in particular their exit ramps, are important enough to the commerce of boomburbs to have come up multiple times in conversations with boomburb elected and economic development officials. When asked about their city's economic development tools, many of the people connected with boomburb business promotion responded that they could use more freeway access. In fact, most of the nation's biggest urban freeway expansions completed since 2000 lie in boomburbs. Examples include the Foothills Freeway in Southern California's Inland Empire, which runs through Ontario, Rancho Cucamonga, Fontana, and San Bernardino. Phoenix's Loop 202, which is still under construction, links Tempe, Mesa, Gilbert, and Chandler, while the recently finished Loop 101 connects Scottsdale, Peoria, and Glendale. In Denver, the 470, the region's eastern beltway, was just finished in Aurora; and in Las Vegas, the still-under-construction 215 beltway passes through North Las Vegas and Henderson.

Freeways are an especially important element of growth for boomburbs in the Dallas Metroplex. Describing the role played in promoting office development in Houston and Dallas, Robert Lang says,

> Office development occurs along freeway corridors more in Texas than perhaps anywhere else in the country. The Texas freeway system, which features long stretches of frontage road running parallel to the highway, has facilitated this type of growth. These [frontage] roads function as local lanes to the freeway's express lanes, allowing motorists to leave the freeway and drive alongside it for miles. . . . The frontage road functions as a quasi-extra lane and has multiple points of entry to the highway, helping to elongate [commercial] development into corridors.[7]

Aerial Views of Boomburbs—Then and Now

Panoramic view of Naperville, Illinois, 1869. Photo shows Naperville as a bustling post–Civil War village. Western boomburbs and baby boomburbs were for the most part either too small or did not yet exist at the time the panoramas were in vogue. (Landslides Aerial Photography)

McMansions from above. This upscale subdivision in Plano, Texas, shows large homes nearly consuming relatively modest lots. Even in the wide open spaces of Texas, boomburb lots tend to run small, although most homes shown here have pools filling what little space is not taken up by the house. (Alex S. MacLean/Landslides Aerial Photography)

Boomburb Housing: Old and New

Victorian-era house, downtown Naperville, Illinois. Some of Naperville's older housing downtown is being torn down in order to build larger homes. (Jennifer LeFurgy)

New condominiums on the outskirts of Naperville, Illinois. Attached dwellings are common in most boomburbs—even up-scale ones. (Jennifer LeFurgy)

Broad Acre Realized

As architect Frank lloyd Wright predicted in his Broad Acre model, superhighways would shape the future American metropolis. The just completed interchange linking Superstition Freeway and the 202 Loop in east Mesa helps spread Broad Acre-style development in Phoenix's East Valley.

Scottsdale's Taliesin West. When Wright's Taliesin West was constructed in the 1930s, Scottsdale was a tiny speck of a town that did not even warrant mention in the Arizona WPA Guide. Wright thought he had moved far enough from the city to ensure long-term tranquility, but subdivisions now sweep around the site along Frank Lloyd Wright Boulevard. Wright, the visionary who imagined the boomburbs, had his rural sanctuary consumed by one.

(Except as noted, all photos by Robert Lang.)

Large lot for sale, east side of Mesa, Arizona. The one-acre lot in the photo sits at the end of a gated cul-de-sac and includes all water and utility hookups.

House with surrounding wall, Vialetto section, Aliante, Nevada. The dwelling consumes most of the lot, so that the walls constitute the view and lie almost in an arm's reach of the house.

Big Names, Small Lots

Large, single-family homes on tiny lots, Rancho Cucamonga, California. This subdivision occupies some of the last buildable land, as development of the Inland Empire presses against the San Gabriel Mountains.

Common driveway in the Dos Lagos master-planned community, Corona, California. Three upscale, single-family homes with zero lot lines share a common driveway.

Gates

Broken gates, Mesa, Arizona. Many boomburb rental gated communities are easy to enter because their gates are either not in use or broken.

Private, gated residence in the "cluburb" of Paradise Valley, Arizona. Upscale, large-lot homes in the East rarely feature such gates across driveways, but houses in the Western cluburbs often have a more fortressed look.

Life on the Strip

Kitschy spindles and a faux gaslight on a Santa Ana, California, Mexican restaurant. The contrast reflects perhaps that between the several communities in this new Brooklyn. (Jennifer LeFurgy)

Most new strip shopping in the boomburbs comes with a greater emphasis on pedestrian space. A minimall in Tempe, Arizona, with ample outdoor seating and courtyard areas.

Signs

The Camp, Costa Mesa, California, and its rustic signage. This can be seen as the developer's attempt to "blur the boundaries between the outdoors and everyday life" and to bring green development to Orange County. (Jennifer LeFurgy)

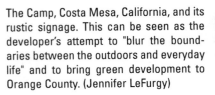

Megachurch marquee in Peoria, Arizona. Despite their newness, many boomburbs have seen some of their older retail areas recycled into other uses. In this case, a mall has become a megachurch, with, among other offerings, day care, conference facilities, and a school.

Downtown and New Town

Sleepy downtown Irving, Texas, contrasts sharply with Irving's new town of Las Colinas shown below. Most boomburbs have tiny downtowns relative to overall size.

Residential tower in the mixed-use new town of Las Colinas in Irving, Texas. High-rise buildings are changing the skylines in the more densely built boomburbs.

Light Rail

Transit-oriented development at a station stop along the Dallas Area Rapid Transit (DART) line in Plano, Texas. Rail is literally just steps away from an adjacent apartment building and lies within a short walk of revitalized downtown Plano.

Phoenix Metro System under construction in North Tempe's edgeless city. This site will be a station stop in a low-slung office landscape that was designed around the automobile. Future infill projects will substantially increase density in this still suburban environment.

Civic Centers

Reflecting the new urbanist style, the civic center and retail core of Verrado, a large master-planned community in Buckeye, Arizona. In keeping with the image of a professionally run government, some boom-burb civic centers are in leased office space.

City Hall in an office building, Chandler, Arizona. Chandler's municipal government shares space with other tenants, including a business college, in this "downtown" office building.

Urban Scenes

Downtown Santa Ana, California, loft. The growth of such housing signals a shift to a more urban plan for built-out boomburbs

H.E.A.T. (Help Eliminate Auto Theft) van visiting Trillium at Rio Salado in Tempe, Arizona. Auto theft is a serious problem in areas close to Mexico, where stolen cars are taken to be sold for parts.

The issue of frontage roads came up in a conversation with Bob Day, mayor of Garland, Texas. According to Day, Garland may be the largest city in the United States without a regional mall. He believes that the lack of retail development in Garland is a problem of access. Garland has no frontage roads on the LBJ Freeway, which prevents the strip development typical along other Dallas freeways. Day notes that the nearby boomburb of Mesquite has half the population of Garland and generates double the sales tax. To quote Day: "You get exits, you win the retail game."[8]

The city of Arlington has the same concern about freeway access. One strategy Arlington will employ to generate more development involves building three more exit ramps off Interstate 30, which runs from the center of Dallas west to downtown Fort Worth and right through Arlington. The new exits will better connect the Arlington Stadium (home of the Texas Rangers) and Arlington's downtown to the freeway.[9] The use of the freeway as an economic development tool for Dallas boomburbs is another case for what Bruce Katz refers to as the exit-ramp economy.[10] The miles of freeway frontage a boomburb builds and the number of exit ramps it constructs will certainly shape its growth patterns and may help determine its economic fortune.

A boomburb's residential and economic development potential may also be determined by whether or not the city lies within a region's favored quarter. The real estate consultant Chris Leinberger developed the favored-quarter model of regional development to explain the fact that, for the most part, wealthy households, high-end retail stores, and suburban corporate offices seem to spread disproportionately through one quadrant of the metropolis.[11] The idea has its roots in the work of Homer Hoyt, an economist with the Federal Housing Administration in the 1930s. Hoyt found that high-cost housing radiated from the core of a region in one wedge—often beginning at the corner of the downtown that contained the region's financial district.[12] Hoyt's "sector hypothesis" was empirically based on tracking the origin and evolution of wealthy urban and suburban neighborhoods in 142 American cities in 1900, 1915, and 1936.

This pattern certainly holds true in the Dallas Metroplex. High-priced homes, up-scale shopping, and class A office space spill mostly north out of the central business district. This pattern began early in the twentieth century with the establishment of wealthy in-town residential areas such as Highland Park and rich suburbs such as University Park (home to Southern Methodist University).[13] This wealth wedge starts in the northern parts of Irving, runs through Carrollton and Plano, and ends in Garland. The wealth also radiates out of these more established places to such baby boomburbs as Flower Mound and Lewisville and such exurbs as Allen and McKinney.[14] Boomburbs that lie within Dallas's favored quarter have mostly benefited in terms of business development.

Many people connected with boomburbs—mayors, economic development folks, and local business owners—like to talk up downtown, but when one finally locates an actual boomburb downtown they may be reminded of the Peggy Lee hit song, "Is That All There Is?" It is remarkable. Boomburbs with 200,000 and 300,000 residents can have centers that look like they belong in cities one-tenth their size. Part of the relative obscurity of boomburbs surely has to do with their lack of a center.

Mesa, Arizona, for example, has more people than Atlanta, Minneapolis, St. Louis, or Miami. But Mesa's size advantage does not translate into a bustling downtown: Atlanta has over 30 million square feet of office space in its downtown, and Miami has about 13 million; downtown Mesa?—less than 1 million. To a pedestrian downtown Miami feels like a big city, Atlanta feels like an even bigger city, but Mesa seems like a midsize suburb. Boomburb downtowns are less production centers than consumption centers. The most attractive downtowns are lifestyle oriented rather than business oriented. They seem to work best as small, pedestrian-friendly neighborhoods that offer alternative environments to the typical suburban subdivision. Examples include Scottsdale, Plano, and Orange.[15]

Some boomburb mayors find that the ultimate value of downtown may be public relations, in that an amusing and attractive downtown can help brand the city. Boyd Dunn, mayor of Chandler, Arizona, believes that historic preservation and urban revitalization in downtown is especially important to boomburbs in the Phoenix region, so that places such as Chandler can keep their identity. Otherwise, he observes, boomburbs blend right into to one another and become one large, spread-out city. Downtown housing and mixed-use development promote the idea of the town. And who knows, it could even indirectly help sell homes in the boomburb's many single-family subdivisions. People moving into the sprawl can at least point to the center of their town and say, "There is a there there."

Boomburb boosters have other reasons for promoting downtown development. Nearly every person interviewed for this book who was connected with a boomburb was completely sold on the idea of transit-oriented development (TOD). In its modern form, TOD had been developed and promoted by the new urbanist planner Peter Calthorpe.[16] The idea is that station stops on rail lines—including light rail—should be developed as dense, mixed-use, and mixed-tenure places. It is easy to understand the acceptance of this thinking in a place such as Gresham, Oregon (a baby boomburb), whose town center was developed around this model. As a Portland suburb, Gresham falls within the region's urban growth boundary and must comply with land use regulations that mandate such a practice. TOD has caught on even in what would appear to be the least friendly of places—the heart of Texas and Arizona's Goldwater country.[17] Most people connected with downtown boomburb revitalization apparently see economic value in transit, specifically its potential to encourage high-value real estate development.

Boomburb mayors and economic development folks do not like just any kind of transit; they specifically want rail. In their minds, rail stops become places of importance, which create value. Whether or not rail is an efficient form of transportation is pretty much a secondary concern. The people invested in a boomburb downtown want to be able to point to a real core. They are looking less for urbanity than a competitive advantage over the emerging baby boomburbs and exurbs at the fringe of the metropolis. For whatever reason, light rail will expand significantly over the next twenty years. The motive, ironically, may be less about moving people than anchoring them.

The Dallas–Fort Worth Metroplex

Dallas and Fort Worth are not really twin cities like Minneapolis and St. Paul. Dallas and Fort Worth are about thirty-five miles apart from downtown to downtown. At the time of the 1939 WPA *Guide to Texas,* the two urban clusters were not treated as part of a single metropolis. Sure, they were just down the road from one another; yet the region was not unified.

The urban unification (read, sprawl) that made the Dallas–Fort Worth Metroplex emerge is a post–World War II phenomenon. For Dallas and Fort Worth to go from two metropolises to one required interstate highways, air conditioning, and boomburbs. The boomburbs around Dallas–Fort Worth are regional filler: they link distant places in the Metroplex and give the region its definition. All of the space between Dallas and Fort Worth is filled in by three boomburbs: Irving, Grand Prairie, and Arlington. Minus these boomburbs, the Metroplex would be a duplex—two places side by side but mostly unlinked.[18]

The federal government played handmaiden to suburbia's development (see chapter 2), but one federal agency in particular helped shape the Dallas–Fort Worth Metroplex: the Federal Aviation Administration (FAA). In the 1960s Dallas and Fort Worth were insisting on separate airports, despite the fact that the cities were so close to one another. As part of a cost-saving measure, the FAA ruled that there be only one joint airport for the region. A compromise was worked out to place the new Dallas–Fort Worth International Airport (DFW) halfway between the two cities, at the line of the counties of Dallas and Tarrant.

After DFW opened in the early 1970s, the Dallas and Fort Worth urban areas rushed toward each other. The Dallas side of the region developed faster. The airport is in Dallas's favored quarter, as was its old airport, Love Field.[19] The area east of DFW, in Irving, quickly filled with hotels and offices. When airlines shifted to hub-and-spoke routes, DFW became a major hub. The significance to the region's economic development has been tremendous. According to *USA Today,*

> Dallas-Fort Worth International Airport has unleashed massive devel-
> opment around it. Las Colinas is the biggest. A 12,000-acre commu-
> nity that's larger than most downtowns and is geared to businesses
> and residents needing quick airport access, Las Colinas has 27 million
> square feet of office space, 8.5 million square feet of light industrial,
> 1.3 million square feet of retail, hotels, restaurants, and 13,300 single-
> and multifamily homes. Its commercial space and [its] population of
> 25,000 rival downtown Dallas.[20]

John Kasarda dubbed this airport-driven urban growth "aerotropolis" and refers to Irving as "an airport city."[21] DFW so changed the face of Irv-ing that the new official city history is titled *Irving, Texas: From Rails to Wings, 1903–2003.*

The Dallas–Fort Worth Metroplex is also a major business center. In a study for the Brookings Institution that looked at global business net-works, Peter Taylor and Robert Lang found that, among U.S. metropolitan areas, the region was the ninth most networked city in the world's pro-ducer service economy.[22] Through a network analysis that tracks the global distribution of a hundred leading firms, the study shows how "world cities" connect to the global economy of advanced producer services.[23] Dallas ranks behind Sunbelt rivals such as Miami (fifth) and Atlanta (sixth) in this measure but just ahead of Houston (tenth) and miles ahead of Phoenix (thirty-seventh).

The Market for Office Space

Boomburbs and baby boomburbs have plenty of office development. There are well-established markets in such diverse places as Bellevue, Washing-ton, Olathe, Kansas, Plymouth, Minnesota, Beaverton, Oregon, Sugar

Land, Texas, and Pleasanton, California, to name but a few. The single biggest cluster of office space in any boomburb (and indeed in any suburb) is in Irvine, the edge city around John Wayne Airport in Orange County, California.[24] This market contains almost 30 million square feet of office space, or approximately as much as Dallas's downtown.[25] Were it a downtown, the John Wayne Airport area (also called South Coast, in reference to its big anchor mall) would rank about tenth in the United States, just behind Dallas and Atlanta but ahead of Denver. Irvine is home to several Fortune 1000 headquarters: Standard Pacific, Allergan, Broadcom, and Westcorp. The design shops of several major car makers are in Irvine.

Scottsdale, Arizona, also serves as headquarters for major firms: Allied Waste Industries, Giant Industries, Meritage, and Dial. Scottsdale's office market surpasses that of Phoenix, the downtown at the center of its region. The Phoenix region's office markets and business development patterns are different from those of the Dallas Metroplex.

Dallas

Dallas currently has the eighth largest regional office market in the country, with nearly 172 million square feet of inventory.[26] This puts Dallas ahead of such other major Sunbelt markets as Atlanta (156 million square feet), Houston (157 million), and Phoenix (63 million).[27] According to *Black's Guide*, Dallas also has the highest vacancy rate of any major market in the nation, with just over a quarter of the region's office space lying empty. As would be expected given the high vacancy rate, very little new space is being built. As of 2003 the Dallas region only had 2.3 million square feet of new office space under construction.

Table 4-1 shows that, combined, the seven Dallas boomburbs in 2003 had more office space than did the main central business district. Downtown Dallas has just over 30 million square feet of space, while office space in the boomburbs exceeds 37 million square feet. The rest of the Dallas region has over 104 million square feet of office inventory remaining, with the vast bulk of it lying within the city of Dallas. Just over 62 percent of the office development in the Dallas metropolitan area is in the central city.[28] This high percentage is attributed to the city's relatively large size and to the fact that much of the region's beltway passes through Dallas proper, which allowed it to capture much of the office development outside the central business district.[29]

Because the city of Dallas alone has about 105 million square feet of office space, the rental offices outside of incorporated Dallas equal about 67 million square feet. The city of Fort Worth accounts for about 6.4 million square feet of this space. Thus the boomburbs contain well over half

Table 4-1. Metropolitan Dallas Office Space, 2003

Office market	Square feet of office space	Percent of metropolitan office space	Number of buildings	Average square feet
Central business district	30,050,277	17.5	77	390,263
Outside of central business district	104,487,701	60.9	1,430	73,068
Boomburbs	37,112,248	21.6	374	99,231
Arlington	4,208,802	2.5	79	53,276
Carrollton	1,340,694	0.8	25	53,628
Garland	836,432	0.5	21	39,830
Grand Prairie	597,831	0.3	9	66,426
Irving	21,385,912	12.5	139	153,855
Mesquite	733,688	0.4	6	122,281
Plano	8,008,889	4.7	95	84,304
Total	171,650,226	100.0	1,881	91,255

Source: *Black's Guide to Office Leasing: Dallas/Fort Worth Office Space Market* (Gaithersburg, Md.: Black's Guide, 2003).

(about 60 percent) of the region's suburban office development, or over a fifth of the total office market in the Metroplex. The edge city of Los Colinas is home to Irving's single biggest cluster of office space, at nearly 8 million square feet of class A and B office space in 1999.[30] The office market produces tremendous taxes for the city, which is therefore able to tax residential property at the low rate of $4.90 per $1,000 of market value.[31]

As chapter 1 indicates, Irving has the most high-rise office buildings (with sixteen of them above twelve stories) of any U.S. boomburb other than Irvine (which has nineteen). The tallest building in Irving is the Williams Square Central Tower, at 358 feet and twenty-six floors. According to Emporis (a real estate firm that tracks office buildings), the building is the tallest in the Metroplex outside of Dallas or Fort Worth proper. It is located in the Los Colinas development and is noted for its sculpture of bronze horses. The building is also the tallest office tower by far for all fifty-four boomburbs. Irving may feature Dallas's only boomburb high-rise skyline—and with ten buildings above 200 feet the most impressive for any boomburb—but it does not rival the city's cenral business district in either the height or size of offices. Dallas's downtown offices average 390,263 square feet. The downtown also has two dozen buildings taller than the Williams Square Central Tower. Even the smaller Forth Worth downtown features six building above this height. Irving is as good as it gets for boomburb skylines, and yet it is trumped by the Metroplex's smaller city.

The rest of Dallas's boomburb office development (with the exception of the development in the edge city of Los Colinas) is in edgeless cities, "a form of sprawling office development that does not have the density or cohesiveness of edge cities."[32] A look at data from both *Black's Guide* and the publications of the real estate firm Cushman and Wakefield reveals that the vast majority of the office space in the fifty-four boomburbs can be found in edgeless cities.[33] This figure is perhaps 90–95 percent of the total building inventory.

Table 4-2 highlights the changes in the Dallas boomburb office markets from 1980 to 2003. Note that this is a historical analysis of existing inventory as opposed to a longitudinal analysis that takes a snapshot of data at different points in time. It looks at the age of existing buildings and projects them back by a decade. The *Black's Guide* data were gathered only for 2003. Before the late 1980s, the guide did not survey Dallas, so it would have been impossible to find these data for earlier periods. However, *Black's Guide* data do include the year that each building was constructed. It cannot be known from current inventory the exact office figures for any one decade because some buildings that existed in 1980 or before may have subsequently cycled out of the current inventory. But this is not really much of a problem for most boomburb office markets, because they are so new that very few buildings will have fallen out of use.

Based on when Dallas boomburbs' current offices were built, the 1980s were indeed a boom time. This is also reflected in the population data covered in chapter 2. About half (46 percent) of the 2003 boomburb office stock was constructed in the 1980s. By contrast, about a quarter of the inventory was added in the 1990s. This slowdown in the 1990s was not limited to Dallas. The entire Dallas region added about 40 million square feet of new office space in the 1990s, well under the 85 million built in the 1980s.[34] The current decade would seem to be on pace to exceed the growth in the 1990s, as indicated by just the first three years' performance; however, given the high office vacancy rates in the region and the slowdown in new construction, that may not happen. Much of the office growth since 2000 was driven by the late 1990s' hot economy, which has since cooled.

The average life span of office buildings is about fifty years.[35] Almost 66 percent of Irving's office space is pre-1990s; put another way, much of Irving's office inventory is approaching, or may be over, twenty years old. That may not sound old in terms of buildings in traditional cities, but in the disposable world of suburbia, that is midpoint in the life cycle. One of Irving's edge cities, Los Colinas, saw a dramatic slowdown in office construction during the 1990s: only 657,185 square feet of its 1999 office inventory was built during the decade.[36] Conversely, almost ten times that amount of

Table 4-2. Dallas Boomburb Office Space, 1980–2003

Boomburb	2003		2000–03		1990–99		1980–89		Before 1980	
	Square feet	Percent	Square feet	Percent	Square feet	Percent	Square feet	Percent	Square feet	Percent
Arlington	4,208,802	11.3	490,424	9.5	1,180,371	12.9	2,407,699	14.1	130,308	2.3
Carrollton	1,340,694	3.6	506,815	9.8	261,544	2.9	528,220	3.1	44,115	0.8
Garland	836,432	2.3	25,440	0.5	27,382	0.3	665,610	3.8	118,000	2.1
Grand Prairie	597,831	1.6	n.a.	0.0	100,682	1.1	379,149	2.2	118,000	2.1
Irving	21,385,912	57.6	1,665,373	32.1	5,004,951	54.7	11,237,932	65.9	3,477,656	60.8
Mesquite	733,668	2.0	n.a.	0.0	n.a.	0.0	103,496	0.6	630,172	11.0
Plano	8,008,889	21.6	2,494,591	48.1	2,575,798	28.1	1,740,117	10.2	1,198,383	21.0
Total	37,112,228	100.0	5,182,643	100.0	9,150,728	100.0	17,062,223	99.9	5,716,634	100.1

Source: See table 4-1.

space (or 6,252,982 square feet) was built in Los Colinas during the 1980s. This means that Irving's edgeless cities account for most of Irving's office growth during that decade. In contrast to Irving, Plano has much newer office space. Just over a third of Plano's office space was constructed before 1990. That means the city's typical building is in the ten-year-old range. Plano's office market is now growing faster than Irving's. The city added over 800,000 square feet more office space to its stock from 2000 to 2003 than Irving did for the same period.

Dallas's four baby boomburbs of Denton, Flower Mound, Lewisville, and North Richland Hills also have had some office growth since 1980. Interestingly, two of these places—Flower Mound and Lewisville—are starting to emerge as decent-sized office markets. Their growth hints at greater diffusion of commerce in the Dallas Metroplex, away from boomburbs and into smaller, newer, and more remote suburbs. From 2000 to 2003 Lewisville added almost 1.7 million square feet of office space—a figure that surpasses Irving's—and this in a city that has only about 3 million square feet of total inventory. That means that over half of Lewisville's office space dates to just 2000. Flower Mound is seeing similar growth. Although this baby boomburb has only 723,711 square feet of office space, it added 616,800 of this since 2000.

Phoenix

The Phoenix metropolitan area is not highly ranked in terms of its network link to other world cities. The region likewise has relatively few major producer service companies relative to Sunbelt peers such as Atlanta, Miami, Dallas, and Houston. Most of Phoenix's accounting, law, media, finance, and management consulting firms handle regional business only. But Phoenix is a fast-growing region in a fast-growing state, so local demand for these services is high. Thus, the region does have considerable office development—but below the level of its Sunbelt rivals, whose offices are filled with firms that export their producer services, or services used by businesses, to the rest of the nation and the world.

Phoenix had nearly 63 million square feet of rental office space in 2004 (table 4-3).[37] The amount of space falls well below that of the Dallas Metroplex. Phoenix is a less populous region than Dallas, but even in per capita terms it has less than half the space of Dallas. Phoenix also has a much smaller downtown than Dallas: it accounts for only about 10 percent of its region's office market.

Phoenix, like Dallas, has a favored quarter; it runs north out of the downtown. In fact, the city's midtown corridor runs straight out of downtown

Table 4-3. Metropolitan Phoenix Office Space, 2004

Office market	Square feet of office space	Percent of metropolitan office space	Number of buildings	Average square feet
Central business district	16,942,275	26.9	135	125,498
Downtown	6,441,270	10.2	41	157,104
Midtown	10,501,005	16.7	94	111,713
Outside of central business district	23,474,736	37.3	423	58,967
Boomburbs	22,519,217	35.8	437	51,531
Scottsdale	12,312,069	19.6	222	55,460
Tempe	6,467,471	10.3	130	49,750
Mesa	2,570,970	4.1	63	40,809
Chandler/Gilbert	1,168,707	1.9	22	53,123
Total	62,936,228	100.0	995	63,252

Source: Cushman and Wakefield, Global Real Estate Solutions, *The Phoenix Office Market, Spring 2004* (Phoenix, 2004).

along Central Avenue. Even Phoenix's central business district sprawls for several miles along a main boulevard. Beyond the midtown office market lies affluent north Phoenix. This area includes the Camelback Corridor office district (near Camelback Mountain). North Phoenix had about 8 million square feet of office space in 2004.[38]

The boomburb of Scottsdale lies northeast of downtown Phoenix, inside the region's favored quarter. About a fifth of the Phoenix region's office space may be found in just this one boomburb. But Scottsdale office development does not cluster in any one place, least of all its downtown. And Scottsdale has only one office building above twelve floors.[39] That building—the Amtrust Tower—just barely surpasses the high-rise minimum of eleven stories. By 2007 the Scottsdale Waterfront Tower will be finished, to become the tallest building in Scottsdale (at thirteen floors).

The biggest single concentration of office space in Scottsdale is in the Scottsdale Airpark, next to the city's small corporate airport; it has around 4.5 million square feet. According to Scottsdale's website:

Scottsdale Airpark, the 2,600-acre commercial area which surrounds the Airport, has become a national model for airport-based business parks. This model has been achieved through the efforts of numerous City of Scottsdale civic and community leaders. Several important factors have contributed to the success of the Scottsdale Airport/Airpark—It is headquarters for over 25 national/regional corporations; home to more than 2,200 small- to medium-size businesses; workplace of more than 42,000 employees; and has easy airport access and seven miles of taxiway access. The workforce within its boundaries has tripled in the past decade, making it the second largest employment center in a community of approximately 212,000.[40]

The passage shows the power of even a small corporate airport to spark economic development. Keno Hawker, mayor of Mesa, noting Scottsdale's success, hopes that his city could do the same for its Falcon Field airport, which has runways long enough to take spillover commercial freight traffic from the overburdened Phoenix Sky Harbor.[41] He is even more hopeful that the Phoenix-Williams Gateway Airport, a recently decommissioned military base with three runways, can serve Phoenix's East Valley the way Ontario Airport serves Los Angeles's Inland Empire.[42] Or better still, the boom in passengers at Williams could trigger office development in the way that John Wayne Airport in Orange County has helped anchor the big edge city, Jamboree, at Jamboree Road in Irvine and Costa Mesa.

Yet even with a large concentration of development at the Scottsdale Airpark, Scottsdale will not qualify as an edge city under Joel Garreau's criteria, which require 5 million square feet of space and a mix of uses, including 600,000 square feet of retail space.[43] The boomburb of Tempe, Arizona, looks as though it too could become an edge city, but its office development is divided between at least two submarkets in the northern and southern parts of town. Even by stretching the edge city definition a bit and throwing in the Camelback area, less than a fifth of the office space lies in large, noncentral, business district clusters.

It is ironic that there are so few edge cities in Phoenix, considering that this is the region where the edge city concept began in a 1984 planning document written by Chris Leinberger.[44] The report argues that, rather than letting its office development sprawl, the Phoenix region should develop higher-density urban village clusters that mix high-rise offices, multifamily housing, and major retail stores. The report notes that doing this would take planning, because market forces alone would produce only sprawl. Several of the Phoenix region's boomburbs were identified as ripe for such planning. The idea of building urban villages may have died had Leinberger, along with Charles Lockwood, not written an influential article based on the concept for the *Atlantic Monthly* titled "How Business Is Reshaping America."[45] The article so impressed the *Washington Post* reporter Joel Garreau (who had a new beat covering growth) that he used the urban village concept as the basis of a book.[46] Garreau kept all the criteria that Leinberger proposed but relabeled the idea "edge cities."

The five boomburb markets contain nearly 36 percent of the Phoenix region's office space, or a much larger share than the boomburbs of the Dallas Metroplex. Most of this space is in Tempe and Scottsdale, but small markets exist in Mesa, Chandler, and Gilbert. Of the latter three, only Mesa has plans to add significantly more space, especially around its airports, Falcon Field and Williams, along the still-under-construction Gateway 202 Loop. Mesa also has the tallest high-rise office tower among the Phoenix boomburbs, with the sixteen-floor, 225-feet-tall Bank of America building.[47] Phoenix office space not in the central business district is just over 37 percent of the total market in the region. The majority of this office space, as in Dallas, lies within the expansive land area of the city proper. But the boomburbs of Glendale and Peoria also have some of this space.[48]

While downtown Phoenix has a small office space market for such a big city, its buildings are much taller and larger (at an average 155,104 square feet) than the area's boomburb offices (with an average of 51,531 square feet).[49] In fact, downtown Phoenix's offices are almost three times the size of those in Scottsdale, the boomburb with the largest average building size. Even downtown Phoenix, which is one of the smallest major downtowns in the United States and has equally small buildings, still has a larger average building size than the leading boomburb of Irving, Texas.

Business and the Exurbs

A concern expressed by many boomburb leaders is that a new ring of exurbs (including some baby boomburbs) is now in a position to draw businesses from the boomburbs as the boomburbs once had from central cities. Boomburbs are by now so big and so often diverse that they are starting to take on some characteristics of central cities. Many have distressed sections, and others are challenged by having to educate the children of foreign-born residents in multiple languages.

And like central cities, boomburbs are now becoming vulnerable. The costs of doing business in many boomburbs are rising. Boomburbs are starting to invest in more expensive types of infrastructure such as public transit. At the same time these places are aging—not a good thing for most suburbs. No longer new, not old enough to be quaint, some boomburbs are stuck in the middle, which may not be the best position to compete from. Even successful boomburbs face challenges as communities at the edge of the region go after their share of commercial development.

For example, consider the city of Plano, Texas. It is the second most affluent community among the fifty-four boomburbs, after Naperville, Illinois. Plano also is home to seven Fortune 1000 headquarters and has over 8 million square feet of office space. What could Plano possibly have to worry about? As it turns out, plenty. According to Mayor Pat Evans, the business of Plano is under threat from such nearby exurbs as Lewisville (a baby boomburb), Frisco, Allan, and McKinney. The reason is that these places have a tax advantage that was intended to promote economic development in rural areas. But even though these exurbs are now fully part of a large Dallas metropolitan economy, they retain these advantages.

Under a state law known as 4A/4B remote cities can use a penny of each dollar of their sales tax to promote business development. Texas boomburbs such as Irving, Plano, and Garland cannot do the same. Besides, the latter have already dedicated a penny of their local sales tax revenue to pay for DART (Dallas Area Rapid Transit system). People in the Dallas exurbs of course also use DART but thus far have been unwilling to pay to extend service to their towns. Instead, exurb residents park at the terminals in the boomburbs and take DART from there.

Exurbs can use sales tax money to develop property and lease space at low cost to tenants. The sales tax revenue can also be used to directly subsidize businesses. Mayor Evans described a specific case: a small firm that spun off EDS (Electronic Data Service) was planning to locate in Plano in a built-to-suit building, and the mayor arranged for the company to get a $7,000 tax abatement as part of a business retention package. But the city of Frisco offered the firm a $700,000 package to locate in Frisco. The $700,000 came from the sales tax boon. Mayor Evans notes that office developers are now expressing doubt as to the future market in Plano, given that the city cannot compete successfully against its exurbs.

Mayor Evans finds that the tactics used by Frisco to poach businesses from closer-in suburbs also put a strain on regional cooperation. The question is, Why cooperate when you cannot trust the exurbs not to steal businesses? But the city of Frisco claims it does not recruit firms from Plano. The businesses "just come to us." This is indicative of how American metropolitan areas are growing. They push into increasingly remote locations and use legislation intended to promote rural economic growth to steal businesses from older, more developed suburbs.

Boomburbs are mostly successful for now, but there are some dark clouds on the horizon. As Mayor Joe Putnam of Irving notes, places such as Frisco, Allan, and McKinney "are the Irvings of tomorrow—they are now where we where we were in the 1970s."[50]

5

Big Skies, Small Lots
Boomburb Housing and Master-Planned Development

Yes the lots are small, but look up and see the skies—they are big!

SALES AGENT,
ALIANTE MASTER-PLANNED DEVELOPMENT

From Coral Springs, Florida, to Costa Mesa, California, land is at a premium in most boomburbs. The result is that many developers of master-planned communities build increasingly larger homes on smaller lots and create dense residential clusters. Some open-space relief is afforded these places by common amenities such as parks, pools, and nature trails. But the bottom line is that many boomburbs seem crowded. This chapter explores the housing and community development world of boomburbs. It highlights some surprising patterns of growth, including a wide variation in the use of gated and walled developments.

Housing and community development is at the heart of boomburb business and identity. Before boomburbs attracted professional sports franchises, theme parks, high-technology firms, and corporate headquarters, they were almost exclusively residential. Even with their entire commercial, retail, and entertainment growth, housing development often still drives boomburb economies. Furthermore, the population gains made by boomburbs due to rapid residential expansion will anchor subsequent rounds of businesses locating in these cities as they seek proximity to new labor markets.

Chapter 5 examines housing conditions in the boomburbs from multiple perspectives, including the opportunities to own homes in these places. Housing affordability in boomburbs depends mostly on in which region of the country the city is found—Texas boomburbs are the most affordable, while those in California are the least affordable. In general, boomburbs have somewhat less affordable housing than the nation as a whole. This chapter includes an analysis of boomburb occupancy numbers, building permit data, and the age of the housing stock. It also examines housing "hardship," affordability, ownership rates, and 2006 boomburb home values. Boomburbs are often home to master-planned gated communities; therefore, trends, data, and case analysis of such developments are covered, with a focus on the Phoenix and Las Vegas regions. The chapter concludes with a section on the evolution of housing types in boomburbs, including a review of various forms of residential gating.

The Business of Housing Growth

Boomburbs may be stealth cities for much of the public, but they are well-known turf to the nation's biggest home builders. The national associations for developers, such as the Urban Land Institute and the National Association of Home Builders, have hundreds of members who make good livings from constructing boomburbs. In a sense, the primary business of most boomburbs is growth itself. This is most true for the newest and fastest-growing boomburbs.

Master-Planned Community Development

Boomburbs, especially those around Los Angeles, Denver, Phoenix, and Las Vegas, are home to some of the nation's largest master-planned communities. In fact, Irvine, California, home to Irvine Ranch, is essentially one large master-planned community. The scale of construction—and the wealth it is generating—in some places is tremendous. Large sections of many boomburbs are literally under construction, including the whole northern half of North Las Vegas, Nevada, much of Chandler and Gilbert, Arizona's, southern and eastern fringes, and the foothills east of the 805 Freeway in Chula Vista, California.

The five largest home-building firms (ranked by realtytimes.com) are all active in the fastest-growing boomburbs. The big home builders are Centex Homes, D.R. Horton, Kaufman & Broad (or KB Home), Lennar, and Pulte Homes.[1] Combined, these firms sell well over 100,000 housing units a year. These home builders often work with master-planned community developers as subcontractors of multiphase projects. The home builders will take a "builder pod" as a subsection of a much larger planned project and construct dozens or even hundreds of homes at the site.

A survey of the five largest national home builders' websites indicates that they are all actively developing new residences in boomburbs.[2] As one would expect, activity is greatest in the exploding Phoenix and Las Vegas areas. Dallas-based Centex Homes listed seventeen projects under construction in May 2005 in the Phoenix region, fourteen of which were in boomburbs. The company also has twelve developments started or planned in North Las Vegas. D.R. Horton has four developments under way in Henderson, Nevada, and three more in North Las Vegas. In the Phoenix region the firm has two new communities in Scottsdale and three in Mesa. KB Home has eight developments in North Las Vegas and six more in Henderson.[3] In Phoenix, KB is building three new communities in Mesa, two each in Gilbert and Chandler, and one in Peoria. Pulte Homes is constructing residences at four communities in Chandler, two in Peoria, and one in Mesa. The company also has five projects in Henderson and three in North Las Vegas.

Considering that the building activity mentioned above comes from just five big national companies, one sees the massive scope of boomburb growth. Note also that home building in many regions is a fragmented field and that there are plenty of smaller players at both the national and metropolitan levels that are also busily constructing houses in these markets.

Building Permit Data

National housing data for 2004, provided by the U.S. Census Bureau, indicate that five boomburbs issued permits for over 3,000 new units.[4] Boomburbs with the most new permits in descending order are North Las Vegas (5,096), Henderson, Nevada (4,869), Chandler, Arizona (4,658), Gilbert, Arizona (3,862), and Chula Vista, California—south of San Diego—(3,143). Mesa, Arizona, Irvine, California, and Arlington, Texas, trailed just behind with 2,931, 2,804, and 2,724 permits, respectively.

The biggest share of the 2004 permits issued is for single-family dwellings. The boomburb of Gilbert issued permits for only single-family homes, while Chula Vista approved 1,006 permits for multifamily units. Irvine and Riverside, California, issued the largest number of multifamily permits, with 1,742 and 1,329, respectively. These multifamily gains in California are especially impressive because they come in a state that, as Dowell Myers and Julie Park note, suffered a "collapse of multifamily housing in the 1990s."[5]

Twenty-two of the fifty-four boomburbs issued over 1,000 housing unit permits in 2004, indicating that many boomburbs were still growing strongly by mid-decade. The figure for all boomburbs was 67,117 new housing permits issued, with 49,703 for single-family residences and 17,414 for multifamily dwellings. As Anthony Downs of the Brookings Institution points out, the total number of permits issued in boomburbs is a small fraction of housing starts nationally.[6] This does hint at a possible overall slowdown this decade in these long-growing places. In addition, it shows that many diverse boomburbs, especially in California, are gaining population by more intensely using existing dwellings by, for instance, the doubling up of families. Still, when compared with older cities of equal size, most boomburbs remain very much works in progress.

When people first occupy newly built homes, they typically cram them with consumer items and appliances. New homeowners often purchase furnishings, electronic goods, and yard and home improvement items by the pallet load. Residents of brand-new communities demand a host of services, from haircutters to medical doctors. They also need public services such as schools and roads.[7] The multiplier effects from growth are tremendous. The business generated from housing development remains a driving force in the economic development of most boomburbs.

Home Prices in the Boomburbs, from Zillow.Com

The website zillow.com maintains the most comprehensive current estimation of the nation's home prices. The data can be gathered at any unit of analysis, including individual properties. An analysis of boomburb and baby boomburb housing prices was conducted in March 2006.[8] In most cases, zillow.com's market information is based on a proprietary formula using house comparables matched against current sales. In the few cases in which such an estimate cannot be performed due to insufficient data, tax assessments are used. Of 140 boomburbs and baby boomburbs, fewer than a dozen places had only tax information. Only one place—Chesapeake, Virginia—had no data.

Using a median of medians approach, zillow.com shows that a mid-priced boomburb house stood at $365,910 in 2006. This compares to the zillow.com median U.S. value of $213,900. As expected, the highest-cost homes are in California, especially the Bay Area. Sunnyvale—in the heart of the Silicon Valley—registers the highest median value, at $780,436. In Southern California, Orange County boomburbs top the list. Irvine's median-priced home is $689,224, followed closely by neighboring Costa Mesa, at $684,917. Even the once affordable Inland Empire boomburbs in

Riverside and San Bernardino Counties now have high-cost homes. But these places still offer some price relief compared with Los Angeles's coastal communities. This is especially true for San Bernardino, where the median home price is just $292,941. In Riverside County, bargain boomburbs include the city of Riverside (with a $404,498 median) and Moreno Valley (with a $368,156 median).

In 2004 and 2005 house price spikes dramatically lifted median values in the until-just-recently affordable Las Vegas and Phoenix metropolitan area boomburbs. According to data from the National Association of Realtors, the two regions experienced a 50 percent price gain in just one year. In Las Vegas, that jump came in 2004, while in Phoenix it occurred in 2005. Due to the big Las Vegas housing boom, prices in Henderson, Nevada (with a $338,781 median value), are now comparable to Los Angeles's Inland Empire. Scottsdale, Arizona (with a $459,197 median-value home), has prices now equivalent to the lower-cost towns of Orange County, California.

People who cash out Southern California homes and move to Nevada and Arizona have bid up house prices there because they often carry over enormous amounts of home equity to the purchase. For years Phoenix and Las Vegas boomed by offering a lower-cost alternative to California. However, this gap has closed somewhat, which could slow future out-migration from California to Arizona and Nevada and affect growth rates in the Las Vegas and Phoenix boomburbs.

By early 2007 this trend reversed slightly as homes in Phoenix and Las Vegas boomburbs lost as much as 15 percent of their value. Yet bargain boomburbs remain in other parts of the country, especially around Dallas. Mesquite, Texas, maintains the lowest median boomburb house value in the nation, at just over $100,000. It is followed closely by other boomburbs in the Metroplex, such as Grand Prairie (with a $104,658 median value) and Garland, where the median home runs $104,878. Even an upscale Dallas boomburb such as Plano (with a midpriced home under $200,000) has a median value that is just a fraction of equivalent California communities and even well below Arizona and Nevada upscale boomburbs.

Housing Affordability for Owners and Renters

According to an analysis by Robert Lang, housing in boomburbs is slightly less affordable than in the nation as a whole, especially for homeowners.[9] Housing is widely considered unaffordable if a household spends more than 30 percent of its gross income on housing costs. By this definition, in 2000 the share of boomburb renters with affordability problems slightly exceeded the share of all U.S. renters with affordability problems (44 percent versus

42 percent). Among owners, the gap between boomburb and national affordability rates was somewhat greater: 27 percent of boomburb owners faced excessive housing costs, compared with 22 percent of all owners.[10]

The most affordable owner-occupied homes are located in the Texas boomburbs. In Mesquite, Arlington, and Irving, only 17–18 percent of owners had excessive housing costs in 2000. By contrast, nearly 40 percent of homeowners in Hialeah, Florida, paid more than 30 percent of their income for their homes.

The boomburb rental market—like the owner market—is most affordable in Texas boomburbs.[11] In Carrollton and Irving, three in ten renters pay more than 30 percent of their monthly incomes for housing. In contrast, more than five in ten renters in San Bernardino, California, and Hialeah, Florida, shoulder unaffordable housing costs.

Housing Hardship Index

The Fannie Mae Foundation estimates "housing hardship" for all U.S. communities.[12] The calculus is for households earning up to 80 percent of their region's median income. The housing hardship index reports the percentage of households in this earning range that pay more than 30 percent of their gross income for housing. The higher the percentage paying this share of income, the greater the community's housing hardship.

Housing hardship data exist for all fifty-four boomburbs and eighty-six baby boomburbs. Ten boomburbs have a housing hardship score above 70 percent. Note that some boomburbs with the nation's most expensive housing do not have the most hardship. For example, only one of seven Orange County boomburbs—Irvine—makes the list. Yet two boomburbs in the lower-cost Inland Empire of Riverside and San Bernardino Counties have high levels of housing hardship. In fact, Moreno Valley, a city with a reputation for affordable housing, has a score that matches Irvine's. That is because there are two components to the hardship measure—income and housing costs. Irvine is expensive, but its residents have high incomes. By contrast, Moreno Valley is both less affluent and less expensive.

While six in ten of the boomburbs with the most hardship lie in the Los Angeles region, no communities in the San Francisco Bay area or San Diego County make the list. However, two South Florida boomburbs—Hialeah and Coral Springs—have high housing burdens. The two scored above 70 percent in this measure for reasons similar to those of Irvine and Moreno Valley. Coral Springs is affluent but with high housing costs, while Hialeah is poorer yet has less expensive housing. The boomburbs with the lowest housing hardship can be found in the Dallas region, which includes

Grand Prairie, the only case to fall below 50 percent (with a 48.7 percent score).

The median housing hardship for all boomburbs is 63.8 percent. By contrast, the median figure in baby boomburbs is slightly lower, at 60.9 percent. The U.S. median is 58.7 percent, meaning there is somewhat greater hardship in boomburbs and baby boomburbs than for the United States as a whole. The baby boomburb with the highest level of hardship is Davis, in suburban Sacramento; its index is 78.6 percent. With a branch of the University of California, Davis is a college town, which may be elevating this statistic somewhat due to modest student income. The least hardship is found in St. Charles, west of St. Louis; St. Charles is followed closely by Olathe, outside of Kansas City. These two Midwestern baby boomburbs have scores of 46.3 and 46.4 percent, respectively. In total, seven baby boomburbs have housing hardship figures below 50 percent. These are mainly found in the Midwest and are typically places with relatively high incomes and low housing costs.

Homeownership

For all fifty-four boomburbs combined, the homeownership rate is lower than for the nation as a whole (62.5 percent versus 66.2 percent). As with other area characteristics, however, the rate varies widely across the areas, ranging from 84.9 percent in Gilbert, Arizona, to 37.2 percent in the new Brooklyn of Irving, Texas. Homeownership rates in several other new Brooklyns, including Sunnyvale and Santa Ana, California, are also relatively low (47.6 percent and 49.3 percent, respectively).

Overcrowding

Interestingly, some boomburbs with relatively few housing starts still managed to grow significantly. Higher occupancy rates, especially in rental units, appear partly responsible for this growth. A housing unit is generally considered overcrowded if it has more than one occupant per room. By this standard, 21 percent of boomburb rental units are overcrowded, compared with 11 percent of all rental units nationwide. Southern California boomburbs, in particular, have crowded rentals, with 35 percent of renters in such fast-growing boomburbs as Oxnard and Ontario living in overcrowded conditions.

Some slower-growing new Brooklyns also appear to be squeezing more residents into existing housing. In Santa Ana, more than 60 percent of renters live in overcrowded housing, and in Hialeah, almost 40 percent of renters live with more than one person to a room.

Age of Housing Stock

The housing stock in most boomburbs is newer than in the nation as a whole. At the time of the 2000 census, one-third of the nation's housing stock was twenty years old or less. By contrast, half of the boomburb housing stock was built after 1980. Gilbert, Arizona, and Henderson, Nevada, have the newest homes: roughly 90 percent of each area's housing stock was built within the last twenty years.

While boomburbs overall are newer places than the rest of the nation, their housing was built only eight years more recently than the U.S. average (1979, versus 1971). Seven boomburbs have housing that is older than the national average. In general, baby boomburbs have newer housing stock, with a median building year of 1981.

According to Arthur Nelson and Robert Lang, housing is a legacy development. Homes last on average about 150 years, which greatly exceeds the lifespan of all commercial structures, especially retail.[13] Thus, much of the built environment in boomburbs, of which housing composes the majority share, will last well into this century. The patterns set by the boom in housing development from this decade and the several preceding it will lock boomburbs into an urban form for years to come and may be a significant drag if there are major shifts in taste and technology that make such communities obsolete.

Behind the Housing Data: Gated Community Development in Las Vegas and Phoenix Boomburbs

Las Vegas and Phoenix are lands of walled and gated communities, and its boomburbs are chock full of them. According to the first-ever American Housing Survey (AHS) of gated communities, Las Vegas has the highest percentage of such places for any large metropolitan area in the United States, followed closely by Phoenix.[14] While gated communities compose a relatively small share of the nation's housing stock, they are sufficiently well represented in the boomburbs around Los Angeles, Denver, Phoenix, and Las Vegas to warrant a special focus. They are ubiquitous enough in some boomburbs that much new housing construction lands within their walls.

Background on Gated Communities

The term "gated communities" for most people conjures up images of exclusive developments with fancy homes and equally fancy lifestyles. At the gates stand guards who screen all nonresidents or the uninvited. Much of the popular and academic literature on gated communities promotes this view.[15] These authors also focus on how some gated communities closely control the lives of residents, including extreme examples such as limiting the number of guests they can bring in or the types of vehicles they can park in their driveway.

Gated communities are also easy targets for social critics who point to their walls as the physical manifestation of a long-standing exclusionary impulse among rich people to shut out the less fortunate (including a big chunk of the middle class).[16] Such criticism extends to popular culture, including an *X-Files* episode several years ago in which a monster eats those who fail to follow the homeowners association rules, or a *Twilight Zone* episode where unruly teenagers are turned into fertilizer.

While much of the attention has focused on the demographic characteristics and geographic distribution of upscale gated communities, little attention has been devoted to other types of enclosed communities, those inhabited by lower-income renter households. Recent data released by the U.S. Census Bureau as part of the 2001 AHS show that lower-income renters are more likely than affluent homeowners to live in walled or gated communities.[17] Because class and race are correlated, the owner-renter distinction translates into a separation of higher-income from lower-income developments and whites from minorities. While affluent, white homeowners in gated communities have been extensively profiled, the gated low-income, nonwhite renters have not. The case studies below cover both types of place.

The 2001 AHS added forty new questions, covering type of home financing, country of origin for household members, and communities' attributes. For the first time the national sample included questions to distinguish gated communities, two of which are, Is your community surrounded by walls or fences preventing access by persons other than residents? Does access to your community require a special entry system such as entry codes, key cards, or security guard approval? Las Vegas and Phoenix have both types of place. Much new development in these regions is walled, but only part of the walled space is gated. Furthermore, some places, especially rental communities, have gates but never use them, a not uncommon practice in Las Vegas and Phoenix boomburbs.

Gates and gating came up in discussions with numerous boomburb mayors, planners, and developers. This is not unexpected given the extent of gates the authors saw on tours of rental communities or the finding by Thomas Sanchez, Robert Lang, and Dawn Dhavale that a higher proportion of renters than homeowners are behind gates.[18] But when they were asked about the prevalence of rental gated units, the officials gave some surprising answers. As it turns out, gates on apartment complexes may be less driven by renters than by public policy. Security issues raised by police and NIMBY (not-in-my-back-yard) opposition to multifamily residences by nearby homeowners are the two most significant reasons for gating. The police specifically seek to curb auto theft, which is a major crime problem for apartment complexes.

The issue raised by homeowners is a bit more complex but is mostly out of concern that proximate multifamily units will lower home values. Whether this charge is correct or not is mostly irrelevant—if homeowners believe it to be true, they will act on that belief. One way to at least partly mitigate this fear is by making rental multifamily housing look inter-changeable with all master-planned community development. Gates and walls are therefore used to signify that rental units are upscale. It also helps if pools, gyms, and other resort amenities are part of the package.

Many boomburbs now carry ordinances that rental housing should if possible be gated, while some places ban them for homeowners.[19] Based on a literature review and case analyses of gated communities, Karen Danielsen determined that gates may also serve several "positive functions."[20] Chief among these is the capacity to manage racial and income diversity at very close proximity. It also facilitates building at greater density than would be possible without the gates. These findings confirm preliminary analysis in the 1990s by Robert Lang and Karen Danielsen.[21]

Below are three case studies of gated and walled communities in the boomburbs of Henderson and North Las Vegas, Nevada, and Tempe, Arizona. The first two are homeowner communities, while the last is a rental. The first case study comes from secondary accounts of the large, upscale, master-planned development of Green Valley in Henderson, which was substantially built in the 1990s. The second case is a visit to Aliante in North Las Vegas, which is a new, walled (and sometimes gated) development begun in 2003.[22] Finally, Trillium at Rio Salado, a new (finished April 2005) apartment complex in Tempe, is profiled as an example of a gated rental community.[23]

Green Valley in Henderson

Green Valley is a highly regarded gated community in Henderson, Nevada, and has been the object of great fascination among social critics and researchers since it was begun in the 1980s. Because Green Valley figures so large in the literature, it is worth a short review of observations made in the 1990s regarding its development and lifestyle.

Green Valley's first national exposure came in a long and highly critical 1992 *Harper's* article by David Guterson.[24] Guterson's tale of Green Valley mostly focuses on what motivated middle-class Americans to—as he calls it—"incarcerate" themselves in their new walled city. He finds that in Green Valley walls dominate the landscape and are "the first thing visitors notice."

The walls provide residents with much more than physical protection: they offer psychological protection as well. Their message is subliminal and at the same time explicit. Controlled access is as much a metaphor as a reality. Controlled access is also a two-way affair, because "both coming and going are made difficult."[25] In gated communities, the walls are there to delineate status and provide security; they do not signify a collective understanding.

What erects these walls, as emerges from Guterson's interviews, is a free-floating anxiety about the world beyond them. According to one couple with children who moved to Green Valley from San Diego, "There were these . . . forces, if you know what we mean. There were too many things we could not control."[26] These unspecified forces were sufficiently distressing to compel this family to trade their life in California for the security of Nevada's desert.

But Green Valley today is nearly complete and seems a bit less like the *Brave New World* dystopia that Guterson depicted over ten years ago. Perhaps it is that the shock of the new is now over and that Green Valley seems like so many other walled developments in the region.

There is also an eight-page description (again somewhat critical) of Green Valley in the first academic book on Las Vegas, written by Mark Gottdiener, Claudia Collins, and David Dickens.[27] These authors review the specifics of its development and get in a few digs at Green Valley's social life in the process by citing Guterson's account at length. The overall theme is that Green Valley is exclusionary but is not an impenetrable fortress. There was an element of shock to 1990s gated communities that seems to have worn off a bit in this decade. The reality is that people living in gated communities are not necessarily seeking to wall the world off. In fact, the case analysis that follows points to more mundane reasons for gates, including deterring auto theft and giving the impression of resort lifestyle, as noted above.

Aliante in North Las Vegas

Aliante is a big, gate-ready, master-planned community—on land previously held by the Bureau of Land Management—just off a beltway so new that it did not appear on a 2004 Rand McNally atlas.[28] This is about the boomingest part of a boomburb, or as Dolores Hayden would call it, a zoomburb.[29]

As is common for upscale gated communities, Aliante is a themed development rather than a standard subdivision.[30] The theme here is nature park. In fact, Aliante's address is on Nature Park Drive. In keeping with this image, the development's signs are similar to those used by the U.S. Park Service to guide people through national parks and monuments built around native ruins. Thus, entering the site one might expect a visit to a national park—were it not for the sea of walls and of houses under construction. Why the native imagery is hard to say, given that there are no Indian ruins in the immediate area, and we can only hope that the development does not cover an ancient Piute burial ground.

Aliante's information gallery even looks as if it could be a U.S. Park Service entrance building. The structure has an art deco (or moderne) Pueblo Bonita look—complete with small flat stones as one would find at the Pueblo Bonita ruins in Chaco Canyon, New Mexico.[31] Adjacent to Aliante's information gallery is its Nature Discovery Park. The kids' play section is "archeological themed" and includes features such a "fossil wall" and "dinosaur eggs."[32]

Opened in May 2003, Aliante will take five years to build and will eventually have 7,500 homes. The project is a partnership between American Nevada Corporation and the Del Webb Corporation, the former of which built Green Valley in Henderson. Del Webb once specialized in retirement communities, most famously the Sun City developments. Del Webb has now diversified and is building what the company calls active adult, country club, and family living communities.

Aliante contains 428 acres of land. Just over a fifth (or 22 percent) of the land is for recreational and public use. This land encompasses a municipal golf course, city parks, an arroyo, and a trail system. The Del Webb community is built around an eighteen-hole municipal golf course.

Las Vegas's still-to-be-completed beltway splits the development.[33] The highway was so recently built that it is composed of an asphalt slab that features "temporary" lights at the major intersections. Even by May 2006 much of the road through Aliante was not finished. In time, all of these lights will be replaced by exit ramps as the highway shifts to a limited-access, four-lane interstate. The developers of Aliante paid for an interchange at the center of the development to link to its main arterial, Aliante Parkway.

On the north side of the beltway, Del Webb is developing the age-restricted Sun City Aliante. The north section also contains a large area for future residential development that is not age restricted. South of the belt-way, Aliante is composed of nine separate builder pods, four of which are gated. Only one of these will have "attached" single-family homes; not a single multifamily or rental unit is planned for the entire development.

Among the first phases of Aliante under construction is the Vialetto sec-tion, built by Pulte Homes. According to the sales literature (as of March 2004), homes here run from 1,520 to 2,284 square feet and cost between $384,000 and $440,000 (which is an upscale price range by Las Vegas standards). By May 2006 prices had not budged (according to an analysis using zillow.com). Prices for homes over 2,000 square feet ran in the low $400,000s, while those below this size were in the mid- to high $300,000s. While there was no gate at the entrance to this development, Vialetto is completely encircled by a wall, and future residents could easily vote to install gates. The section was partly occupied by 2004 but already had some "For Sale" and "For Rent" signs up, which indicates that some peo-ple bought the houses as speculative investments.

The lots in Vialetto are remarkably small. Some of the floor-to-area ratios are just less than 1.0 (which means a one-story home would cover its entire lot). Such lot coverage would violate the building code in many Eastern sub-urbs but is not uncommon in new boomburb developments. There are cases in which narrow "racetracks" of open space around the dwellings are barely wide enough for a person to walk through. Many of the views, including even those in the virtual tours on Vialetto's website, are of walls. Some walls are so close that people can just about reach out a window and touch one.

Interestingly, most of the imagery used to sell Aliante is of wide-open spaces—the stars at night and mountain vistas in the distance. Given its desert location, it is easy to see the connection. But as with many boom-burbs, North Las Vegas is a land of big skies and small lots. Look up and see the stars at night the way the Indians did, but look over and you may see a neighbor staring back at you. Perhaps Aliante is more in the tradition of the West's mining camps, where houses pressed tightly together and peo-ple sometimes feared the night and one another.

Aliante is what could technically be called a mixed-use development, in that retail spaces and offices will be built proximate to residences.[34] But Aliante's urban design could hardly be described as pedestrian oriented. Home, stores, and businesses are separated by walls and gates. As is typical in master-planned development, each builder is given a pod (with an inter-nal network of streets) that links to the main arterial road through just one entryway. Again, this walled development pod may or may not be gated.

Ironically, Aliante easily achieves the built densities—even though it has no multifamily dwellings—that could support a more traditional street system complete with pedestrian-accessible shopping. In fact, people could live literally a stone's throw (over a wall) from a store. But given the circulation system within the development they could be stuck walking a mile just to reach a destination that sits no more than 50 or 100 yards away. It is more than likely that people will simply get in their cars and drive to grab a paper or a quart of milk—something that a slight shift in urban design would have made easy to do on foot.

Trillium at Rio Salado in Tempe

Trillium at Rio Salado is an upscale, gated rental community that was finished in the spring of 2005 on the north side of Tempe's Town Lake.[35] The development contains 466 apartments, with 259 one-bedroom, 138 two-bedroom, and 69 three-bedroom apartments. The three-bedroom units run 1,500 square feet, while the two- and one-bedroom apartments are about 1,200 and 900 feet, respectively. In spring 2006 rents went for just over a dollar per square foot per month. Trillium is built in two sections and is split by an exit-entrance ramp onto the Red Mountain Freeway (or the 202 Loop). The complex is constructed on land leased from the Salt River Project, which makes it unlikely that this rental development will ever turn into a condominium complex.

Trillium residents are mostly young and include a large number of Arizona State University students. There are also many airport workers. The development is so close to Phoenix Sky Harbor that Trillium runs a courtesy van to the airport. The complex is well equipped with recreational amenities, including two pools, two hot tubs, a full gym, and a large entertainment room with a small private movie theater. Tempe Town Lake figures in the marketing of Trillium. The complex rents out jet skis and occasionally has one on display in the sales office.

Trillium lies on one of the Phoenix region's major thoroughfares—Washington Avenue—but it created a new street, the bucolically named Parkside Drive, to provide it a different identity. As of spring and summer 2006, the Phoenix light-rail system, which runs down the center of Washington Avenue for miles, was actively under construction next to Trillium. When finished, it will provide Trillium residents with direct access to a system that connects to Phoenix Sky Harbor as well as the downtowns of Phoenix and Tempe. The nearby station stop will be at Priest and Washington Streets, putting it at just under a half mile away.

Trillium is quasi-urban. Its residents, in addition to being able to take light rail, can walk to Tempe Town Lake, a Starbucks, a pizza place, a Mexican restaurant, and Papago Park Center—a 522-acre, mixed-use office development, which even includes a preschool. But the landscape also features freeway exit ramps and boulevards that are so wide that it makes for an uninviting pedestrian environment. The mixture of land uses around Trillium is more diverse and finely grained than the Aliante master-planned community, but the area lacks an urban streetscape. Perhaps the beginning of light-rail service and infilling the vacant properties adjacent to Trillium will shift the perception of auto dominance a bit, yet this section of Tempe has a long way to go before it achieves the pedestrian friendliness of a traditional city neighborhood. Vibrant downtown Tempe is a twenty-minute walk away, across Town Lake Bridge.

Gates are everywhere in and around Trillium. Each of Trillium's four buildings has its own security system, so that residents of Building B cannot gain entry to Building C. Each building also has its own parking garage, with a gate that can be opened only by its residents. A separate fence wraps around all of Trillium, enclosing all of it behind a secure perimeter. Thus, to enter a parking garage, residents must first open the gate to the general complex and then the gate to their own building. Those walking around the complex can enter the pool area and the gym but are cut off from other buildings.

The description of the gates alone makes Trillium sound like a fortress, yet that is hardly the case. The reality is that gates break—often. When the gates jam they must be left open to allow access. And the gates may stay open for long periods. For example, Trillium's main gate and the gate to Building B remained wide open for a month, from February to March 2006. While it was eventually fixed, gate repair remains a periodic problem.

In February 2006 a car was stolen from a Trillium garage. The event sparked much concern among residents and prompted a visit from Tempe's HEAT (or Help Eliminate Auto Theft) task force. As noted above, many police forces in Western boomburbs recommend that new apartment complexes be gated to eliminate auto theft. The proximity of places such as San Diego, Phoenix, and Las Vegas to Mexico is one concern, because stolen vehicles can be easily driven across the border and stripped for parts. The theft occurred when one of the gates was stuck open, which made some residents especially angry.

In general, gating is a far more complex process that the early literature on the topic revealed. The reasons for gating, the way the gates work, how difficult they are to defeat, vary tremendously from project to project. The meaning of these gates to residents also seems to vary. In rental units, it may signify that a development is a high-amenity complex (because gates are often packaged with pools and gyms) and that a resident's car is safe (provided the gates do not break). In homeowner communities, the gates may exclude nonresidents, but these places are often so large and diverse that the world inside and outside the gate may be quite similar. To be sure, boomburbs have some very exclusive gated communities. DC Ranch in Scottsdale, Arizona, is one such example. But gates are now so ubiquitous in many boomburbs that they have lost some of their cachet.

Housing Types in Boomburbs, 1900 to Present

Boomburbs are widely scattered enough throughout the United States that they contain no signature housing design. Yet the range of homes that one finds in these places is more limited than in suburbia in general. Given their Western tilt, boomburb housing is generally more horizontal than vertical. The typical single-family home has only one floor, in contrast to the more common two-story houses in the East. But boomburb dwellings have evolved over the years and are now converging with suburban home design elsewhere in the United States. This includes a shift to two-story luxury homes and even multilevel townhouses. Below is a historic sampler of these homes from the past century. While the types covered here do not capture all variations of single-family boomburb houses, they nonetheless represent most residences in these places. This knowledge of boomburb home design comes from the authors' over three years of fieldwork in dozens of new developments and older neighborhoods.

Craftsman, 1900 to 1940

Given the newness of boomburbs, their very oldest residential architecture typically dates only to the early twentieth century. The common boomburb home then was a Craftsman-type home, or bungalow. Craftsman homes originated in Southern California in 1903.[36] Their design departed significantly from that of the Victorian homes dominant in the period.[37] They were low-slung, modest, and easy to construct buildings with minimal detail. Like other vernacular styles, the Craftsman design was spread through pattern books and magazines such as *Western Architecture*. Craftsman homes can be found in boomburbs from Miami to Seattle. Many of the smaller houses that could be bought via mail order from department stores such as Sears were Craftsman designs.[38] New Craftsman dwellings often contained just four first-floor rooms and had an unfinished

Figure 5-1. Floor Plan of a Typical Craftsman House

Note: Plan is not to scale.

second floor for expansion (figure 5-1). Some of them ran as little as 600 square feet, and most did not exceed 1,000 square feet. Building lots were as small as 50 feet by 80 feet, or 4,000 square feet.

Older boomburbs do contain the occasional Victorian house. The typical larger Victorian homes are from very late in the nineteenth century and are often either stick or Queen Anne style. There is also a smattering of the smaller-scaled folk Victorian and other classic vernacular styles in the very oldest boomburb neighborhoods.

Ranch, 1935 to 1975

According to *A Field Guide to American Architecture*, the ranch house also originated in California (the style is based loosely on the Spanish colonial) and quickly spread to the rest of the Southwest.[39] The ranch may be the single most common home type in the boomburbs of the 1950s and 1960s, such as Anaheim, California. The ranch is bigger than the Craftsman and could be significantly bigger if added on to. Also, while the Craftsman home typically faced the street gable (or short) end, ranch homes were turned sideways to expose their full length. The addition of garages and carports made these expansive fronts even longer. The ranch is seldom found on lots smaller than 100 feet by 100 feet, or 10,000 square feet. Almost all ranches have just one floor, and most feature very little ornamentation.

As noted in *A Field Guide to American Architecture*, the "rambling" ranch also reflects the switch to a less compact urban form fueled by the widening use of cars at mid-twentieth century:

> The popularity of the "rambling" ranch house was made possible by the country's increasing dependence on the automobile. Street car suburbs of the late 19th and early 20th century still used relatively compact house forms on small lots because people walked to nearby streetcar lines. As the automobile replaced street cars and busses as the principal means of transportation in the decades following World War II, compact houses could be replaced by sprawling designs on much larger lots. Never before had it been possible to [be] so lavish with land, and [the] rambling form of the ranch house emphasizes this by maximizing façade . . . which is further increased by built-in garages that are an integral part of most ranch houses.[40]

The boomburb ranch house, which is found even outside the Southwest, has an open floor plan (see figure 5-2). The living room, dining room, and kitchen fill one side of the house, in one continuous space, while the bedrooms are found off short halls at the other end of the house. Most early ranch houses had at least six rooms, including three bedrooms, with larger versions of the house running eight to nine rooms. The typical ranch contained 1,000 to 2,000 square feet. These were therefore big homes by post–World War II standards but below the size of average single-family home today (which are about 2,500 square feet).

Midcentury Modern, 1940 to 1970

Modern architecture had a much bigger impact on the commercial architecture of boomburbs than on their residences. In fact, much of the post–World War II strip development, which characterizes much of the office and retail space in boomburbs, is almost entirely modern. Only now, as the "new urbanist" style exerts influence on "lifestyle centers" such as Victoria Gardens in Rancho Cucamonga, California, are neoclassical nonresidential structures popping up. At the same time, there is far more modern home architecture in boomburbs than in suburbs of the Northeast and Midwest.

Figure 5-2. Floor Plan of a Typical Ranch House

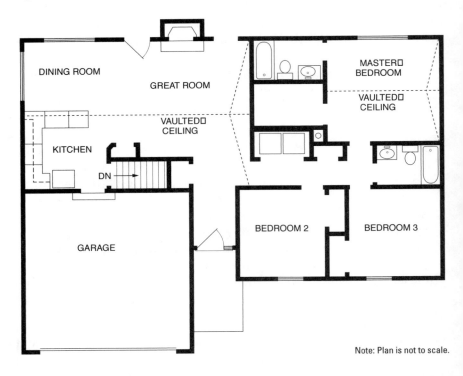

Note: Plan is not to scale.

The midcentury modern home is also essentially a high-concept ranch house. Forms of this style are found in most boomburbs, but it is most common in California and the Southwest. A wide range of structures fall into this category, from craft builder "art homes" such as Eichler homes around the Bay Area to more vaguely modernist dwellings found in virtually any boomburb neighborhood built in the 1950s and 1960s.[41] The common features are a single story, a very low-pitched roof, abundant floor-to-ceiling and banded windows, exposed and vaulted ceilings, and a complete lack of ornament. These houses were mostly scaled to the size of ranch homes, but up-market versions could easily exceed 2,000 square feet. Lot sizes varied and could run to a half acre or more.

Some modern homes were essentially more contemporary versions of ranch homes while others introduced innovative floor plans that, for example, wrapped around interior courtyards. Figure 5-3 shows an Eichler plan of a wraparound residence.

Figure 5-3. Floor Plan of an Eichler Wraparound House

PATIO

BEDROOM

LIVING

DINING

HOBBY &☐
LAUNDRY

KITCHEN

BEDROOM

ATRIUM

MULTI-PURPOSE

BEDROOM

BEDROOM

GARAGE

CARPORT

Note: Plan is not to scale.

Neo-Mediterranean, 1970s to Today

By the 1970s there was a widespread rejection of modern styles in suburban residences.[42] Home sizes also began to climb. In 1970, according to the
National Association of Home Builders, the average new home was less
than 1,500 square feet, but by the mid-1980s it was nearly 2,000 square

feet.[43] Bigger and fancier suburban homes needed a new architecture, and they mostly found expression in classic revivals.[44] In Northeastern and Midwestern suburbs this meant styles such as French château, or neo-Victorian, or more formal classicism. But in Sunbelt boomburbs, the neo-Mediterranean—especially Tuscany-style homes—dominated upscale subdivisions. These homes are eclectic and vary widely, but most incorporate Spanish elements such as tile roofs (now made from composites rather than clay), stucco walls, and rounded windows. In much of the Southwest, there is also a subvariant of this general style in designs such as adobe revival and mission territorial.

Even though many neo-Mediterraneans remained one-story, ceiling heights soared to enclose a greater volume of space. The exterior high massing of these structures also creates a very different profile from low-slung ranch and modern homes. The number and types of rooms also shifted. Family rooms became the norm as did a minimum of four bedrooms. Thus typical new homes ran eight rooms with at least two full baths and a two-car garage. Interestingly, lot sizes remained almost unchanged and in many land-constrained markets, such as California, began to shrink. Therefore the amount of the lot covered by these new, larger homes began to shoot up. The crowding of neighborhoods was managed by an increased use of walls, which are now ubiquitous in all but large-lot, luxury subdivisions.

Neoeclectic McMansion, 1980s to 2000s

Data from a 2002 study by the National Association of Home Builders indicate that home sizes have been growing since 1970.[45] In 1987 the size of the average new home was 1,900 square feet; by 2001 this had increased by 20 percent, to an average of 2,300 square feet. The percentage of new homes larger than 3,000 square feet has almost doubled, according to the U.S. Census Bureau.[46] In 1988, 11 percent of new homes constructed exceeded 3,000 square feet; by 2003 this number had grown to 20 percent. Pulte Homes, one of the nation's largest home builders, reports that its average new home is growing by 150 to 200 square feet every few years.

By the mid-1980s a new home type emerged—the McMansion. This housing style essentially extended the luxury of the neo-Mediterranean by adding more rooms, bigger and more plentiful bathrooms, giant closets, and an extra garage bay (see figure 5-4). The McMansion also often overrides vernacular tradition. It is now common for second floors to appear in even boomburb versions of these homes. Even in homes without an actual

Figure 5-4. Plan of the First Floor of a Typical McMansion

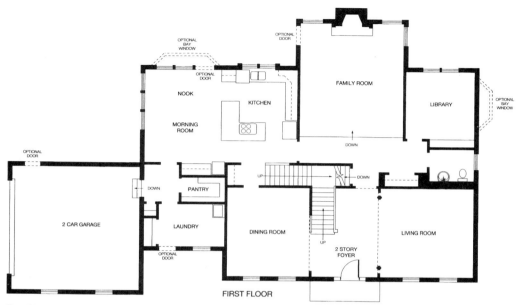

Note: Plan is not to scale.

second floor, the ceiling heights are now so lofted as to give the outward appearance of there being two stories.

The "Mc" in McMansion connotes that the luxury these homes offer is rather faux. The reality is that many of these homes are big boxes made of the same basic materials found in more affordable projects. Lots have also remained constant or have shrunk, which means McMansion-dominated neighborhoods have a distinct vertical feel.[47] In fact, when someone builds such a dwelling to replace, say, a torn-down ranch in a 1950s neighborhood, it provokes a great outcry from nearby homeowners, who declare that such houses ruin the context of the existing community.[48] Paul Knox labels the McMansion trend "Vulgaria," in that the display of wealth in such homes matches Thorstein Veblen's definition of "conspicuous consumption."[49]

While the exterior of most new homes has taken on classic features, the interiors still maintain and even enhance the open floor plan of the ranch. This is especially true of the vast space that now makes up the kitchen–family room complex. Also, very little of the classic details found on exteriors translates into home interiors. Houses now often have dual styles—traditional exteriors, modern interiors.

A McMansion in a boomburb now looks much like one built in a typical upscale suburb in the Northeast or Midwest, but some design differences remain. In many McMansions the formal space has been shrunk to such an extent that living rooms and dining rooms seem almost vestigial. In the East builders have been reluctant to dispense with these rooms, but that is less true of Sunbelt builders. In many boomburbs the newest McMansions have seen the old separate living and dining rooms become incorporated into the kitchen–family room or great room and open core of the house. Finally, while many boomburb McMansions may appear to have multiple floors, this space is often a loft or even decorative space simply meant to make the house more imposing. By contrast, McMansions in Northeastern and Midwestern suburbs often have a full second floor, in keeping with the general tradition of vertically oriented homes in these regions.

Townhouse, 1980s to 2000s

The last boomburb housing type covered here is the most recent and—in many boomburbs—the fastest growing. Townhouses have a long history in urban areas but are new to suburbs and especially boomburbs. Boomburbs emerged in the post–World War II era as perhaps the quintessential antiurban space in America. In this book, a case has been made that boomburbs are accidental cities in that they were never planned—or at least not intended to reach the scale and intensity of traditional big cities.

Yet one more sign that boomburbs are actually cities is the boom in high-density, attached housing. Some boomburbs, especially those in the built-out parts of Southern California, are simply out of land, and townhouses are the only real option for residential growth. In boomburbs that have opted for transit-oriented development, such as Plano, Texas, townhouses have sprouted up at station stops. While a few boomburbs flat out resist townhouse development—a notable case being Gilbert, Arizona—the majority of boomburbs either have townhouses or plan to build some in the near future.

Boomburb townhouses have diverse style, size, and target market. Some are as big as midrange new homes and may even cost more per square foot than the conventional detached single-family home. Others are intended as an affordable alternative to detached units. At the midprice point, these homes typically run under 2,000 square feet and have three bedrooms. But most feature the same open floor plan in the living/dining/kitchen areas as a standard new home in a subdivision (see figure 5-5). The exteriors of townhouses also vary. Homes built in new urbanist greenfield (open-space)

Figure 5-5. Open Floor Plan, Typical Townhouse

Note: Plan is not to scale.

developments tend to have classical exteriors. More modern styles appear in redevelopment and infill sites.

Beyond townhouse developments, loft developments and even high-rise condominiums are appearing throughout the boomburbs of South Florida, Dallas, Phoenix, and Los Angeles. Examples include the new Santa Ana Lofts in Santa Ana, California, and the Hayden Landing high-rise condominium at Town Lake in Tempe, Arizona. In Anaheim's Platinum Triangle, an 800-acre industrial area south of Disneyland, the city plans a mix of high-density and high-rise residences. It has significantly boosted the number of homes allowed per acre: "Previously, the city [of Anaheim] capped housing density at 36 units per acre for apartments and 18 units per acre for ownership projects. The Platinum Triangle will have densities up to 100 units per acre and all housing is attached. The district will also have a greater mix of uses than elsewhere, as the city is mandating first-floor retail on some key streets."[50] Even the once sleepy town of Oxnard is getting into the high-rise act. A developer there has proposed building three residential towers at nineteen, twenty-eight, and thirty-seven stories.[51]

Contemporary Variations in Boomburb Housing

Given their number and size, boomburbs and baby boomburbs exhibit tremendous variation in housing. As noted earlier, there are differences in the percentage of single and multifamily homes, but generally boomburbs have more single-family homes than comparably sized traditional cities. Beyond this, even the subvariation in the type and style of home and community setting is worth noting. One commonality is an abundance of walls and gated communities, including even gated trailer parks. Below is a sample of notable housing types, along with examples of where such housing exists.

McHousing.

—McMansions, or large homes that are scaled much bigger than conventional suburban residences. These can come in greenfield settings (for example, Plano, Texas) or as infill and tear-down housing (for example, Naperville). In Naperville, McMansion replacements of teardowns have become so common that the city developed a pattern book to minimize the impact on neighborhoods.[52]

—McLofts, or downtown loft space in cities that never had a loft district (for example, Santa Ana, California). These open-plan, multifamily housing developments may have live-and-work units that include first-floor commercial space.[53] The owner buys the home using a residential mortgage and has the option of renting out the work area or using it for a home business.

Gated and Walled Housing.

—Gated rental communities. These range from luxury rentals to affordable housing (sometimes within the same development). Examples include much of the northern areas of Rancho Cucamonga, California, where the Lewis Family Company has developed a string of these places in several price ranges. Boomburbs and baby boomburbs in particular have a high incidence of these places.

—Gate-ready walled communities. Many new single-family subdivisions in Western boomburbs come with walls. Often, the walls are left ungated and the decision to install gates is left to homeowners associations. An example is the Aliante master-planned community in North Las Vegas, Nevada, developed by the American Nevada Corporation. However, the typical high-end development within a master-planned community with multiple housing segments is almost always gated from the start.

—Gated cul-de-sacs. Most people think of upscale gated communities and imagine large-scale developments that include golf courses. Upscale boomburbs such as Scottsdale, Arizona, can have dozens of big, luxury, gated communities (an example is DC Ranch by DMB Associates in north Scottsdale). But gating is so common in boomburbs that it comes in several—and often unanticipated—forms. These include some cases of microgating, where several, or even one, cul-de-sacs are gated. Gated cul-de-sacs mostly appear in the rapidly developing boomburb fringe. For example, in northeast Mesa, where the city is building out against low mountains, there are multiple gated cul-de-sacs. The gates seal off building lots that are intended for custom homes. The land is often fee simple, with the only common area being the roads and the pad-entry gated area. Many individual lots in these luxury zones also have gates, but the gating of an individual street can save buyers the time and cost of gating their individual residences.

—Gated trailer parks. The less affluent parts of some boomburbs and baby boomburbs contain manufactured housing in gated trailer parks. Examples of such communities can be found in Palmdale, California. The gates in trailer parks have a different purpose and significance than they do in luxury communities. In fact, they may not even reflect the interest of residents and may instead be placed there as part of an agreement with municipal interests, such as the police, as is sometimes the case with more upscale gated rentals.

Boomburb Housing Summary. Despite the variation, some general statements hold true for much boomburb housing. The typical home has just one floor, although much new construction may be so high that it gives the impression of two floors. The one-story plan reflects the locations in which boomburbs are mostly found—the Western Sunbelt and South Florida. Related to this locational influence is the fact that most boomburb single-family homes occupy more modest lots than comparable dwellings in other suburbs.

Boomburbs: Exclusionary but Not Exclusive

Boomburbs are big, complicated communities with considerable variation in income within the municipality. While some boomburbs are affluent, none can be definitively called exclusive. Places that reach 100,000 residents, or even 50,000 residents as in the case of the baby boomburbs, are simply too large to contain only wealthy households. The next chapter deals with the policies that many boomburbs use to expand their share of affluent neighborhoods, but as a preview consider the relationship that an upscale place such as Scottsdale, Arizona, has with two nonboomburb neighbors—Fountain Hills and Paradise Valley.

Paradise Valley and Fountain Hills border Scottsdale; the former lies west and the latter east of the city. Both places are small towns compared to Scottsdale—Paradise Valley has less than 14,000 people and Fountain Hill has just under 24,000 residents. And as opposed to Scottsdale's ambitious expansion goals, neither place plans to grow much. Finally, unlike Scottsdale, Fountain Hills and especially Paradise Valley can be described as exclusive.

There are rich people within the Phoenix region—especially long-time residents—who favor Paradise Valley and Fountain Hills over Scottsdale. What the two smaller satellites offer is neighborhood stability in a rapidly changing metropolis. These places are small and manageable. They do not want high-rise residential development, unlike Scottsdale, and feature no office districts. More important, Paradise Valley and Fountain Hills lack a downscale south Scottsdale, which dampens the reputation of the whole city in the regional housing market.

This is not to say that Scottsdale does not have a generally strong reputation for a high quality of life. It maintains luxury resorts and fancy shops; in fact, whole parts of the city are indeed exclusive. But wealth in Scottsdale means walls and gates more routinely than in, say, Fountain Hills. Fountain Hills is tucked in a nice corner of the Phoenix region between Indian land and a regional park, and its lack of easy access makes the city physically exclusive. Most of Fountain Hills is not gated, and the lots are generally larger than those in Scottsdale. While superwealthy subdivisions lie within Scottsdale that outclass any in Fountain Hills, the boomburb also has poverty. In a way, a boomburb's housing reflects a more traditional city in that it provides shelter to rich and poor. By contrast, Fountain Hills is composed almost exclusively of upper-middle-income households. Or to sum up the view of one realtor, when pressed on the question: "There is no bad part of Fountain Hills."[54]

The Small Town Politics of Big Cities

6

Boomburbs are now technically big cities but have often arrived at this status accidentally. Chapter 4 shows how this is true for the boomburb business landscape. The boomburbs' commerce, unlike that of more traditional cities, is not centered in downtown but lies instead along major highways and exit ramps. Many of the elements of a big city economy are typically there but arrayed in a pattern that few would recognize as urban. The same accidental imagery applies to boomburb government—they are big cities yet are run in many ways as small towns. Chapter 6 shows that this big city–small town governance split is both a strength and weakness for boomburbs.

Boomburbs offer a surprising mix of governance. Residents seek both more and less government than residents of suburbs around big cities in the Northeast and Midwest.[1] Boomburb municipal governments are usually much smaller than those of comparably sized old-style big cities, but filling the gap are often private governments, such as homeowners associations, and various shadow governments, such as special improvement districts.

Almost all boomburbs have part-time mayors, who work under a professional city manager–council system. That boomburbs have part-time mayors is not a shock considering that many Sunbelt core cities such as Dallas and San Diego use the same system.[2] But most big Sunbelt cities that maintain part-time mayors are debating the switch to full-time officeholders, or to the so-called strong mayor system.[3] Within this decade many big Western cities will be run by full-time mayors. No similar debate over a strong mayor is occurring in boomburbs. It is likely that these cities will have part-time (and technically nonpartisan) political leadership well into this century.

Boomburbs are inventive places that devise numerous strategies to adapt governments intended for small towns to the realities of big cities. In many cases, private solutions lessen the burden of urban management. Boomburbs are fortunate in that their rise occurred at the moment when multiple alternatives to traditional government also appeared. These accidental cities are testing labs for quasi-government instruments that complement municipal management. For now the system is working, but a day of reckoning may not be far off in some of the largest and more densely built boomburbs. At some point, big boomburbs may be forced to switch governance methods as service demands overwhelm their small staffs.

Chapter 6 covers the various ways that boomburbs are managed and publicly financed. It touches on a range of topics in both the public and private spheres. The blend of public and private worlds makes the boomburb an especially complicated, although interesting, political terrain. From condo boards, to city hall, to the state legislature the debate over growth also defines boomburbs. The big issues include where growth will occur, what form it will take, and who will pay for new development—especially its costly infrastructure. Chapter 6 ends with a look at the impact that boomburbs have on regional cooperation and governance.

The Biggest Small Towns in the World

For cities with over 100,000 residents, boomburbs feature rather modest governments. Most residents prefer it that way; there is no groundswell for radical change. How this system came into existence and compares to the governments of other suburbs in major metropolitan areas that lack boomburbs is key to understanding how boomburbs are run. Of course, not all boomburbs are governed the same, but there is enough commonality among them for key themes to emerge.

The City Manager System and Reform Government

The city manager system dates to the early-twentieth-century Progressive Era.[4] Big city governments in the East and Midwest were often corrupt and captured by political machines that used public revenues for patronage or personal gain. As Western and Southern cities developed at the turn of the last century, they adopted reform governments that hired professional management to run city affairs and limited political leadership to part-time (essentially volunteer) jobs.[5] The reforms mostly worked. Western central cities, and later boomburbs that also use this system, were typically not plagued by the type or level of corruption sometimes found in the East.

The more than two dozen boomburb mayors interviewed for this book were all competent people who generously gave their time and clearly have the best interest of their respective communities at heart. But the early-twentieth-century reform version of civic government may be broken—or at least may not fit the current structure of boomburbs. For one, boomburbs are usually far more diverse than is reflected by many of the mayors, who are usually white men. Second, the mayors are all affluent volunteers. Volunteering is certainly noble, but if boomburbs offered decent mayor's salaries, people seeking the office could be drawn from a wider income spectrum.

Also, despite the fact that boomburb mayorships are technically part-time jobs, the demands of running a big city are really starting to stretch the term "part-time," even though there is a full-time city manager. The mayor of Arlington, Texas (an obstetrician), acknowledged that having only part-time mayors does exclude those who are not in jobs that pay well and offer flexibility.

Virtually all boomburb city council members are elected at large and can live anywhere in the city. That means boomburbs are not divided into roughly equal-sized wards, in which council members live in and represent the interests of their wards. Again, the at-large council structure comes from reforms in early-twentieth-century government. One problem with a ward system is that council members swap projects with each other—say a new bridge in Ward 1 for a new park in Ward 2—which can raise the cost of government.[6] In an at-large system, the idea is that each member has the interests of the whole city at heart.

When boomburbs were mostly small and socially homogeneous places, the at-large council structure worked. But boomburbs are now big and diverse. And as this book shows, there is also a spatial dimension to boomburb diversity. There are rich and poor parts to just about every boomburb. Yet at-large council members tend to be drawn predominantly from the wealthy sections. There are even some cases—based on discussions with boomburb officials—in which all council members live in the same upscale neighborhood. Thus, the interests of lower-income and minority parts of boomburbs often remain underrepresented. At this stage, the risk of corruption and inefficiency may be less worrisome than the likelihood of alienating whole sections of the city. After much debate, Phoenix switched to a ward system in part because the continued disenfranchisement of the city's south side was so controversial. The result has been a greater focus on problems in Phoenix's poorer wards. Some larger and more diverse boomburbs will soon follow big Sunbelt cities in this transition to the ward system.

Ward systems may drive up the cost of local government, as council members swap pork projects, yet the cost of not switching to the ward system may be the systematic disenfranchisement of diverse neighborhood interests. Several boomburbs, such as Fontana, California, are now debating a switch to ward-based councils. This is one more sign that boomburbs' nonpartisan professional management system is starting to break down. Given the rate at which boomburb populations and interests are diversifying at the neighborhood level, it is likely that many of these places will shift away from at-large city councils in the near future.

Another problem in boomburb governance concerns the strong tug of partisan politics at the state and national levels, which pulls mayors into the kind of party loyalty that the reform system sought to avoid. Most boomburb mayors interviewed did not run for office under a party label, yet all but one admitted to being a Republican. Interestingly, some of the more moderate Republicans expressed concern that they were expected to toe a conservative party line on a host of issues that they did not feel comfortable with or thought were completely irrelevant to the management of their city.[7] If boomburb mayors are really in political parties and are in fact pressured to take positions based on their affiliation, they might as well run for office as Democrats and Republicans.[8]

Putting Boomburb Governance in Context

Examining how other suburbs in major metropolitan areas outside the Sunbelt are administered puts boomburb government in a larger context. Big Eastern suburbs provide equivalent scale to the boomburbs, yet no individual Eastern suburban city directly compares to any boomburb in size, so one must look instead at major suburban counties. Two Eastern suburban counties that match boomburbs are Bergen County, New Jersey, and Fairfax County, Virginia.[9] The counties are also very different from one another and offer interesting alternatives in governance.

Bergen County: Weak County, Strong Cities. Bergen County is a large, close-in suburb of New York City, with nearly 900,000 residents in 2005. All of Bergen's 234-square-mile land area is incorporated, but it fragments into seventy-one separate municipalities. Like the rest of New Jersey, Bergen has strong municipal and weak county governance. The county's boroughs and cities run all local services and the schools, with most of the revenue generated by residential property taxes. The quality of service is therefore determined by each municipality's fiscal capacity. Looking at the county in 2002, Myron Orfield determined that Bergen is dramatically split.[10] In the affluent northern sections of the county, fiscal capacity is very high, while in southern Bergen it is much lower. The split lines up almost perfectly with income and home values at the municipal level.

Fairfax: Strong County, Weak (or Even No) Cities. Fairfax County is a large mature suburb of Washington, with a 2005 population of just over 1 million. Most of Fairfax's 395 square miles are unincorporated and consolidate into one large county government.[11] Like the rest of Virginia, Fairfax has weak (or nonexisting) municipal and strong county governance.[12] The state runs the county's roads, while Fairfax manages and mostly funds the schools and other services like the police. Fairfax divides into several large ministerial districts, but the quality of local service is essentially uniform because taxes raised even in affluent parts of the county are shared with poorer areas. This includes even the revenue generated in Fairfax's large commercial districts such as Tysons Corner and along the Dulles Toll Road. Myron Orfield determined that all of Fairfax maintains very high fiscal capacity.[13]

Boomburb Model: Strong Counties, Strong Cities. Boomburb location varies to some extent, but most can be found in what Robert Lang and Megan Gough refer to as MEGA counties.[14] Nearly all MEGA counties have strong governments and, like Fairfax County, run the schools.[15] Boomburbs are, then, incorporated places within these strong counties (unlike Fairfax) and assume local responsibility for infrastructure such as streets. In addition, many boomburbs in the Southwest have large, master-planned communities complete with homeowners associations, which monitor code enforcement and pay for a host of local services such as garbage collection. Many of these associations also pick up the cost of local streets. Thus, boomburbs are strong cities in that they are incorporated, but they may offer relatively light and low-cost government because they are helped on the upper end by strong counties and below by active homeowners associations.

The Politics of Growth

There is a big literature on the politics of growth.[16] From the critical side, John Logan and Harvey Molotch identify what they call a growth machine that advocates politically for rapid regional development because it enriches companies that benefit from providing goods and services to expanding housing markets.[17] Large developers and construction companies are part of this machine because their business is growth. The opposite view on the growth machine is expressed by Joel Garreau, who in his book *Edge City* comments on the many improvements that metropolitan (in particular suburban) development brings to a region and the nation.[18]

A more balanced view on the politics of growth is provided by William Fulton, who in his 1997 book *The Reluctant Metropolis* describes the complicated political landscape surrounding development in metropolitan Los Angeles, the greatest growth machine of all.[19] In Fulton's view, the corporate growth machine is breaking down, as citizen resistance and the environmental movements join to stop housing development.

There are some obvious upsides and downsides to metropolitan development. This book does not judge growth but instead documents and describes it in the nation's fastest-expanding group of cities. That means exploring many dimensions of growth that are part of the ongoing debate without explicitly coming down on one side or the other as to its politics. The point here is to understand the constantly shifting political landscape of growth. But some of the discussion that follows does critically address certain forms of government and municipal organization that exclude lower-income households. If a bias exists in the analysis, it reflects the belief that boomburbs are easy targets and are often misunderstood by Easterners.[20]

The Homevoter and Growth Politics

An economist at Dartmouth College, Bill Fischel, has developed the concept of the "homevoter."[21] Fischel argues that homeowners are an especially conservative bunch because what is typically their single largest asset is at risk. Homes are at risk because they cannot be moved, which means that they are linked to the fate of the neighborhood. Further, there are only limited insurance policies that one can use as a hedge against depreciation in the value of a home.[22]

The solution is to always vote in local politics in the interest of your home—thus the homevoter. And how do you vote? To stop all land uses that can potentially devalue your property, which is to say basically all change. The reason is that all change carries some risk to most people's principal investment, and thus it is in a homeowner's perceived self-interest to fight all neighborhood transformation—even potential improvements.

The homevoter has different tools to use in different parts of the country. In a place such as northern New Jersey, where a very high level of municipal fragmentation exists, homevoters can use local government to serve their interests. The homevoter is a far more potent force than the growth machine in local New Jersey (or any Northeastern state) suburban politics.[23] For one, there is slower growth in the Northeast than the Sunbelt; further, the fragmented nature of municipal government is the right scale for homevoter action.

Consider again a place such as Bergen County. Bergen divides into dozens of municipalities, none of which has over 50,000 residents, with many smaller than 10,000. Most towns in the northern part of the county are exclusive bedroom communities, with expensive homes and sky-high real estate taxes. Northern Bergen's towns also have little or no multifamily rental housing. Therefore, to gain entry to such places one must be wealthy.[24]

Municipalities in Bergen County, such as Haworth, with just 3,390 residents (in 2005), are essentially run as private clubs.[25] This number of residents could easily be accommodated in just one phase of a master-planned community in the West. The school systems in northern Bergen County are de facto private because of the high entry price into its communities.[26] In fact, these places are so close to being private clubs a good label for them would be "cluburbs."[27] In such a small-scale and exclusive community, homevoters rule, and they rule directly by capturing the public sphere.

Walls surround Haworth, but they are not physically manifested. Rather, they are income barriers that prevent less affluent households from living there. These invisible walls may be much more effective than the real thing in keeping lower-income people out.[28] A poor person can drive through Haworth, which may not be the case in a gated or walled community, but he or she can forget about joining the club.

The Western equivalent of Haworth includes two towns discussed in the previous chapter—Paradise Valley and Fountain Hills, Arizona. But one of these exclusive places—Fountain Hills—offers much broader housing options than Haworth, especially in the form of multifamily condo units and gated rental communities.

In contrast to cluburbs such as Haworth, boomburbs, even baby boomburbs, are too large for a determined group of homeowners to completely take over. Even affluent boomburbs are hardly exclusive—and they are certainly not like the cluburbs of northern New Jersey. At least some affordable rental opportunities exist in these places. There are, for example, lower-cost sections in the mostly affluent cities of Costa Mesa, California, Coral Springs, Florida, Plano, Texas, and Scottsdale, Arizona. Yet there are whole towns in northern New Jersey—Haworth being but one—without a single downscale neighborhood. In the boomburbs at least, the growth machine still trumps the homevoter.

But people living in upscale boomburbs have another option—private government, or homeowners associations.[29] The bottom line for a homevoter is the maintenance of home value. In the absence of a small and totally compliant municipal government, a private one will do. Yet while homeowners associations offer safety and control at the neighborhood level—and often exclusion—they do not control other vital services, such as schools. Most boomburbs are part of a countywide school district. Fairfax County, Virginia, also runs a county school system. But Bergen County has municipal-level school districts and funding (except for the state share). A child who does not live in an upscale, master-planned community, but resides in the boomburb of Scottsdale, can go to a Maricopa County school. Likewise, a less affluent child in Fairfax County can go to a county school—including the system's highly regarded honors high school. These schools are funded by a very wide revenue base, including major commercial developments. In Haworth, there are no poor children (other than a small handful who have parents that scraped and found the money for a house).

The point of the comparison between suburbs is to show the complicated and variable ways that services such as schools are delivered under different types of suburban arrangement. It also highlights the various ways that a place can exclude poorer residents. On the surface, the lack of gates and the small town feel of Haworth seems much less elitist than a gated community in Scottsdale. Gates are a visible and dramatic form of exclusion. Yet ungated Haworth lacks poverty, while heavily gated Scottsdale maintains considerable income diversity among its residents.

One could imagine a contented Haworth citizen reading an account of the West's gated communities in the *New Yorker* or *Harper's* and thinking, "Wow! These places are rather harsh, with their walls, gates, and extensive rules—I would certainly not live in a guarded compound." But Haworth residents need not resort to walls and gates, because a private government in a segregated enclave is unnecessary when you run the public sphere as an exclusive club—especially one ruled by rich homevoters.

Privatopia: The Politics and Importance of Boomburb Homeowners Associations

Given that boomburbs lack a strong homevoter potential, homeowners associations take on a special significance as a mechanism whereby homeowners mitigate risk and maintain home value. The political scientist Evan McKenzie, who dubbed places dominated by these associations "privatopias," was among the first researchers to understand that the real power in many new suburbs lies in land covenants that place tight restrictions on residents.[30] Also called common-interest developments, homeowners associations are found most commonly in the exact Sunbelt places where boomburbs flourish.[31] But for the invention of such associations in the late 1960s, boomburbs almost certainly would be governed more like traditional cities of similar size. These associations enable boomburbs to maintain their part-time mayors and small staffs by providing a free and highly effective private government in place of a costly and often less effective public one.

How important are homeowners associations to boomburb governance? Consider the fact that some boomburbs allow no new development outside of homeowners associations. Boomburbs fitting this description include Coral Springs, Florida, Henderson and North Las Vegas, Nevada, and Chandler and Gilbert, Arizona. Other boomburbs are trying to retrofit a homeowners association structure for existing neighborhoods with fee simple land tenure. The reason boomburbs promote such associations is hardly altruistic; rather, most boomburbs recognize the efficacy and economy that homeowners associations provide to local government.

In fact, new cities that are competing with boomburbs have even taken the process one step further by outsourcing city hall altogether. The new master-planned communities of Weston, Florida, Sandy Springs, Georgia, and Centennial, Colorado, are now "contract cities."[32] These places hire private companies or other governments to run city services. So complete is the contracting of services that Weston—a city of nearly 70,000 people—has just three employees.[33]

Homeowners Associations in the Las Vegas Region

A good example of how critical homeowners associations are to the basic functioning of boomburbs is North Las Vegas. In fact, the current mayor of North Las Vegas, Michael L. Montandon, got his start in politics as the president of the Hidden Canyon homeowners association.[34] The mayor describes Hidden Canyon of the mid-1990s as "a starter-home neighborhood." He was elected association president by default for the first five years and notes that not only did he run unopposed, he "could not give the job away." According to Montandon, the attitude in Hidden Canyon's early years was "leave me alone—I signed the CC&R [covenants, conditions, and restrictions], but screw you." There was no real civic interest in working together. Then suddenly, as people started to sell homes, they came to Montandon and said "clean up my neighborhood." Overnight there was tremendous civic engagement (as would be predicted by Fischel's homevoter hypothesis). The experience taught Montandon a key lesson—homeowners associations matter most when the stakes are highest.

As North Las Vegas's mayor, Montandon aggressively promotes homeowners associations. While the city cannot directly mandate that all new development have such associations, it can create code requirements that virtually ensure that associations will form. For example, Montandon wrote a new code prohibiting a community from building a wall at the very edge of its property line. The code required a ten-foot setback between the subdivision's wall and the city's property. The mayor claims that this was done for aesthetic reasons—drivers in new neighborhoods saw nothing but unbroken walls. According to Montandon, "It was getting ridiculous—nothing but walls as far as the eye could see."

Yet not only did the new wall code require a ten-foot setback, it also charged property owners with the responsibility of maintaining this perimeter space. Without directly requiring a homeowners association, the city code nonetheless strongly encourages it. The reason is that individual property owners would be better off forming an organization to maintain this land than doing so individually. And that organization would most likely be a homeowners association. And it would not need to be a full-blown association, which is expensive in part because it requires a professionally managed and bonded corporation, according to state law. It may take half the dues just to manage such an organization. Instead, one could use the light version, or what Nevada calls a "landscape management association," under a new state law. The bottom line, however, is that every new North Las Vegas development now has some form of common-interest development.

North Las Vegas, like so many boomburbs, has both rich and poor sections. The divide here is I-15, which runs north out of Las Vegas and splits the city in two. The largely built-out area east of I-15 is low income and composes about a third of North Las Vegas. The still-booming space west of I-15 is higher income and accounts for about two-thirds of the city. In a new twist on the old concept of the "wrong side of the tracks," boomburbs now often feature the "wrong side of the freeway."

New projects approved in the new parts of North Las Vegas are more upscale than the existing neighborhoods in the east. The mayor argues that the city needs to do this to balance the city's income, but the more pressing issue for Montandon is that North Las Vegas's east neighborhoods create enormous costs in code enforcement. The problem is that the east side of the city has few homeowners associations to manage relations between feuding neighbors and the local government must be brought in to settle disputes. This requires hiring municipal employees to do the settling, and that raises taxes.

Mayor Montandon is especially dismayed by the chain-link fences in low-income neighborhoods. He notes that "when the little chain-link fence goes up, the engine block goes up, the used furniture goes in—it is totally predictable." The city is now experimenting with strategies to create neighborhood organizations that do their own code enforcement. But there remains such a strong ethos for unfettered land use that it has been a slow and difficult process.

Interestingly, homeowners associations did not dominate North Las Vegas even as little as ten years ago. But almost all post-1997 construction has included homeowners associations in its development code. In 1997 the city had 83,000 people, and at most 5 percent lived in developments with a homeowners association. Since that date, 90 percent of the construction has required them, and the city now has 175,000 residents. North Las Vegas is rapidly approaching a point where at least half of its population lives in developments with homeowners associations, and the plans for the city's buildout include the objective that all new residential developments form associations.

What is true for North Las Vegas also holds for the region's other boomburb, Henderson, home to master-planned communities such as Green Valley. In their book on Las Vegas, Mark Gottdiener, Claudia C. Collins, and David R. Dickens note that homeowners associations do more than provide for nice lawns and shared amenities:

> Many homebuyers are attracted to the master-panned communities of Green Valley and Summerlin, not just for their beautifully landscaped parks and walking trails but because they want protection from neighbors who might disassemble a car in their driveway or pile junk around their house. These "neighborhood nightmares," featured regularly in the *Las Vegas Sun*, can go on for years, even decades, because of slow-moving city or county code enforcement. In short, they seek services and protection they can no longer expect from municipal government.[35]

Homeowners Associations in the Phoenix Region

Homeowners associations also figure prominently in the governance of three Phoenix East Valley boomburbs—Chandler, Gilbert, and Mesa. In Chandler,

Mayor Boyd Dunn sees homeowners associations as very important because they relieve much of the cost burden on the city. Gated developments even have private streets that they maintain. According to Dunn, if these associations went away, "it would be disastrous for the city." They are so important that Chandler, like North Las Vegas, is trying to get neighborhoods that are fee simple to adopt them. Chandler even supports such associations directly by giving them small grants for improvements, and the city also uses these grants as inducements to start new associations in fee simple neighborhoods.

Again, one key benefit is code enforcement. Like other boomburbs, Chandler has a big management problem in settling disputes in fee simple neighborhoods. Homeowners associations, because of the developments' private covenants, take care of such disputes directly. In addition, they can demand higher codes and tighter neighborhood restrictions than the city can, so there is much less concern on the part of city officials that real estate will lose value.[36]

One fear expressed by Mayor Dunn, and shared by Mesa's mayor Keno Hawker, is that some old associations will run short on funds and fail.[37] These neighborhoods would then become a burden on the city. One problem is that even though the responsibilities of defaulting associations would become a direct municipal burden, these associations are regulated at the state level. So cities are at the mercy of the state, and they can only prod the state to set rules that ensure associations remain sufficiently funded. Some boomburb mayors are not confident that the state legislature fully understands the impact that these associations have on local government and what costs they would impose on municipalities should they fail.

Mesa's Mayor Hawker sees homeowners associations as so important that his city actually tracks them in a database. He also assigned someone to be Mesa's point person on issues related to the associations. Mesa estimates that there were nearly 500 associations in the city as of 2006. The mayor also notes that much of Mesa's leadership comes from board members of the associations, and he suspects this is true for all boomburbs in greater Phoenix.[38]

Gilbert is another Phoenix boomburb that relies heavily on homeowners associations. According to Mayor Steven Berman, Gilbert used to be famous for its single-family homes on one-acre lots.[39] But those days have now passed. Gilbert requires a new residential development to have a homeowners association if it includes any commonly owned area.[40] However, on fee simple, one-acre lots there is no such requirement. That would seem like a loophole were Gilbert still seeing such development, but according to Mayor Berman no stand-alone homes have been built since 2001. Effectively, Gilbert is now a homeowners-association-only community, and nothing on the horizon should change that as the city builds out over the next twenty years. In the end, Mayor Berman wants 80 percent of Gilbert to have homeowners associations with strong covenants, conditions, and restrictions.

Boomburb mayors find that by performing labor-intensive, neighborhood-level management, homeowners associations free cities to concentrate on providing big infrastructure, economic development, and long-range master planning. In sum, the associations help boomburbs function with a governance structure intended for places just a fraction their size. Were these associations to lose their enforcement capacity, boomburbs might descend into political chaos. At the very least, they would need to hire more employees and increase taxes to pay for expanded government. The associations do have some lobbying power in the form of the Community Association Institute in Alexandria, Virginia, but some of their biggest local advocates are boomburb mayors.[41]

State Politics and Homeowners Associations

In 1994 Evan McKenzie noted that very little legislation had been passed to regulate homeowners association rules and management.[42] In recent years this situation has changed as especially Sunbelt state legislatures take up the subject of homeowners associations. More important, association critics are finally gaining traction in the state legislature. For example, the Arizona legislature in 2004–05 (Forty-Sixth Legislature, second regular session) passed ten bills regarding the regulation of homeowners associations. The laws mainly diminish the authority of these associations and require that they disclose to residents the dense details of covenants, conditions, and restrictions using more common language. This legislation touches on some of the most controversial powers of the associations, including the ability to foreclose on those who fail to pay fines.

The reality is that some of these associations got carried away in attempting to regulate anything that could possibly diminish home values. They also became trigger-happy and ready to foreclose on residents for the failure to pay fines for tiny infractions. This has resulted in some well-circulated horror stories about how granny went to visit the grandkids and came home to find her home sold at auction because some notice to pay a fine or back dues got lost in the mail. The overzealousness on the part of some associations could cost these organizations their greatest power—the ability to enforce codes by threat of foreclosure. Absent that capacity, they are reduced to garden clubs. Thus, the stakes could not be higher for boomburbs in the next several years as state legislatures consider what curbs to place on the associations. So far, they have maintained their basic power, but the future remains more uncertain.

Consider Arizona. In 2004 Arizona House Bill 2402 passed: the bill "would not allow a planned community that does not maintain any portion of the homes to foreclose unless it first waits three years [and] would not allow foreclosure of fines under any circumstances." The bill forces associations to secure court orders before placing liens on homes. It seems a reasonable reform, which guards against too rapid a foreclosure but does not prevent an association from exercising its ultimate enforcement power.

Other recent bills that passed the Arizona legislature focus on less significant but still divisive elements of homeowners association power. These include one law that allows political signage to appear on properties forty-five days before an election and another that lets residents park motor vehicles with advertising and business names on them in their driveways. These may seem like relatively small matters, but they have been a source of immense irritation over the years. The journalist Joel Garreau noted in his book *Edge City*, as far back as 1991, that people in the Phoenix region were already tiring of these types of rule. This long-simmering frustration finally worked its way through the political process over a decade later.

In 2005 California passed several bills impacting homeowners associations. Like Arizona, one law protects homeowners from nonjudicial foreclosure for the failure to pay association dues or fines. Senator Ducheney from San Diego introduced the bill, which gives homeowners the right to redeem their properties for ninety days after a nonjudicial foreclosure and requires a minimum amount of $1,800 in unpaid assessments. Legislation was considered that would allow homeowners to run up as much as $50,000 in unpaid dues and fines until an association could take foreclosure action, but it was defeated. Such a law would have all but doomed homeowners associations in the Golden State; one group that lobbied against it was the California League of Cities, which includes a large number of boomburbs and baby boomburbs.

In California, homeowners associations are now more tightly regulated by the Department of Real Estate. All associations must register with this department. New legislation (2005) also created an ombudsman position to manage disputes between associations and residents.

Homeowners Associations: Who Pays for Development Impact?

One of the more politically contested boomburb issues is determining who pays for the cost of growth. Historically, suburbs have had real challenges with free riders, who benefit from infrastructure improvements but do not pay the full share of these costs.[43] But today there is growing sophistication in calculating true development expenditure and finding ways—through impact fees or special improvement districts—to charge them directly to homeowners.[44] This serves to drive up the cost of housing and at the same time trigger voter anger.

One problem with homeowners associations is their growing cost. It can easily run residents well over $100 in monthly fees just to have one. There are often three layers:

—This starts with special improvement districts. Most new development in the West has an assessment for such districts. This is an innovation of Las Vegas's Summerlin homeowners association, which charges a flat rate for each acre developed. Special improvement districts pay for the big infrastructure, such as a freeway interchange or, in the case of Las Vegas, the freeway itself.

—Next are master-plan association fees. These are used to build and support the main amenities and major arterial streets within the master-planned community. Even schools can come out of this fee.

—Finally, there are the home builder fees. There are individual builder pads within a larger master-planned community, and builders pay fees to fund grounds, streets, and even pocket parks within their pods.

From Levittown, N.Y., where homeowners paid nothing but the cost of the house while the county provided all the infrastructure, to North Las Vegas sixty years later, where a homeowner pays for everything, including the freeway to get to work, suburbia has moved toward a more direct-impact system—and homeowners associations shoulder the brunt of the cost.

The Future of Homeowners Associations

In general, residents, communities, and state legislators have grown more sophisticated regarding homeowners associations. One keen observer of this world, Brent Herrington, vice president of DMB (a master-planned community builder in Scottsdale) remarks that "in the late 1980s and early 1990s, most consumers just did not get" homeowners associations."[45] The rules found in covenants, conditions, and restrictions at that time varied considerably from association to association. States were not yet in the business of regulating these associations, and standards had yet to emerge. But according to Herrington, "things are very different now." The consumer may belong to his or her third or fourth homeowners association, and state legislatures increasingly regulate the rules they can impose. Very few people are now shocked by the covenants, conditions, and restrictions they sign, and thus there is much less friction between residents and their homeowners associations.

Herrington also finds that these associations have developed an increasingly sophisticated governance structure. There is now what Herrington calls the "software" of community, which does not focus on rules but instead develops governance methods that increase civic engagement and build social capital. Herrington sees three parts to the structure of homeowners associations in high-end developments: there are the covenants, conditions, and restrictions (and in Herrington's mind we are doing this better); the community-building entities (civic grass-roots volunteerism); and even a nonprofit organization, which allows the association to fund philanthropic efforts.

Many upscale associations now have a built-in 501(c)(3) organization.[46] In the past, homeowners associations were entirely insular, concerned only with their own interests. But some of these associations now seek engagement with the larger community. As benevolent as these philanthropic efforts are, they also make good business sense. Homeowners associations that excite people's interest and draw them in may develop very effective community leadership and could also improve a development's reputation for being friendly and active. Such an identity in the larger community can help distinguish one master-planned development from another and could even result in a price premium for homes in places that feature high civic engagement.

Homeowners associations are now so woven into the fabric of boomburbs that they should remain active for some time. But as noted here, these associations are changing. Future associations may have a few less teeth in terms of rules, but they also should evolve into more multidimensional organizations that even further shape the politics and governance of boomburbs.

County versus Boomburb

A key governmental relationship for most boomburbs is that with their county. Boomburbs are incorporated municipalities, but within their borders often are unincorporated parcels of county land. The county serves as both a partner with and a rival to boomburbs. Boomburbs often need counties to run schools and to manage large-scale infrastructure. But counties also compete with boomburbs for economic development, such as major retail centers, and can also attract some high-end housing developments away from boomburbs.[47]

Clark County, Nevada, and the Lost Boomburbs

Clark County, home to the Las Vegas region and the boomburbs of Henderson and North Las Vegas, has perhaps the most complicated county governance structure in the United States. This starts with the fact that the county contains the region's key economic asset—the Las Vegas Strip. Years ago the city of Las Vegas attempted to annex the Strip, which prompted Clark County to seek help from the Nevada state legislature.

Help came in the form of a law that enabled Clark County to form unincorporated "towns," which still paid taxes into the county but were now protected from annexation by incorporated cities such as Las Vegas and its boomburbs. But Clark County did not want these places to become cities, or again it would have lost valuable tax ratables, so it left them as unincorporated. Any Clark County town created before 1984 cannot be annexed. The town of Enterprise was formed in the late 1990s and therefore got partly annexed by Henderson in 2004, but it is not likely to lose any more land in the future because the county stepped in in its defense. By this action, Clark County has locked up Henderson from further expansion.

Three Clark County towns are best described as Las Vegas's "lost" boomburbs. In 2003 Robert Lang and Dawn Dhavale did an analysis of all census-designated places (CDPs) above 50,000, which they dubbed reluctant cities.[48] CDPs are unincorporated areas but, according to the Census Bureau, serve as proxies for cities based on a central-place model. Some CDPs are simply large master-planned communities that lie on unincorporated land, such as Reston, Virginia, in Fairfax County. But the three largest CDPs in the United States, and the only ones to exceed 100,000 residents, all lie in Clark County. The three towns would easily qualify as boomburbs based on the criteria used in this book, but these places are not just accidental cities; rather, they are reluctant cities in that they failed to incorporate.

The largest lost boomburb is Paradise, Nevada, with over 200,000 residents. Paradise also contains most of the Las Vegas Strip. Most tourists who visit the Strip assume they are in Las Vegas. Most Las Vegas tourists could care less about what city they are in—or in this case even if they are in a city at all—because the Strip offers faux versions of New York, Paris, and Venice. Guests at say the New York–New York Hotel and Casino are staying in a city type so obscure that it is known only to Clark County officials (who insisted that the Strip not be in an actual city), census analysts (who invented the statistic to describe places such as Paradise), and the occasional urban planning professor (who is simply trying grasp why Paradise even exists).

In addition to Paradise, the other lost boomburbs of Las Vegas are Sunrise Manor and Spring Valley. Case visits were made in 2004, 2005, and 2006 to all three Las Vegas CDPs for purposes of comparison with official boomburbs. This included a 2005 visit to the Sunrise Manor "Town Hall" to meet with Russell Davis. Davis is the community liaison for Sunrise Manor to Clark County and is the closest thing to a mayor Sunrise Manor has. It is an appointed position. There is also a citizen's advisory council, to which residents are appointed by the county for two-year terms. The council serves as a conduit for local citizens to raise issues with the county. Davis attends these meetings, which are held in Sunrise Manor Town Hall.

The town advisory board meets twice a month. The county staff provides background on the key issues. Most issues discussed involve land use. Building variances and use permits in particular are a big problem. In fact, any land use that does not conform to the Sunrise Manor master plan is hotly debated. But like boomburbs, much of Sunrise Manor belongs to homeowners associations, so most rules are specifically spelled out. Were it not for these associations it might have been necessary for Sunrise Manor to incorporate. Part of Davis's job is to provide a forum for homevoters who fail to get satisfaction through their association. Much of the discussion he has with residents is heated. But given the weird governance structure of Las Vegas's lost boomburbs Davis can understand their frustration. As he jokes—you can't fight city hall, especially when there *is* no city hall.

County Land within Boomburbs

Due to some quirks of annexation, small chunks of county land remain within at least two dozen boomburbs. This issue came up with several boomburb mayors and planners, because it creates some complicated governance issues. Most notable among these is a free-rider problem, which involves residents of the embedded county parcels using city services but not paying taxes to the boomburb. The question is, How do boomburbs treat these people? One solution is to invite them to join the city, but many people turn down the offer to pay for something that they already get free.

Steve Berman from Gilbert is particularly angry with the county's free riders. According to Berman, people who live on unincorporated land are, to put it bluntly, a "pain in the ass." He notes that homeowners in these unincorporated parcels refuse to join Gilbert, yet they use the city's parks, libraries, and fire protection without being taxed for them. The state of Arizona recently ruled that cities do not have to provide fire protection for unincorporated areas, but they do have to provide other services. The mayor thinks once a couple of homes burn down, the owners of unincorporated parcels peppered throughout Gilbert may have a change of heart about joining the town.

On several occasions, the question of people who live on unincorporated land embedded in cities has come up in discussion between Robert Lang and the media. At one point, *USA Today* entertained the thought of doing a story on the resisters, focusing on Gilbert. Commenting on Gilbert's holdouts, Paul Overberg of *USA Today* observed, "Somewhere out on the desert there is an invisible line, the corporate limit. Five saguaros farther into the desert squats a rugged individualist who insists on his right to live free of the massive strangling government of Gilbert, Arizona, probably as efficient and minimal a government as information technology and privatization can build. Is this a great country or what?"[49]

Overberg's point is right on target. Gilbert offers one of the most minimal and cost-efficient governments possible, and yet there are those who still resist living in this boomburb. The Gilbert unincorporated holdouts point to a bigger issue with respect to the general relationship between counties and boomburbs. Boomburbs live by grabbing land. Counties often thrive on land that remains unincorporated. To the extent that counties provide a workable alternative to boomburbs, more and more metropolitan development could wind up outside of cities. While boomburbs may be accidental cities, they remain cities nonetheless. Their biggest future competition may come from reluctant cities.

Municipal Fragmentation and the Potential for Regional Cooperation

Because of their size, boomburbs are gaining recognition and standing in their respective regions. As noted in chapter 1, about half of boomburbs are now defined as principal cities by the U.S. Census Bureau. Like all municipalities, boomburbs have a stake in regional cooperation on key issues, including environmental quality and transportation capacity. Most boomburbs used for case analysis in this book were active members of the regional councils of government. Almost all mayors interviewed mentioned that, on many issues, they worked in cooperation with both the main principal city and smaller suburbs.

The South's suburbs comprise mostly small, fragmented municipalities that capture tiny fractions of metropolitan population. The difference in municipal structure between the East and West Sunbelts has important policy implications.[50] The East's fragmented municipalities will likely produce more fragmented responses to regional problems. If, as many now argue, regional cooperation is becoming more essential to take on such problems as sprawl, then the South's lack of boomburbs may put the region at a disadvantage.

The majority of boomburbs are found in the West. Western metropolitan areas, while featuring some municipal fragmentation, have the majority of residents living in cities of 50,000 people or more. This coalescence into larger places reduces the number of local governments that must cooperate in order to get a regional response to problems. In some cases, the mayors of just a dozen or so places—traditional cities and boomburbs—can meet with most residents in the region at one table. In a structural sense, this should favor cooperation based on simple group dynamics. The fewer the parties, and the more people they represent, the greater the probability for coordinated action.

Consider, for example, the difference between Phoenix and Atlanta in structural opportunities for regional cooperation. The two metropolitan areas are exemplars of their respective halves of the Sunbelt. During the 1990s Phoenix and Atlanta registered the largest percentage gains among the nation's biggest metropolitan areas, growing 45.3 percent and 38.9 percent, respectively.[51] Both have continued to boom.

Phoenix, a region with over 4 million people, has seven boomburbs. The city of Phoenix and its boomburbs combined have over 80 percent of the region's population. To have just eight municipalities account for so large a share of their metropolitan population is very unusual. Atlanta, by contrast, has just 17 percent of its population living in the eight largest cities. In fact, all of Atlanta's seven largest suburbs add up to a far smaller population than Mesa, Arizona.

Also note that Atlanta's municipalities are physically smaller than Phoenix's.[52] Roswell, Atlanta's most populous suburb, is just 32.6 square miles. Meanwhile, Mesa spreads over 108 square miles. Tempe, the physically smallest boomburb in the Phoenix metropolitan area, would rank second in land area and first in population were it a suburb of Atlanta. Interestingly, the seven big suburbs of Atlanta and the seven boomburbs of Phoenix have similar total density, with 1,579 and 1,687 people per square mile, respectively. It appears that the large size of Phoenix's boomburbs allows them to capture such growth and accounts for a major share of the region's population.

Given that Phoenix's largest eight cities contain over four-fifths of the metropolitan area's residents, regional action requires only that the leaders of these places work together. The mayors of Atlanta's big cities could also cooperate, but it would impact less than a fifth of the region's residents. In fact, the Phoenix region has recently seen a good deal of regional cooperation, including unified action on such issues as regional light rail and water management. Thus, the emergence of Phoenix's boomburbs gives it a distinct structural advantage for regional solutions over Atlanta, where municipal fragmentation greatly complicates metropolitan-level action.

Also, given their scale, boomburbs may have an easier time relating to larger principal cities than do smaller suburbs. For now, boomburbs remain a bit hard to place as cities. But as they grow and diversify, their citylike qualities will become more manifest. It is likely that, within a decade or so, many boomburbs may become coalition partners of big cities at both the national and regional levels simply based on converging interests. Metropolitan areas with abundant boomburbs may find it easier to take cooperative actions on a number of regionwide issues, which could advantage these places as economic competitors.

Eminent Domain and Regulatory Takings

At the time of this book's writing there is a national debate over the use of eminent domain as a tool to redevelop cities. Much of the controversy stems from the 2005 ruling by the U.S. Supreme Court in the case of *Kelo* vs. *New London*. In a five-to-four decision the court ruled that the city of New London, Connecticut, could condemn a moderate-income neighborhood to make way for a luxury mixed-use project that would yield considerably more tax revenue. The ruling struck a nerve and was immediately seized on by property rights advocates as a symbol of a government with too much power.

The politics of *Kelo* played out in some unusual ways, as noted in an investigative article by Ray Ring in *High Country News*.[53] The immediate reaction by property rights advocates was to seek more restrictive eminent domain legislation at the state level. However, the bigger prize sought by people in the so-called wise-use land movement was to use the public outrage over *Kelo* as a battering ram against what the group sees as excessive use of municipal zoning.[54] In particular, property rights advocates focus on regulatory takings by municipalities in the downzoning of land uses. A downzone reduces the intensity at which private property can be used, such as lowering the floor-to-area ratio that a structure may use of a land parcel.[55]

Consider, for instance, the use of an overlay zoning district that downzones the lot coverage of homes. In much of the United States the debate over McMansions in older neighborhoods of smaller homes has resulted in overlay districts that create greater regulation at the neighborhood level in an effort to curb large infill houses that are seen as out of context. Such a special district may satisfy the interests of the majority of residents but represents regulatory takings from the person who is denied the right to build a McMansion on a particular lot.

But help is on the way. Legislation similar to Oregon's Measure 37 (passed in 2004 in response to the state's restrictive land use plan that denied people who own land outside a designated urban growth boundary the right to build subdivisions) recently appeared on the ballot in five other Western states (Arizona, California, Idaho, Nevada, and Washington).[56] In Oregon, regulatory takings must be compensated by the government doing the downzoning, or the regulation will be waived.[57] The results so far have been to waive the rules rather than pay compensation.

Now consider Arizona's Proposition 207, which combines eminent domain reform with a takings provision that mimics Oregon's.[58] The proposition passed in 2006 and severely limits the municipal capacity for zoning changes. Boomburbs such as Scottsdale, which employs overlay districts in some older neighborhoods to prevent the spread of McMansions, now face the prospect of abandoning this strategy or risking stiff costs from private takings claims.

As cities exceeding 100,000 residents, boomburbs are increasingly diverse and complicated places that need all the tools possible to manage change in older neighborhoods. The rise of regulatory takings and eminent domain reform comes at an especially bad time for built-out boomburbs, which can grow only by preserving vibrant neighborhoods and redeveloping declining ones. The new laws serve as a one-two punch against government-led efforts to remake older boomburbs: they may help increase the built density in neighborhoods seeking more open space, while preventing cities from condemning land that could be much more intensely utilized.

Conclusion: Accidental Politics?

Boomburbs may have reached their quasi–big city condition accidentally, but there is not much left to chance in their governance. Boomburbs have highly targeted politics. They are governed lightly in the public realm and precisely in the private sphere. The mix allows these places to offer cost-effective government, where volunteers (from the mayor's offices to the homeowners associations) do most of the heavy lifting. So far the blend of private and public is working, but there are clouds on the horizon.

One looming issue is equity. Boomburb governance assumes a basic commonality of interest among residents. But as boomburbs become big cities, this is no longer valid. Boomburbs need to retain the element of government that has made them so attractive for decades but at the same time adjust to new realities. Perhaps boomburbs will lead the nation in a new round of civic reform that enables them to broaden enfranchisement without inviting corruption. Boomburbs that fail recognize their growing diversity through the political process risk alienating their future residents.

7

Boomburbs at Buildout

Boomburbs occupy an in-between niche in the suburban landscape—they are not typical inner-ring suburbs nor are they exurban. Most are the products of the post–World War II building boom, and they continued to grow horizontally through the 1970s, 1980s, and 1990s. However, some now find themselves in competition with their exurbs, facing neighborhood disinvestment, demographic shifts, and limited growth options. These former bedroom communities now have big-city needs that they must balance with a suburban environment based on low-density, single-use subdivisions.

The boomburb boom may not be sustained, and some are seeing a slowdown in population gains.[1] Population growth rates rest on several factors, including the amount of buildable land available; the number, type, and size of the new housing units that will be built on this land; the ethnic background of people who migrate to the city; and the age, education, income, and life plans of both existing and new residents. Based on this mix, some boomburbs have decades more double-digit growth ahead. However, there are also boomburbs where these factors weigh against significant future population gains, and a few boomburbs have already stopped rapid growth.

Yet given the boomburb trend toward low density, changes in the nation's building patterns may also affect the dynamics of how these places can expand. If sprawl has hit the wall, as it has in several big regions around the country, then slower-growing boomburbs may see new life as more densely built urban areas.[2] A key is how boomburbs plan for the future. Some are rushing to fill their remaining space with new development that is even lower density than the old. Meanwhile, other boomburbs are beginning to explore being denser and more traditional cities.

Most boomburbs are not only more populous than they were several decades ago, but because of annexations, they are also physically larger. Western boomburbs were especially eager to annex surrounding lands to access their water rights. Data on land area are available for the forty-three boomburbs that existed in 1960. Between 1960 and 1990, the average size of these cities increased from fifteen square miles to fifty square miles.[3] Comparisons of population across time, however, can be tricky because the places annexed usually contained some population. For example, San Bernardino, California, annexed land in the 1950s and 1960s; the 1950s annexations added 12,803 people to the population by 1960, and the 1960s annexations added 6,092 people by 1970. But it is not known how many of these people were there to start with and how many moved into the annexed parts after the land was added to the city. Another fact complicating population comparisons is that some boomburbs were formed through combining existing towns or unincorporated places, which can result in a large initial population. For example, Chesapeake, Virginia, was created in 1963 as the result of a merger between the city of South Norfolk and Norfolk County.[4] The new city had an estimated population of 78,000 in 1963 and an enumerated population of 89,580 at the time of its first decennial census in 1970.

This chapter considers how boomburbs expect to build out. The methods used to determine their plans were phone interviews with planning departments, visits to over two dozen boomburbs, interviews with the mayors of these cities, and an analysis of planning documents posted to municipal websites. The result is a multifaceted portrait of how boomburbs expect to develop in the next several decades. For smart-growth advocates, boomburb buildout plans are both encouraging and sobering. Many boomburbs expect denser, mixed-use development to be built around light-rail stations. But it appears that the majority of new growth will feature typical subdivision and strip development—with perhaps only slightly higher densities than have been common in the past.

Boomburb Buildout Plans

Buildout refers to the point at which development either has reached a city's borders or has exhausted large-scale greenfield options. Many cities survey the area that remains available for new growth and estimate the date at which current development trends will consume this space. Some boomburbs also calculate their final buildout population. Because of planned annexation, some cities may produce two scenarios—one with and another without the expected additional land. Several variables factor into buildout analysis. Perhaps the most important of these is the intensity at which land will be used. Cities with just a small portion of land left may plan to develop the space at a higher density than existing development, which could translate into significant new population and commercial growth. Conversely, cities may zone remaining land for very-low-density development or may even seek to preserve it. Therefore, the issue is not just how much land remains but also how it will be used.

Redevelopment potential also figures into buildout estimates. Some boomburbs have such low density that plenty of potential remains to infill and renew existing developments in a way that will add significantly to the metropolitan feel. A few boomburbs—such as Tempe, Arizona, Hialeah, Florida, and Lakewood, Colorado—despite their being essentially at buildout, still offer opportunities to developers seeking to build denser projects.

Buildout estimates are important because they help frame debates over how and where to grow. Some boomburb personnel surveyed for this chapter raised objections to the term *buildout*, because they believe that it sparks controversy. Several refused to provide data on buildout, arguing that the term is misleading because—to paraphrase—no place is ever really finished building. It may be that indicating a growth limit invites a critical reexamination of current development patterns. In that light, even mentioning a buildout date or estimating how much land remains is a potential political liability.

All 54 boomburbs and 86 baby boomburbs were contacted about their buildout plans. Data were provided for 130 of these places. Although in many instances the data were incomplete, there is full information for 87. Cities often do not produce buildout plans per se; rather, they make estimates as part of their general plan. Thus, getting full information on boomburb buildout required multiple methods. The most comprehensive data were gained by direct phone calls to boomburb planning offices. Planners were asked the following:

—What percentage of city land is left?

—What year will the city's buildout occur?

—What will the population be at buildout?

—Will new developments be denser or less dense than existing development?

—Are there plans for passenger rail?

—Are there plans for transit-oriented development?

—Are there plans for mixed-use development at the project level?

—Are there plans for annexation?

To provide quality control and confirm the information provided in the surveys and interviews, the authors checked boomburb websites. Information regarding rail service was checked against transit system websites that show maps of lines and stations. The sites yielded a few cases in which the boomburb reported having passenger rail when in reality it was one town over.

Table 7-1 lists five characteristics of buildout for the eighty-seven boomburbs for which full data are available and then divides the boomburbs into three categories: those that are embracing compact building, those that have a mix of densities, and those that do not want to become more "urban." Four of the characteristics specifically capture land use change, while the inclusion of rail shows the extent of plans for transit-oriented developments. The characteristics represent thresholds, the presence of which indicates that a boomburb is maturing as a city. A boomburb registering all five characteristics is near buildout, has little remaining land, expects to grow denser as it nears buildout, is done annexing land, and has a rail stop either existing or planned. Eight boomburbs have all five characteristics. Having none of them indicates that the boomburb is still developing and may not mature for decades. Only three boomburbs meet this condition (Escondido, California, Peoria, Arizona, and West Jordan, Utah). Many boomburbs have just two of the characteristics.

Well over half of boomburbs (forty-seven of the eighty-seven) expect to be at buildout by 2020. All of these have been booming for decades, with many registering double-digit growth for each census since 1940—or at any rate, since their incorporation date. The fact that over half of these cities expect to fill their existing space within the next fifteen or so years signals a dramatic shift: some of the fastest-growing cities in America are about to slow down—or at the very least alter their development pattern. This change in direction is confirmed by the fact that thirty-five of the eighty-seven report that less than 10 percent of their land is left to build on. In addition, fifty of the eighty-seven expect to grow denser as they reach buildout. And many (thirty-one) plan no additional annexation. After this point, all new additions will be due to infill and redevelopment.

Finally, forty-one of the boomburbs in the table either have or plan passenger rail. Many also report plans for transit-oriented development. The finding shows how rapidly rail (especially light rail) is proliferating in metropolitan America. In the 2004 elections, fifty-five transportation-related initiatives were on the ballot.[5] Of these, forty-two (or 80 percent, and

Table 7-1. Boomburb Buildout

Category and boomburb	Buildout by 2020	Less than 10 percent of land remains	Becoming denser	No plans to annex	Rail exists or is planned[a]
Built out and building up					
Hillsboro, Oregon	✓	✓	✓	✓	✓
Lakewood, Colorado	✓	✓	✓	✓	✓
Mission Viejo, California	✓	✓	✓	✓	✓
Oceanside, California	✓	✓	✓	✓	✓
Palatine, Illinois	✓	✓	✓	✓	✓
Santa Ana, California	✓	✓	✓	✓	✓
Sunnyvale, California	✓	✓	✓	✓	✓
Tempe, Arizona	✓	✓	✓	✓	✓
Town and country					
Anaheim, California	—	✓	✓	—	✓
Beaverton, Oregon	✓	—	✓	—	✓
Bellevue, Washington	—	✓	✓	—	—
Boca Raton, Florida	—	✓	✓	—	✓
Boynton Beach, Florida	—	—	✓	—	✓
Burnsville, Minnesota	✓	✓	✓	✓	—
Carrollton, Texas	—	✓	✓	—	✓
Chesapeake, Virginia	—	—	✓	✓	—
Chula Vista, California	—	—	✓	—	✓
Clearwater, Florida	✓	✓	✓	—	—
Davie, Florida	✓	✓	✓	—	—
Eagan, Minnesota	—	✓	✓	—	—
Elgin, Illinois	—	—	✓	—	—
Fairfield, California	—	—	✓	—	✓
Federal Way, Washington	—	—	✓	—	—
Fontana, California	—	—	✓	—	✓
Frederick, Maryland	—	—	✓	—	✓
Fullerton, California	✓	✓	✓	—	✓
Garland, Texas	—	—	✓	—	✓
Gresham, Oregon	—	—	✓	—	✓
Henderson, Nevada	—	—	✓	—	—
Irvine, California	✓	✓	✓	—	✓
Irving, Texas	—	—	✓	—	✓
Miramar, Florida	—	—	✓	—	—
Missouri City, Texas	✓	✓	✓	—	—
Moreno Valley, California	—	—	✓	—	✓
Murfreesboro, Tennessee	—	—	✓	—	—
Oxnard, California	✓	✓	✓	—	—
Palmdale, California	✓	—	✓	✓	✓
Pembroke Pines, Florida	✓	✓	✓	✓	—
Plano, Texas	✓	—	✓	✓	✓
Plymouth, Minnesota	—	—	✓	✓	—
Roseville, California	✓	—	✓	—	—
Round Rock, Texas	—	—	✓	—	—
San Bernardino, California	—	—	✓	✓	✓
Sandy, Utah	—	—	✓	—	✓
St. Charles, Missouri	—	—	✓	—	—

(continued)

Table 7-1. Boomburb Buildout *(continued)*

Category and boomburb	Buildout by 2020	Less than 10 percent of land remains	Becoming denser	No plans to annex	Rail exists or is planned[a]
St. Peters, Missouri	—	—	✓	—	—
Sunrise, Florida	✓	✓	✓	✓	—
Tamarac, Florida	✓	✓	✓	✓	—
Waukesha, Wisconsin	✓	—	✓	—	—
Westminster, Colorado	—	—	✓	—	✓
The Holdouts					
Arlington, Texas	—	—	—	✓	—
Aurora, Colorado	—	—	—	—	✓
Brooklyn Park, Minnesota	✓	—	—	✓	—
Carlsbad, California	—	—	—	✓	—
Chandler, Arizona	✓	—	—	—	—
Coral Springs, Florida	✓	✓	—	✓	—
Corona, California	—	—	—	—	✓
Costa Mesa, California	✓	—	—	✓	—
Davis, California	✓	✓	—	—	✓
Deerfield Beach, Florida	✓	✓	—	✓	✓
Delray Beach, Florida	✓	✓	—	—	✓
Eden Prairie, Minnesota	✓	✓	—	—	—
Edmond, Oklahoma	✓	—	—	—	—
Escondido, California	—	✓	—	—	—
Folsom, California	✓	✓	—	—	—
Fremont, California	✓	✓	—	—	✓
Gaithersburg, Maryland	—	—	—	—	✓
Gilbert, Arizona	—	—	—	✓	—
Glendale, Arizona	✓	—	—	—	—
Lancaster, California	—	—	—	—	✓
Maple Grove, Minnesota	✓	—	—	✓	—
Margate, Florida	✓	—	—	✓	—
Mesa, Arizona	—	—	—	✓	✓
Mesquite, Texas	✓	—	—	—	—
Milpitas, California	✓	—	—	✓	—
North Las Vegas, Nevada	✓	—	—	—	—
North Miami, Florida	✓	✓	—	—	—
North Richland Hills, Texas	✓	✓	—	—	—
Olathe, Kansas	✓	—	—	✓	—
Ontario, California	—	—	—	✓	✓
Peoria, Arizona	✓	—	—	—	—
Plantation, Florida	✓	✓	—	—	—
Rancho Cucamonga, California	—	—	—	—	✓
Riverside, California	✓	✓	—	—	✓
Scottsdale, Arizona	✓	—	—	✓	—
Tustin, California	✓	✓	—	—	✓
West Jordan, Utah	—	—	—	—	—

Source: Authors' research.

a. Planned rail means that there is a high probability that a line will be built, based on committed funds or a recent public referendum. Many boomburbs have conducted feasibility studies and are actively lobbying for rail, but these are not indicated in the table as having or planning rails.

totaling some $30 billion in bonds) were approved.[6] Metropolitan areas such as Denver, Phoenix, San Diego, and Austin passed light-rail measures, ensuring that many of the planned rail stops in boomburbs will be built. All but one of the twenty-four boomburb mayors interviewed held a favorable view of rail. Most were less interested in rail for mobility purposes (such as relieving traffic congestion) than for its economic development potential.

Buildout Holdouts

A significant share of all boomburbs reported using buildout as a way to shift toward more upscale development. In some instances, the boomburb plans to use its remaining space to upgrade the town's image and attract more affluent residents. The boomburbs discussed below are seeking to remain low density even as they approach the end of greenfield development.

Gilbert, Arizona

Gilbert is in the Phoenix metropolitan area, south and east of downtown. Since the 2000 census it is the fastest-growing city with a population above 100,000 in the United States.[7] Oddly, however, the census still identifies Gilbert as a town. As it turns out, this is not an accident but a conscious choice—and speaks volumes about how Gilbert sees itself. Mayor Steven M. Berman was asked about Gilbert still being called a town. The mayor responded that Gilbert could have been considered a city once it had more than 5,000 residents, according to Arizona rules, but he believes that people in Gilbert want the place to be called a town—and more important, to remain a town.[8] "I don't think there are ten people in Gilbert that want to have it called a city." Gilbert's goal, he said, is "to be the only 300,000-person small town in America." It is a reluctant city.

Mayor Berman completely rejects the idea of light rail in Gilbert, arguing that slow-moving trolleys running down the middle of boulevards would not improve mobility. He is the only boomburb mayor interviewed who did not see the side benefit of light rail spurring real estate development at station stops.

Because of its rapid growth, Gilbert is only about twenty years away from buildout despite having an ample land supply. The town has "strip annexed" seventy-six square miles of land.[9] All of Gilbert's external borders are defined, and there is no way to change them unless other places are de-annexed. Gilbert had verbal agreements with Mesa and Chandler not to annex land at the edge of the region, but according to the mayor the town was subsequently "burned" by both cities. Williams U.S. Air Force Base, which will soon be decommissioned, is a case in point. Mesa and Gilbert struck a verbal agreement not to annex around the base, but Mesa went back on the deal and did annex. When Williams is decommissioned, it could be used as a freight-handling airport to relieve the crowded Phoenix Sky Harbor Airport. But Mesa is already committed to making its old military base, Falcon Field, into just such an airport and by annexing the land around Williams prevented Gilbert from using it as an economic development anchor. Gilbert was also "burned" by Chandler, which reached around the south of Gilbert and cut the city off from new unincorporated land.

For now, Gilbert is locked in and can only pick up leftover unincorporated parcels within its existing boundaries. Gilbert is a fully master-planned city. As the mayor notes, "Now it is all about filling in the lines, or painting by numbers" to eventual buildout. Mostly single-family residential development is planned. No mixed-use projects are in the pipeline. There is a retail "town center," but it is cut off from other commercial development, and even the adjacent housing is physically separated from it by walls and fences.

Gilbert does have some higher-density housing development as infill (with fifteen to eighteen units per acre). But the city will allow higher-density residential development only if it is upscale ownership housing. Gilbert has almost no apartment complexes—perhaps as few as ten, according to Mayor Berman. The mayor notes that some developments are zoned for up to twelve units per acre, but he is uncomfortable with anything above four per acre.

Chandler, Arizona

Gilbert's neighbor to the east, Chandler, has a similar "quality-only" buildout strategy. Chandler has even taken the additional step of zoning for larger lots than currently exist in an effort to attract only upscale, master-planned community development. This goal has an interesting impact on the city's buildout plans. Chandler will now build out earlier than was originally anticipated (now by 2020) and will have 50,000 fewer residents than originally planned.

Mayor Boyd W. Dunn argues that "growing cities need to focus on the quality of the buildout."[10] He notes that market research shows that if "you build a big enough house on a big enough lot" people will stay there over their lifetime. Dunn's worry is that low-end housing will age badly and become blighted. He finds that this has happened in the past as people left starter homes when their families grew. The neighborhoods left behind were sold to lower-income residents and are now a drag on the city.

The question was raised with Mayor Dunn about the charge of exclusionary zoning practices that housing advocates could levy at the city for requiring large lots. "Yes," Dunn replied, "but we have also developed a new infill strategy that promotes new housing in built-up areas by lowering regulation and by speeding the approval process." Indeed, Chandler has plans for much denser development at its core, which is a departure from its neighbor, Gilbert. But it's likely that much of this new development will be upscale as well.

North Las Vegas, Nevada

North Las Vegas is a suburb of Las Vegas. After Gilbert, North Las Vegas has been the fastest-growing U.S. city since 2000.[11] In 2003 the city had 144,502 residents and expects to grow to 453,000 residents at buildout in the year 2020, according to Mayor Michael L. Montandon.[12] This is a remarkable growth rate but possible—considering that North Las Vegas grew by at least 25 percent in just the three years from 2000 to 2003.[13] The key variable affecting the city's growth is its ability to annex and develop new land.

Annexation in North Las Vegas is complicated by the fact that the federal government holds virtually all of the area that the city plans to acquire. The land is now in the charge of the Bureau of Land Management (BLM). The BLM has established a "disposal area" around metropolitan Las Vegas. Inside this federally imposed urban growth boundary, the BLM can transfer land to private interests. Because of recent legislation, the money from the sale of BLM land is recycled back into the Las Vegas region in the form of parks and recreation facilities.[14]

At first, according to Montandon, the parcels sold were modest, and the revenue that they generated ($3 million to $10 million) were below the political radar. However, the BLM seeks to sell property worth hundreds of millions of dollars. Environmental groups oppose these large sales, and the mayor notes that some U.S. senators from the East are exploring ways to reverse this legislation. Some Western senators, however, want to extend the practice to their states. The bottom line for North Las Vegas is that the land they hope to annex is increasingly expensive and in addition could become the locked-up prize in a political fight. The costs and uncertainty of BLM land transfers could stall North Las Vegas's growth and alter its buildout plans. But one thing does seem likely—that the city will use whatever land it gets to build upscale, master-planned communities. In part because of high land costs, all development in North Las Vegas is bound to be expensive.

According to the National Association of Realtors, metropolitan Las Vegas's median-priced home more than doubled in just one year (from mid-2003 to mid-2004), the biggest gain for any metropolitan area in the nation.[15] Ironically, Las Vegas would seem to have lots of space to develop, but the transfer of BLM land has occurred too slowly to keep pace with the region's rapid development, and as a result lot prices have shot up. Recognizing this problem, the BLM developed a program to transfer land for affordable housing at deeply dicounted prices. But so far places such as North Las Vegas are not interested. According to the *Las Vegas Sun*:

> The idea looks good on paper: Release land at below-market value—in some cases discounting by as much as 95 percent—to local governmental entities, including housing authorities, so affordable housing can be built. . . . But officials with the local cities, the county, and their housing authorities said . . . there are still more details that need to be worked out, and elements of the program just end up raising more confusion. Officials with some of the entities said they have no interest in the program at all and feel local governments shouldn't have to buy the land.[16]

North Las Vegas is one of the "entities" referred to above. In fact, one city official quoted in the story described being "disgusted" with BLM and accused the bureau of "strictly trying to make a profit off the land."[17] But another issue for North Las Vegas is that affordable housing does not fit into its buildout plans. The attitude in North Las Vegas is that the city already has a high share of poverty, especially when compared to its rival boomburb, Henderson. Therefore, the city is dedicated to finishing out its development with the most upscale, master-planned community development that the market will deliver.

There are two parts to North Las Vegas, divided by I-15. The older core, south of the freeway, is poor and mostly Hispanic. Northwest of I-15 the city is mostly affluent and white. The north is booming, with expensive single-family homes built on former BLM land. Any new BLM land will likely be developed the same way and attract a similar population. North Las Vegas's master-planned communities are often built at a relatively high density because of the land constraints around Las Vegas, but they are seldom mixed use, mixed income, or pedestrian friendly.

Town and Country: Urbanizing the Suburbs

Some boomburbs are following dual paths to buildout. They are continuing to develop single-family homes while at the same time directing some of their growth to mixed-use, transit-oriented development. A national model for this growth pattern is the Washington suburb of Arlington, Virginia.[18] Interestingly, Arlington came up in conversation with several boomburb mayors who admire its ability to preserve conventional, low-density neighborhoods by deflecting more dense growth to targeted transportation corridors.

Garland, Texas

Garland is in suburban Dallas just east of the city. Garland was mostly built between the 1960s and the 1980s and is now near buildout, with just under 90 percent of its land occupied. Garland's mayor Bob Day expects a final population of 250,000 (the city had 218,027 in 2003).[19] While much of Garland is made up of modest single-family homes, the city plans to reach buildout with primarily upscale, master-planned communities. Garland also had a reputation, according to Mayor Day, for affordable garden apartments that house mostly low-income families. Day believes that apartments are now so stigmatized that he refers to them by what he calls the "A-word." Mayor Day notes that traditional garden apartments are now forbidden in Garland and that the city is in the process of condemning and removing some of the oldest stock.

Yet multifamily housing is not entirely banned from Garland. The city plans transit-oriented development at its two planned station stops on the DART system (Dallas Area Rapid Transit light rail). In fact, the land around these stations is zoned at a minimum of fifty units per acre, which is very dense by Dallas area standards. While some of this housing may be mixed income, it is expected to be much more upscale than Garland's old garden apartments. Also, only a small portion of the transit-oriented housing may be rental. Mayor Day says that Garland is "making urban from suburban." He notes that right now in Garland there is a downtown square, but no one lives there. The new thrust is to create downtown living around the DART station similar to what exists in Plano, Texas. According to Day, Garland has to "change our thinking from out to up," as the city builds and rebuilds. He notes that the shift has just happened and that he and other mayors in the Dallas area "now get it." *It* being smart growth.

Plano, Texas

Plano is a suburb north of Dallas that is well known as a corporate head-quarters location. Plano has also been one of the fastest-growing cities in the country over the past half century, going from an unincorporated hamlet in 1950 to a sprawling boomburb of 241,991 residents by 2003. But Plano is starting to plan for a time when its stops booming. The city is exploring ways to create "place." Plano's future centers will combine city and suburban features to produce a new market niche that helps distinguish the city from both Dallas to the south and fast-growing exurbs to the north. Plano is still much less urban than Dallas but feels crowded compared to nearby newer suburbs such as Frisco.

The first step in this new growth model, according to Plano's mayor, Pat Evans, is the transit-oriented development at Plano's downtown DART station.[20] Downtown Plano's redevelopment is much admired in the Dallas region and came up in interviews with the mayors of Irving, Garland, and Arlington as a positive change they hope to repeat in their boomburbs. Plano's shift from start-up suburb to a built-up one is not limited to downtown. The city is also seeing its first-generation office parks redeveloped as more mixed-use and denser suburban town centers. This transition was reported on by *USA Today* in a story about the Legacy office complex, which was begun by H. Ross Perot as a headquarters for his data processing firm EDS.

> When information technology giant EDS began moving its world headquarters in the 1980s from Dallas to this then-remote suburb, employees gazed out at thousands of acres of unspoiled Texas prairie. Longhorns and buffaloes grazed nearby. Unpaved roads surrounded the new corporate campus, one of the first in a 2,665-acre office park bearing the grand name Legacy. . . . Today, pedestrian-friendly streets, upscale boutiques, art galleries, restaurants, theaters, coffee shops, a town square, hotel and 640 apartments are within a five-minute walk from EDS' front gate. They're within a mile of other large employers such as J. C. Penney, Frito-Lay, Dr Pepper/7 UP, Comcast, AT&T Wireless, PepsiCo's information technology division and the Texas Regional Heart Center.[21]

The exurbs (as mentioned in chapter 5) may ultimately impact Plano's buildout options by creating a downward pressure on real estate value and thus creating less incentive to build denser, mixed-use projects. Mayor

Evans wants Plano to be more urban, but market realities may slow its transition from suburb to city.

Lakewood, Colorado

Lakewood is a suburb west of Denver that grew up around the Federal Center—a former World War II weapons plant that now houses several U.S. government agencies. Along with much of the Denver region, Lakewood boomed in the postwar years, especially the 1970s. In the past two decades, Lakewood's growth has slowed, as development around Denver spread to the south and east. In the years following the 2000 census, Lakewood actually lost population and is now unlikely to sustain a double-digit growth rate for this decade, which will be the first time it failed to meet this mark since 1940.

According to Mayor Steve Burkholder, while population growth has stalled in Lakewood, the city actually gained new households.[22] That is because Lakewood's demographics are shifting, resulting in fewer families and many more singles and childless couples. These smaller households still demand new residences but add much less to Lakewood's population than the typical suburban family once did. The result is continued new construction in Lakewood, despite a slight dip in the number of residents.

Lakewood is practically at buildout. By contrast, Mayor Burkholder notes, "Aurora [a boomburb east of Denver] can grow to the Kansas border."[23] But this does not trouble the mayor. He is quite comfortable with Lakewood's status as a rapidly maturing first-ring suburb. Mayor Burkholder is sold on the main principles of smart growth, in particular the idea of building denser, mixed-use projects at light-rail stations. And he now has plenty to work with, given that Denver just passed a $4.7 billion bond to add 119 miles of new track.[24] The West Corridor line on Denver's FasTracks system will run through Lakewood's older, northern neighborhoods. The line will have six stops in Lakewood alone, including one at the Denver Federal Center.[25] The mayor hopes FasTracks triggers an urban makeover of Lakewood similar to what the Washington Metrorail did for Arlington, Virginia.[26] Thirty years ago, before Metro was built, Arlington was a fading older suburb that was losing jobs and people to its western neighbor, Fairfax County. But Arlington used the Orange Line stops along its commercial corridor, Wilson Boulevard, to anchor dense, mixed-use development. Today, the Wilson Corridor offers an alternative urban environment to Washington and an antidote to Fairfax's more sprawling growth.

Plans are for Lakewood to redevelop its light-rail stops based on the Arlington model. According to Mayor Burkholder, most of the areas around the stations along the West Corridor line will either be designed for mixed use or will be de facto mixed use due to existing development. The mayor is especially optimistic about the project at the Federal Center. The Federal Center is built on a square mile of U.S. government land, but its buildings take up only a fraction of the space. Lakewood has been given permission to annex 230 acres of the land and plans to zone the land for a large-scale, transit-oriented development that will include multifamily housing with a diverse income mix.

Lakewood will also do some final conventional suburban buildout in the next decade. On Lakewood's west side is the last major patch of developable open space. It has been zoned for large-lot, upscale development, with about 2,500 single-family homes. As Mayor Burkholder observes, "After that, the party's over." All development thereafter will be infill—which actually pleases the mayor.

The Politics of Buildout

The very term *buildout* is controversial, and the building out of a boomburb is likewise contested. Should a city use its remaining land to attract more affluent residents and thus improve its fiscal capacity and market image? Or should it switch to a more urban development pattern, compared to conventional suburbs? These are hard questions that have been answered by very different strategies, as illustrated above in the case analyses. But there is another and perhaps more subtle political issue linked to buildout.

Many boomburbs have so successfully annexed land that they have put off the immediate question of buildout. In the process, these places have also created vastly differing environments within their borders. Some boomburbs now contain three distinct types of development: older and often declining postwar suburbs, maturing but still vibrant neighborhoods that have grown in the last two decades, and just-built or still rapidly building areas that represent the future. With these spatial divisions comes a corresponding political divide that pits the interests of these three areas against one another. Below are case studies that highlight this tension and point to the difficulties that await places that annex new space and neglect their original neighborhoods.

Scottsdale, Arizona, versus Tempe, Arizona: Cities without Suburbs, or Suburbs without Exurbs?

In 1993 former Albuquerque mayor Davis Rusk wrote an influential book titled *Cities without Suburbs*. In this work Rusk argues that one way that cities can avoid decline is to capture the suburban growth in their metropolitan area through municipal annexation. He illustrates this point by comparing the health of cities with "elastic" boundaries that can easily annex (like Houston) to places that are "nonelastic" and cannot annex (like Newark). Elastic cities are generally more fiscally sound and typically have much less poverty than nonelastic ones.[27]

Rusk's message is taken as conventional wisdom by many boomburb leaders. Yet rather than seeking to be cities without suburbs, the boomburbs are suburbs without exurbs. Boomburbs are often the type of place that a central city would want to annex. The addition of a Plano to Dallas, or a Scottsdale to Phoenix, would expand each city's wealth and tax base. But boomburbs can also gain when they annex unincorporated land and build office parks and upscale master-planned communities. This is exactly what Scottsdale did when it added land to its north as parts of its south side were starting to decline. It is also what Plano would love to do to places such as Frisco and McKinney, given half a chance to do so—even though the city is now planning for a more urban future. Thus, cities want suburbs (or at least the right suburbs), and suburbs increasingly want exurbs. Rusk's thinking about urban elasticity still applies, but the zone for its practice may be farther out than he anticipated. And not all boomburbs are following Rusk's advice. In fact, some have decided to face their buildout now rather than put it off.

According to its mayor, Hugh Hallman, Tempe, Arizona, took a different path from the one Rusk recommends.[28] In the 1970s Tempe had the opportunity to annex much of the land that would eventually come to be part of Chandler. The annexation would have doubled or perhaps even tripled Tempe's size. But city leaders at the time decided not to pursue annexation because they felt it would create a political divide in the town between an "old," or original, Tempe and the "new," yet-to-be-built Tempe. Tempe now lives with the consequences of this decision. It is a city that is essentially at buildout. In the first years of this decade, the census shows its population leveling off. And the mayor notes that Tempe's sales tax revenue is likewise flat; further, its allocation of state aid dropped as the city lost proportionate population share to neighboring boomburbs such as Mesa, Gilbert, and Chandler.

Yet given all the challenges that Tempe faces due to its failure to annex new land, Mayor Hallman still thinks that it was the best strategy. Limiting its space to a relatively modest forty-two square miles, he believes, promotes a sense of community and avoids any old-new split. Buildout also forces the city to confront decline as it happens rather allowing old neighborhoods to languish while new and booming areas mask the fact. Hallman points to Scottsdale as an example of exactly that kind of community split, where new neighborhoods are thriving while the old neighborhoods struggle. The mayor lived for several years as a child in what has become south Scottsdale. Hallman, now in his mid-forties, fondly recalls the 1960s subdivisions of postwar suburbia, which are now the very places in decline. Rather than face the prospect of decline and begin the hard work of renewal, Scottsdale, he says, took the easy way out and simply pursued the Rusk strategy of annexing its still-to-boom exurbs. Political power in Scottsdale has since moved north and has left fewer people to advocate for a decaying southern core.

Tempe and Scottsdale were about the same size in the 1960s, but as Hallman declares, "Tempe does not work on a Ponzi scheme of growth." The city planned for the day it would build out, but, according to Hallman, not enough. Now for the next several years, he fears a revenue shortfall. Tempe may have saved its soul by not annexing land, but it also lost critical new retail development that would have boosted its sales tax revenue. Chandler has a competing retail strip on the very land that Tempe could have added, which is siphoning off a good deal of sales from downtown Tempe—and this in a state and region where sales tax is everything: in 2001 sales tax in Tempe hit a high that it has yet to match and may not any time soon. Revenue is off about $4 million from the peak. As a result, cuts will soon be coming to city services.

By contrast, Scottsdale is banking on its booming north to provide revenue growth for years to come. The city is also unequivocally and unabashedly trying to build at lower density, according to the planner interviewed for this study. Its current housing is mostly low-density, single-family residences. The city is not planning on annexing any new territory, but its planning department estimates that Scottsdale has about 30 percent of its land left to build on. The city is hoping to use nine square miles of that remaining land as a desert preserve, if it can come up with the money. If not, the land will be developed—as luxury, single-family homes, of course.

Riverside, California: A Rusk Case Study

Unlike Tempe's Mayor Hallman, Ronald O. Loveridge of Riverside, California, completely accepts Rusk's arguments in *Cities without Suburbs*.[29] Riverside, which lies east of Los Angeles in the Inland Empire, was seventy-eight square miles but grew to ninety square miles through annexation. According to Mayor Loveridge, the high-end housing going up on these annexed lands has kept up Riverside's tax base and helps place the city in eighth rank among California municipalities in the number of households earning over $100,000 a year. He notes that Riverside is experiencing simultaneous densification and expansion. Hispanics are moving into the city's core, while mostly white families move into the new developments in the annexed land. Without the annexation, Riverside would only be getting denser—and poorer.

Riverside now has three growth streams: a high birth rate among its immigrant population, new residents of the city, and new residents in housing on recently annexed land. Together, these sources of growth have added more than 10 percent to Riverside's population in just the years 2000 through 2003.[30] And the city's growth is bifurcated in terms of income. The booming Latino population is less affluent, while whites continue to move to Riverside from the more expensive coastal parts of Southern California. The rich-poor, white-nonwhite split worried Tempe leaders enough not to annex more land. Places such as Riverside, Scottsdale, and North Las Vegas, however, decided that the revenue gains from an expanding tax base outweigh the risks of a divided municipal politics.

Fontana, California: A Tale of Three Cities

Some boomburbs that have chosen the Rusk strategy of annexing the booming edge to offset declines at the core are now considering the consequences of their actions. One such place is Fontana, California, another Inland Empire boomburb. Like Scottsdale, Fontana is really three towns in one. An article in the *San Bernardino Sun* describes the town: "The story of Fontana, a city split by demographics, three freeways, Interstates 10 and 15 and the extension of Interstate 210, and the pattern of new development, is in many ways a tale of three communities. There's the white-collar, fast-growing north end, the older but still middle-class south end, and the center, the oldest, poorest and most diverse part of the city."[31]

The new land that Fontana annexed to its north has certainly lifted the city's image in the region. A *Los Angeles Times* article for its Inland Empire edition notes the change: "The former steel town that gave birth to the Hells Angels has long endured nicknames as Fontucky and Felony Flats. . . . [But now it is a] new and improved Fontana, a city revitalized by a smoking-hot real estate market and infusion of white-collar families."[32] But discussions with city officials indicate that there is a growing concern for the widening income gaps between the parts of Fontana. The boomburb is exploring some affordable housing developments in its affluent north as a way to even out some of the disparities in wealth but has so far met with resistance from homeowners. California cities—like most places—have a history of resisting inclusionary housing.[33] It is unlikely that enough new affordable housing can be built in the rich parts of Fontana to significantly alter the stratified pattern of growth as the city moves toward its buildout point.

As Tempe's Mayor Hallman notes, the politics of cities with booming sections along with busting sections often sees the balance of power shift to the booming, more affluent neighborhoods. Fontana proves no exception, as the *San Bernardino Sun* reports: "In contrast to the 1980s, when the entire City Council lived in central Fontana, all the sitting council members live in the northern or southern [booming] part of the city."[34] One way to solve the increasing underrepresentation of old neighborhoods is to institute a ward-based system of governance (see chapter 6). But ward government is an alien concept to virtually all boomburbs. By and large, they are governed by city charter systems, with a part-time mayor, professional and nonpartisan city managers, and city councils that are elected at large.

Boomburbs are really reform governments that were set up to prevent the often corrupt and costly pork barrel politics of the strong mayor and ward systems of older, Eastern U.S. cities. Most boomburbs have succeeded in attaining limited and efficient government. But the assumption has been that these places are suburbs and that they do not have the traditional disparities of wealth that are common in cities. As boomburbs mature, they increasingly face big-city challenges that test their logic and structure. The politics of buildout reveals growing tensions that now have some boomburbs rethinking the way they develop. Boomburbs failing to annex may lose some opportunities to develop upscale communities, but those that aggressively add land risk a social fissure between old and new neighborhoods. Given the opportunity, most boomburbs are willing to risk division in order to gain wealth.

8

Emerging Urban Realms and the Boomburbs of 2030

This final chapter looks at two related issues—the emergence of new boomburbs and the division of metropolitan areas into subregional geographic areas called urban realms. Each decade, a new group of cities crosses the 100,000 population mark that the census uses as an informal threshold for big places. The majority of these cities, as this book shows, are in fact overgrown suburbs. The chapter ends with a look beyond 2030 and a short discussion on what forces may constrain the future development of boomburbs.

The new boomburbs of 2030 will mostly be found in rapidly expanding parts of major metropolitan areas. The biggest metropolises have grown so large that they have multiple subregions. Development in some of these urban realms is just taking off. These emerging metropolitan spaces serve as boomburb incubators. Regions often have both built-out urban realms and barely built ones. The following section looks at the future of boomburbs in different types of urban realm and finds that the fate of boomburbs is closely linked to that of its metropolitan subregion. Maturing realms feature slower growing boomburbs, while emerging ones should give rise to new boomburbs by 2030.

Population projections to 2030 are drawn from Los Angeles, Phoenix, and Dallas.[1] All three metropolises have multiple boomburbs and urban realms. These regions also sprawl to such enormous size that each maintains a bigger local identity than the one anchored by the principal city. Greater Los Angeles is referred to more broadly as the Southland; Phoenix, the Valley of the Sun; and Dallas, the Metroplex. These alternate names hint that a single place, even one of the nation's biggest cities, is too small to properly identify all the urban space in its region. At this regional scale, urban realms become evident.

Understanding Urban Realms

The idea of urban realms is well established in geography, starting with James Vance in 1964. Vance argued that major American metropolitan areas had grown so decentralized, due to dispersal of population and economic activity, that they had become a series of semiautonomous subregions, or "urban realms."[2] To Vance, urban realms are natural outcomes when cities grow "one stage beyond that of a metropolis."[3] The core-periphery relationship weakens, as realms become more equal. And the region grows more cooperative as the shared urban and cultural identity of the urban realms creates what Vance calls a "sympolis," rather than a metropolis.

Vance identified realms based on several criteria. One is the size of the region—the bigger the metropolis, the more differentiated the realms. Physical features such as mountains, bays, and rivers also serve to delimit realms by directing the spread of urbanization into geographically defined areas. Realms can also be distinguished by either an overriding economic identity, such as the Silicon Valley in California, or shared employment centers as identified by commuter sheds. The regional geography of transportation, as originally recognized by Homer Hoyt, also plays a role in separating urban realms.[4] This process began with trolley cars but is now centered on interstate highways, in particular metropolitan beltways. Beltways can either define the boundary of an area, as is reflected by the expression of one being located "inside the Washington beltway," or unify a realm, as in the case of the LBJ Corridor in North Dallas.

The urban realm idea relates to other concepts that describe regional variation and integration.[5] One of these is the notion of a favored quarter, the wedge of a metropolis that contains a large share of its region's wealth.[6] The concept is adapted from Homer Hoyt's sector hypothesis, which holds that both wealth and poverty spread from the center to the edge, in quarters.[7] Most large U.S. metropolitan areas have an easily identified favored quarter—the north sides of Atlanta, Chicago, and Dallas; the west sides of Washington and Los Angeles; and the northeast corner of Phoenix.

Urban realms have their own subregional identities, such as South Coast (or Orange County) and the Inland Empire (Riverside and San Bernardino Counties) in the Los Angeles region. The realms around Los Angeles are so distinct that South Coast and the Inland Empire have their own subregional newspapers and airports. On a smaller, but emerging, scale, the East Valley of Phoenix (with such major suburbs as Mesa, Tempe, Chandler, and Gilbert) has its own newspaper and will soon have a national airport. Urban realms also show up in business names, such as South Coast Plaza, Inland Empire National Bank, the *East Valley Tribune*.

Robert Lang and John Hall synthesize the thinking on urban realms and offer four realm types based on social characteristics and development age:[8]

—Urban core realms: the original places of substantial nineteenth- and twentieth-century development, including the region's major central city and downtown.

—Favored quarter realms: the most affluent wedge of a metropolitan area, containing upscale communities, luxury shopping, and high-end office districts.

—Maturing suburban realms: the areas of substantial late twentieth-century and early twenty-first-century development that are rapidly filling in and will ultimately approach the core in scale.

—Emerging exurban realms: extended, rapidly growing, lower-density spaces that contain leapfrog development and will not be full extensions of the main metropolitan development for decades to come.

Realm divisions are not meant to be definitive. Rather, they carve expansive metropolitan geography into reasonably sized urban spaces. The realms identified below also show current conditions and projections of future growth patterns. Yet realms are dynamic and subject to shifts due to new variables such as infrastructure improvements. A key element of realm growth is anchor cities. By 2030 the next generation of boomburbs often will fill this role.

The Southland

Greater Los Angeles breaks into at least five realms.[9] There is the LA Basin, or the area south of the Santa Monica Mountains and west of Puente Hills. South of this area, Orange County (or South Coast) forms a separate realm. To the northwest is a realm that extends from the San Fernando Valley to the western edge of Ventura County (or the West Valley realm). Due north of Los Angeles (but still within the county) lies Antelope Valley. The Inland Empire of Riverside and San Bernardino Counties fills out the Los Angeles region's east side, beyond which is the Mohave. Edward Soja, a geographer who is part of the "LA school" of social science (or those who use the region as the basis for their thinking), developed a similar geography.[10]

The historian Robert Fishman finds that the Los Angeles region was "born decentralized" and thus well suited to the eventual emergence of realms.[11] He attributes this in part to the development of LA's original trolley system, which operated more like an intercity rather than intracity rail.[12] The trolleys linked up semiautonomous cities and villages, which grew into an urban galaxy, with broad spaces of farmland and mountains in between. The boulevards and freeways that followed reinforced this dispersed pattern, even as the spaces between developments filled in.

Los Angeles is so big that four of the realms (excepting Antelope Valley) would each be a major metropolitan area on its own. For instance, both the Inland Empire and Orange County are about the size of metropolitan Phoenix. Each realm has its own climate and feel. Sometimes the differences are quite stark. For example, in the winter commuters from Antelope Valley (a high-desert valley that includes Edwards Air Force Base) can arrive at work in sunny and warm LA with snow on their cars. Joan Didion, in her essay "Some Dreamers of the Golden Dream," sharply delineates the Inland Empire from the LA Basin:

> The San Bernardino Valley lies only an hour east of Los Angeles by the San Bernardino Freeway, but is in certain ways an alien place: not the coastal California of the subtropical twilights and soft westerlies off the Pacific but a harsher California, haunted by the Mojave just beyond the mountains, devastated by the hot dry Santa Ana wind that comes down through the passes at 100 miles an hour and whines trough the eucalyptus windbreaks and works the nerves.[13]

In the tourist's mind, the LA Basin, which includes Hollywood and the Westside beaches, is the real Los Angeles. The other realms are more everyday places, which often do turn up as Hollywood sets for depictions of Anywhere, USA. This is especially true for the West Valley. The LA Basin serves as the region's core realm. It is Southern California's oldest and densest urban area. The Inland Empire and the West Valley are maturing suburban realms, while Antelope Valley is exurban.

There are also divided politics in the Southland. People in the liberal LA Basin sometimes describe residents of the more conservative Orange County as "living behind the Orange Curtain" (in reference to the old cold war iron curtain of Europe). Yet Orange County's politics are changing, as its now majority-minority population turns this once solidly Republican area into a swing district. Orange County, despite its political and demographic shifts, remains the region's favored-quarter realm.

Although freeways connect all of Los Angeles's urban realms, three of the four regions now have their own major airport. The LA Basin has Los Angeles International Airport (LAX), the biggest hub for the Southland.

John Wayne Airport is in the heart of Orange County. Ontario International Airport is in the Inland Empire. Bob Hope Burbank Airport, in the West Valley, is smaller than John Wayne or Ontario but still has some non-stop flights to the East Coast. People in the Inland Empire and Orange County prefer to use their airports rather than getting a direct flight from LAX, even if it means changing planes at a hub.

Four of the five Southland urban realms contain boomburbs. The Inland Empire has seven: Corona, Fontana, Moreno Valley, Ontario, Rancho Cucamonga, Riverside, and San Bernardino. Orange County has six: Anaheim, Costa Mesa, Fullerton, Irvine, Orange, and Santa Ana. The West Valley (including Ventura County) has four: Oxnard, Santa Clarita, Simi Valley, and Thousand Oaks. Antelope Valley (the least-populated realm) has two: Lancaster and Palmdale. The LA Basin, the region's urban core, has none despite being by far the most populous urban realm; this older core area of Los Angeles is not booming in the same way its edges are.

The role that the Southland's urban realms play has gained importance of late in part due to the chronic traffic that clogs Los Angeles's freeways. Commuting between the realms has become such a hassle that people are starting to look more and more to their own realm as a place to work and play. Boomburb leaders know this and are trying to create more diversified environments, which include employment and entertainment centers. For example, Rancho Cucamonga is creating a new city center based on Old Town Pasadena, so as to create a cityscape for its residents.

The Southland's shift from an integrated metropolis to urban realms thus holds promise for its boomburbs. Some boomburbs have the potential to become centers of their realm. Boomburbs serve as the county seats in the Inland Empire and Orange County and as the locations for realm airports. In a sense, these places, along with the other boomburbs in these urban realms, are the central cities of their respective realms.

The Valley of the Sun

The Valley of the Sun contains six identifiable realms.[14] The Central Valley, which is mostly composed of the city of Phoenix, forms the region's urban-core realm. The area includes the downtown and its adjacent neighborhoods and the Central Avenue business corridor. Sky Harbor Airport is also in this realm.

The Upper East Valley of Phoenix constitutes the favored quarter. It contains the upscale communities of Paradise Valley, Fountain Hills, and Scottsdale. On a per capita basis, the Upper East Valley has a larger share of jobs than the any other Phoenix realm, including the Central Valley.

This area is well known for the resorts in and around Scottsdale. Scottsdale also features a cosmopolitan urban arts scene, which draws on the resort crowd and affluent local residents.

Phoenix is also bookended by two maturing suburban realms—the East and West Valleys. The East Valley is by far the more mature and includes Mesa, with nearly a half million residents. Along with Mesa, three other East Valley suburbs top 100,000 residents: Tempe, Chandler, and Gilbert. The West Valley is nowhere near that urban yet, but it is booming. Glendale and Peoria already exceed 100,000 residents. Surprise is well on its way to 100,000, while other suburbs in the West Valley, such as Goodyear and Buckeye, are projected to hit this mark in the next decade.

The East Valley has an increasing share of jobs but still lags behind the Central and Northeast Valleys in terms of employment centers. The East Valley does have perhaps the Valley of the Sun's single most vibrant urban space: downtown Tempe. Both Tempe and Mesa will be linked to the Central Valley via Phoenix's new light-rail system. The East Valley contains nearly a million people, which would qualify just this subsection of greater Phoenix as one of the fifty largest metropolitan areas in the United States. Its population already exceeds that of, for example, Austin.

The West Valley is still too new to contain urban places equivalent to those in the East Valley, but there are plans to build employment centers throughout this realm. These efforts will be driven by a need to balance jobs with housing. Much of this growth will occur along the planned 303 Loop. Also, while newer, the West Valley will be built at densities equivalent to those of the East Valley. For example, Verrado, the 8,800-acre master-planned community in Buckeye, plans mostly small-lot, single-family homes mixed with even denser multifamily dwellings. By the mid-twenty-first century, now-tiny Buckeye could anchor a vast urban realm of over a million residents.[15] In fact, based on water allocations and annexed lands, Buckeye could someday rival Mesa as the second largest city in the Valley of the Sun.

In contrast to the East and West Valleys, Phoenix's two emerging exurban realms are not planned to be unbroken urban spaces, at least not in the short term. The Northwest Valley and the Mid Corridor (halfway down the corridor to Tucson) are developing mostly as islands around Prescott and Casa Grande. Except for urban extensions to the East Valley in Apache Junction and Queen Creek, the Mid Corridor is cut off from the more developed parts of the region by a large Indian reservation. Yet over half the commuters in Pinal County (which approximates the Mid Corridor realm) have jobs in Phoenix's other urban realms.

The Phoenix urban realms are shaped by the loop freeway system, which is still under construction. The 101 Loop helps bound the Central Valley, while the soon-to-be-completed 202 Loop rings the East Valley. Development in the West Valley will be heavily influenced by the future 303 Loop. This is consistent with urban theory, developed by Hoyt and others, that transportation drives metropolitan form.

The Metroplex

As the nation's self-described Metroplex, the Dallas–Fort Worth region was born of urban realms.[16] Dallas and Fort Worth are not twin cities in the manner of, say, Minneapolis and St. Paul or Tampa and St. Petersburg. In fact, as local legend goes these two cities did not care for one another until recently. Dallas saw Fort Worth as a cow town, a label Fort Worth proudly wears. Fort Worth residents felt that Dallas put on Eastern airs and saw itself as better than the rest of Texas. But, as noted in chapter 4, the development of the Dallas–Fort Worth Airport melded the formerly distinct regions into one large Metroplex.

The Metroplex has six urban realms. Its two core realms are Dallas and Fort Worth, although the latter realm is smaller in scale and less built out. Between the two cores is a maturing suburban realm that can be dubbed Midplex. North Dallas is the region's favored quarter, while the Far North (practically to Oklahoma) and the South Metroplex serve as exurban realms. Note that the Metroplex's urban realms are less distinctive than those in the Southland or the Valley of the Sun. The region's flat, open prairie offers few natural divides, in contrast to the mountains and valleys of the Southwest or the mountains and the bay in the San Francisco area. But the realms are identified here in order to provide a consistent comparison with Los Angeles and Phoenix.

The Dallas core realm, which includes the I-635 Beltway and adjacent areas, contains two boomburbs, Garland and Mesquite. The boomburbs of Arlington, Irving, and Grand Prairie fill out the Midplex. Affluent North Dallas is home to Plano and Carrollton. The Far North has no boomburbs yet, and as the analysis below shows, it will by 2030, by the time several baby boomburbs grow past the 100,000 residents mark.

New and Maturing Boomburbs, 2030

Among the three regions—the Southland, the Valley of the Sun, and the Metroplex—at least fifteen new boomburbs could emerge by 2030, according to data from metropolitan councils of government.[17] Fast-growing

Phoenix should lead the pack, with six of these places by that date, followed by five in Los Angeles and four in Dallas–Fort Worth. As the analysis below shows, most of the new boomburbs will be found in emerging exurban realms. The 2030 projections also indicate that many boomburbs now in maturing suburban realms and favored quarters will mostly slow down and match the overall growth rates in their subregions.

The Southland

Antelope Valley north of Los Angeles has two boomburbs, Lancaster and Palmdale. According to data provided by the Southern California Association of Governments, both boomburbs will keep booming to 2030. Lancaster should double, to 259,696 residents, while Palmdale will nearly triple, to 337,314 people. Meanwhile the town of Hesperia in eastern Antelope Valley will become a boomburb by 2010 and reach a population of 179,383 by 2030.

The fringes of the Inland Empire should keep pace with Antelope Valley. A cluster of towns in the southwestern corner of Riverside County—Temecula, Murrieta, and Hemet—will all become boomburbs before 2030. Murrieta will have the fastest growth, jumping from 44,675 people in 2000 to 131,666 by 2030. The only new boomburb to emerge in the more mature section of the Inland Empire is Chino, which will reach 113,977 residents by 2030, or a gain of about 70 percent in thirty years. Places such as Riverside, Fontana, Rancho Cucamonga, Ontario, and Moreno Valley should grow slower than in the past but will likely qualify for a 2030 boomburb list based on growth since 2000.

In contrast to Antelope Valley and the Inland Empire, growth rates in South Coast and the West Valley boomburbs are predicted to drop dramatically by 2030. The cities of Costa Mesa, Fullerton, and Orange (in South Coast) are all expected to gain just 18 percent more residents between 2000 and 2030, meaning that these places will not be boomburbs in 2030. The same is true for some West Valley boomburbs. Thousand Oaks is projected to grow just 16 percent in population, while Simi Valley will gain slightly more at 33 percent.

The Valley of the Sun

Even the slow-growing parts of Phoenix are booming relative to just about any other region in the country. The population data provided by the Maricopa Association of Governments extend this trend to 2030. While most places in Phoenix will make strong gains in the three decades from 2000 to 2030, development in the West Valley and the Mid Corridor should explode.[18]

There are two sections to Phoenix's West Valley. Places like Glendale and Peoria lie east, near Phoenix, while west along I-10 heading to California are a string of what will be new boomburbs by 2030. Growth should be strong enough in the older parts of the West Valley to keep Glendale and Peoria on a 2030 boomburb list. But the big stories in the West Valley are Avondale, Goodyear, Buckeye, and Surprise, all four of which are on track to pass the 100,000-population mark; the latter three may pass 300,000 by 2030. With just 8,615 residents in 2000, Buckeye should gain the most in percentage terms. The town is predicted to grow over 4,000 percent from 2000 to 2030 and total nearly 400,000 people. By 2030 there could be six boomburbs in Phoenix's West Valley, five of which will surpass 300,000 residents. The West Valley urban realm may by that time be home to nearly 2 million people, putting it just below the size of the present-day Las Vegas and Portland regions.

Growth in Phoenix's Mid Corridor, while not quite as strong as in the West Valley, could nonetheless be substantial. Three new boomburbs are projected to appear by 2030—Apache Junction, Queen Creek, and Casa Grande. But beyond these lies state trust land—the massive Superstition Vistas area. As mentioned before, this area is slated for development over the next several decades. Its growth will likely produce two boomburbs by 2030.[19] That would bring the number of boomburbs in the Mid Corridor to five. Upward of 1 million people may live in the Mid Corridor realm in 2030, a figure similar to the current population of the East Valley.

The East Valley should also keep growing but at a much slower rate than either the West Valley or the Mid Corridor. Of the four current boomburbs in this realm—Tempe, Chandler, Mesa, and Gilbert—only Tempe should fall off the boomburb list by 2030 (perhaps even by 2010). The other three boomburbs have some room to expand for now, with Gilbert and Mesa having more space left than Chandler. If predictions hold true, Mesa (with a projected 2030 population of nearly 650,000) is on track to overtake cities such as Boston and San Francisco by 2030. This population would also likely rank Mesa in the top twenty U.S. cities by that date.

Scottsdale, anchoring the Northeast Valley's favored-quarter realm, should slow to a growth rate that just barely keeps it on the 2030 boomburb list. This relatively modest population gain will happen despite the fact that the city annexed a lot of land to its north: much of that land is slated to be preserved as open space or developed at low densities.

The Metroplex

The Dallas–Fort Worth Metroplex should also keep rapidly expanding to 2030, but most of this growth will occur in distant exurbs and will add many fewer residents to existing boomburbs. In fact, all three boomburbs in the North Dallas realm, the region's favored quarter, could drop from a 2030 boomburb list. Plano and Carrollton expect to add only 15 percent more residents by that date, while Richardson will rise by a slightly higher 23 percent. Were these numbers for cities in the Midwest or Northeast, the gains would be respectable, but in the Metroplex it means these boomburbs will fall behind the pace of overall regional expansion. The same is true for the two boomburbs that share the core realm with the city of Dallas. Garland and Mesquite match the growth numbers of the three boomburbs in North Dallas. Likewise the two could easily fall off a 2030 boomburb list.

Growth is a bit stronger in the Midplex, especially in Grand Prairie, which is projected to add 79 percent more residents between 2000 and 2030, according to data provided by the North Central Texas Council of Governments. Arlington, now the second largest boomburb, should grow another 31 percent in the period, lifting its population to 437,862 residents. This would make the city more populous than such major urban centers as St. Louis and Atlanta.

The Far North urban realm is where the region's strongest population growth is predicted to occur. By 2030 the area could have three new boomburbs—Denton, Frisco, and McKinney. The Far North is a nascent favored-quarter realm, which means that it will likely draw people and businesses from the affluent but older North Dallas. This relationship was described in earlier chapters in terms of the rivalry between an older place such as Plano and an exurb such as Frisco. The population numbers now show the size of this shift. By 2030 Frisco is projected to have 227,541 residents, or a gain of 570 percent from its 2000 population of 34,028. This should put the city just slightly behind Plano in that year, with 257,061 residents.

The only other Dallas–Fort Worth boomburb predicted to emerge by 2030 is Mansfield, which is an exurb at the border of the Midplex, just south of Arlington. Looking at the rest of the 2030 projections for the Metroplex shows that most growth will be in smaller exurban towns in all directions (but especially north) out of Dallas and Forth Worth. It appears that the Metroplex will thin out by 2030, as the old core cities and a ring of inner and now former boomburbs lose ground in relative terms to the exurbs and emerging boomburbs.

2030 and Beyond: Will There Be Boomburbs?

Predicting the fate of boomburbs beyond the next two decades is a difficult task. A number of demographic, land use, and resource uncertainties arise that cannot be accounted for by simple extrapolation. These include the possibility of reduced immigration by midcentury, limits on land available for metropolitan expansion due to natural and regulatory barriers, and already diminishing Western water supplies made even scarcer by global warming, which reduces snowpack.[20] Add to these predictions that the world is nearing it peak oil output, and all bets seem off.[21] Further, there is some evidence of shifting consumer preferences for housing types and locations that favor more traditional urban places.[22] In sum, the boomburb, and in a larger sense the expansionist suburban, era may soon draw to a close.

Yet for every no-growth scenario, there are also high-growth ones. If nothing else, the U.S. population remains positioned to keep expanding. Based on current demographic structure alone (excluding immigrants), the United States will likely add at minimum 30 million new residents for each decade until 2050. That is more additional population by midcentury than the estimate for China. In October 2006 the U.S. population reached 300 million. This occurred thirty-nine years after the 200 million mark was passed in 1967. The chances of the country's population getting to 400 million by 2040–50 appear good. Will these people want to live in current and future boomburbs? That is harder to estimate.

A big share of population growth will be immigrants and the children of immigrants. Where these people will prefer to live is uncertain. Some claim that Hispanics and Asians—the bulk of the immigrants—have tastes that are different from native-born Americans' and are more likely to pick cities over suburbs. Yet as this book shows, a new, diverse suburban city has recently emerged, dubbed cosmoburbia. These cities often contain a higher share of foreign-born residents than most traditional cities. The notion that the country will soon be dominated by so-called ethnic housing is a misreading of American history. Imagine in 1906 that developers looked at the village or city of origin of Southern and Eastern Europeans and believed that these people wanted to replicate these places in the United States. How would such a prediction have accounted for the fact that the children of these immigrants would fill Levittown by the mid-twentieth century?

Betting on the demise of suburbia is something of a cottage industry among the new urbanists.[23] The suburban critic James Howard Kunstler in several books predicted just this outcome.[24] Kunstler's assumption began with people rejecting suburbs on the basis of taste and has evolved into his current notion that we are out of oil (as to which his message to suburbanites is, quite literally, tough luck). But Kunstler has always underestimated the social and historical roots of the suburban ethos in America, which writers such as Robert Fishman, Kenneth Jackson, and Dolores Hayden demonstrate so effectively.[25]

At the end of his highly influential book *Crabgrass Frontiers*, the historian Kenneth Jackson raises the issue that the United States may be reaching the limits of suburbanization—and by extension the making of boomburbs.[26] Yet the twenty years that followed *Crabgrass Frontiers'* publication can only be described as a suburban boom. Even in the current decade, despite a recession, a sluggish recovery, and a spike in energy prices, the suburbs—or more specifically the exurbs—continue to boom. Is the United States out of the land, resources, and even willingness to keep the boom going past 2010—or perhaps 2030? Maybe. But Americans could just as easily invent energy-efficient cars and find metropolises with plenty of land and water—and keep pushing the crabgrass frontier for decades to come.

Conclusion: The Reality and Meaning of Boomburb Growth

The not so subtle theme of this book is that boomburbs are a hybrid urban form. There are dimensions in which boomburbs are traditionally urban, for example, in their growing diversity. And yet boomburbs remain mostly horizontally built, with very few physical environments that seem urban. In addition, most lack the public spaces and institutions of comparably sized traditional cities. Arlington, Texas, may be as big as Pittsburgh, but where is its Three-River Park or even its Andy Warhol Museum? Some boomburbs, such as Mesa, Arizona, are gaining new cultural facilities, but the lack of such resources in most boomburbs sets them apart from traditional cities—and may even call into question this definition of *urban*.

The rise of boomburbs challenges planners, developers, and policymakers to rethink what is urban. The U.S. Census Bureau already has done so with its new principal-city category, which recognizes half of the boomburbs as cities. But this designation is so technical that it eludes many urban researchers. A public reframing of the term *city* needs to capture the new reality: that the newest and fastest-growing cities are yesterday's suburbs.

Yet as historians have shown, that has always been the case. Brooklyn, New York, was in many ways the nation's leading nineteenth-century suburb, and now it practically defines the term *urban*. So too will boomburbs mature—some gracefully and others not so gracefully.

This book begins the process of objectively understanding both boomburbs and their unincorporated urbanizing peers such as Fairfax County, Virginia, and Cobb County, Georgia. It joins a growing literature and an academic movement that explore suburbs as legitimate places.[27] Boomburbs are a quintessential American landscape, embodying much of the nation's complexity, expansiveness, and ambiguity. This book only scratches the surface.

Notes

Chapter One

1. The term *edge city* was coined by Joel Garreau, *Edge City: Life on the New Frontier* (New York: Doubleday, 1991); also see Robert E. Lang, *Edgeless Cities: Exploring the Elusive Metropolis* (Brookings, 2003).

2. Observers began to note the trend in the late 1990s. See Haya El Nasser and Paul Overberg, "Suburban Communities Spurt to Big-City Status," *USA Today*, November 19, 1997, p. A4; David Brooks, *On Paradise Drive: How We Live Now (And Always Have) In the Future Tense* (New York: Simon and Schuster, 2004); David Brooks, "Patio Man and the Sprawl People," *Weekly Standard* 7, no. 46 (2002): 19–29.

3. Michael L. Montandon, personal conversation with Robert Lang, March 12, 2004. Interestingly, a referee for this book asserted that North Las Vegas is not comparable with Salt Lake City in part because it "does not confront an array of urban problems" and that Salt Lake City has a "more diverse population." The fact is that North Las Vegas has plenty of urban problems, including a high poverty rate. In addition, North Las Vegas's population is a quarter foreign-born and half minority. In other words, North Las Vegas is considerably *more* diverse than Salt Lake City (which is 70 percent non-Hispanic white) and even than Las Vegas itself. The misread of North Las Vegas by the referee shows that North Las Vegas's mayor was on to something. Apparently no one, not even urban experts who review books, think his city is diverse and has urban problems.

4. Keno Hawker, personal conversation with Robert Lang, March 10, 2004.

5. Jonathon Barnett first used the term *accidental cities,* but he was referring specifically to zoning. Jonathon Barnett, "Accidental Cities: The Deadly Grip of Outmoded Zoning," *Architectural Record* 180, no. 2 (1992): 94–101.

6. Bruce Katz, "Welcome to the 'Exit Ramp' Economy," *Boston Globe*, May 13, 2001, p. A19. Freeway exits as an economic development tool came up in several interviews with boomburb mayors.

7. Jane Jacobs, "The Greening of the City," *New York Times Magazine*, May 16, 2004.

8. The 2000 census marks the first time that a critical mass of suburban cities passed the 100,000-population threshold, and this study is the first-ever book-length treatment of those cities. But see Robert Fishman, *Bourgeois Utopias: The Rise and Fall of Suburbia* (New York: Basic Books, 1987); Garreau, *Edge City*; Carl Abbott, "'Beautiful Downtown Burbank': Changing Metropolitan Geography in the Modern West," *Journal of the West* (July 1995): 8–18; Carl Abbott, *The Metropolitan Frontier: Cities in the Modern American West* (University of Arizona Press, 1993); Carl Abbott, "Southwestern Cityscapes: Approaches to an American Urban Environment," in *Essays on Sunbelt Cities and Recent Urban America*, edited by Raymond A. Mohl and others (Texas A&M University Press, 1990).

9. Robert E. Lang and Patrick A. Simmons, "Boomburbs: The Emergence of Large, Fast-Growing Cities in the United States," in *Redefining Urban and Suburban America: Evidence from Census 2000*, edited by Bruce Katz and Robert E. Lang (Brookings, 2003); Robert E. Lang and Patrick A. Simmons, *Edge Counties: Metropolitan Growth Engines,* Census Note 02 (Washington: Fannie Mae Foundation, 2003); Robert E. Lang and Patrick A. Simmons, *"Boomburbs": The Emergence of Large, Fast-Growing Suburban Cities in the United States,* Census Note 06 (Washington: Fannie Mae Foundation, 2001).

10. Patrick A. Simmons and Robert E. Lang, "The Urban Turnaround," in *Redefining Urban and Suburban America: Evidence from Census 2000*, edited by Bruce Katz and Robert E. Lang (Brookings, 2003); Patrick A. Simmons and Robert E. Lang, *The Urban Turnaround: A Decade-by-Decade Report Card on Postwar Population Change in Older Industrial Cities,* Census Note 01 (Washington: Fannie Mae Foundation, 2001).

11. Kenneth Jackson, *Crabgrass Frontiers: The Suburbanization of the United States* (Oxford University Press, 1985); Dolores Hayden, *A Field Guide to Sprawl* (New York: W. W. Norton, 2004).

12. Simmons and Lang find that, after the 1940s, the 1990s was the best decade for population gains in decliner cities. Simmons and Lang, "The Urban Turnaround."

13. Lang and Simmons originally called such places boomtowns, until it was suggested by Rebecca Sohmer—a co-researcher at the Fannie Mae Foundation—that they call them boomburbs. The new term has a much better ring.

14. *New York Times* columnist David Brooks soon picked up on this fact ("Patio Man and the Sprawl People") and mentions it in *On Paradise Drive*.

15. Robert E. Lang and Patrick A. Simmons, "Tale of the Two Peorias," *Arizona Republic,* June 12, 2002, p. A20.

16. For reviews of this literature, see Lang, *Edgeless Cities*; Robert E. Lang, Edward J. Blakely, and Meghan Z. Gough, "Keys to the New Metropolis: America's Big, Fast-Growing Suburban Counties," *Journal of the American Planning Association* 71, no. 3 (2005): 381–91.

17. See James Howard Kunstler, *Home from Nowhere* (New York: Simon and Schuster, 1996); James Howard Kunstler, *The Geography of Nowhere* (New York: Vintage, 1994).

18. This was done so that almost all boomburbs had full data for their starting point. Many boomburbs were unincorporated places before 1970, making it impossible to track their population changes before that date.

19. Lang and Simmons, in "Tale of the Two Peorias," note that Peoria, Arizona, passing Peoria, Illinois, reflects the shift in population to the South and West.

20. Robert E. Lang and Dawn Dhavale, *Reluctant Cities: Exploring Big Unincorporated Census Designated Places,* Census Note 03:01 (Alexandria, Va.: Metropolitan Institute at Virginia Tech, 2003).

21. Neil Larry Shumsky, ed., *Encyclopedia of Urban America: The Cities and Suburbs* (Santa Barbara, Calif.: ABC-CLIO, 1997).

22. Places such as Olathe, Kansas, and Fairfield, California, were already over the mark by 2004, and it is likely that about a dozen baby boomburbs have by now become boomburbs. By 2010 the figure could reach two dozen.

23. The Las Vegas region's three census-designated places are discussed in chapter 5.

24. Much of the Washington suburban population lives in unincorporated places that do not qualify as boomburbs or baby boomburbs (Lang and Dhavale, *Reluctant Cities*). Even the populous Tysons Corner lies on unincorporated land in Fairfax County, Virginia (Lang, *Edgeless Cities*).

25. Robert E. Lang and Dawn Dhavale, *Megapolitan Areas: Exploring a New Trans-Metropolitan Geography,* Census Note 01 (Washington: Fannie Mae Foundation, 2005).

26. Robert Lang began tracking county growth in 2002 to determine where rapid, sustained development was occurring outside the boomburbs. He found that the two biggest regions for growth that lacked boomburbs were Atlanta and Washington, where counties had gained double-digit population for each decade since 1950. Houston also lacked boomburbs: the city was so successful at annexing unincorporated land that no large cities grew around it. See David Rusk, *Cities without Suburbs* (Washington: Woodrow Wilson Center, 1993). On growth counties research, see Robert E. Lang, *Metropolitan Growth Counties,* Census Note 01 (Washington: Fannie Mae Foundation, 2002); Robert E. Lang and Meghan Gough, *Metropolitan Growth Counties* (Brookings, 2004); Robert E. Lang and Megan Gough, "Growth Counties: Home to America's New Suburban Metropolis," in *Redefining Urban and Suburban America: Evidence from Census 2000,* vol. 3, edited by Alan Berube, Bruce Katz, and Robert E. Lang (Brookings, 2006).

27. In fact, *Money Magazine*'s 2004 survey of the "hottest towns" actually pulls out such Fairfax County ministerial districts as Dranesville (population 110,480), Hunter Mill (population 115,428), and Sully (population 152,169) and ranks them among the hottest places to live in America.

28. Lang and Gough, *Metropolitan Growth Counties;* Lang and Gough, "Growth Counties."

29. Abbott, *The Metropolitan Frontier.*

30. For a full discussion of how the eastern and western Sunbelts differ, see Lang, *Metropolitan Growth Counties.* Lang divides what he calls the "wet and dry" Sunbelts and shows how environmental conditions have shaped development patterns, including the formation of large municipalities in the dry (or western) Sunbelt.

31. Abbott, *The Metropolitan Frontier.*

32. Rusk, *Cities without Suburbs.*

33. William Fulton, *The Reluctant Metropolis: The Politics of Urban Growth in Los Angeles* (Berkeley, Calif.: Solano, 1997).

34. Lang, *Metropolitan Growth Counties;* Lang and Simmons, "Boomburbs"; Lang and Simmons, *Edge Counties;* Lang and Gough, *Metropolitan Growth Counties;* Lang and Gough, "Growth Counties."

35. Graham R. Taylor, *Satellite Cities: A Case Study of Industrial Suburbs* (New York: Appleton, 1915); Ernest W. Burgess, *Urban Community: Selected Papers from the Proceedings of the American Sociological Society* (University of Chicago Press, 1925).

36. James Borchert, "Residential City Suburbs: The Emergence of a New Suburban Type, 1880–1930," *Journal of Urban History* 22, no. 3 (1996): 283–307.

37. James W. Hughes, K. Tyler Miller, and Robert E. Lang, *The New Geography of Services and Office Buildings* (New Brunswick, N.J.: Center for Urban Policy Research, 1992).

38. William Sharpe and Leonard Wallock, "Bold New City or Built-Up 'Burb?'" *American Quarterly* 46, no. 1 (1994): 4.

39. Robert E. Lang, "Labeling America's New Urban Form," Association of Collegiate Schools of Planning/Association of European Schools of Planning, Toronto, Ontario, 1996.

40. Pierce F. Lewis, "The Urban Invasion of Rural America: The Emergence of the Galactic City," in *The Changing American Countryside: Rural People and Places,* edited by Emery N. Castle (University Press of Kansas 1995), p. 61.

41. Robert Fishman, "America's New City: Megalopolis Unbound," *Wilson Quarterly* 14, no. 1 (1990): 24–45; quotation on p. 26. See also Robert Fishman, "Space, Time and Sprawl," *Architectural Digest* 64, nos. 3, 4 (1994): 45–47.

42. Fishman, *Bourgeois Utopias,* p. 25.

43. Jacobs "The Greening of the City."

44. Robert E. Lang, *Office Sprawl: The Evolving Geography of Business* (Brookings, 2000); Lang, *Edgeless Cities;* Garreau, *Edge City.*

45. From Peter J. Taylor and Robert E. Lang, "The Shock of the New: 100 Concepts Describing Recent Urban Change," *Environment and Planning A* 37, no. 5 (2004): 951–58.

46. Hayden, *A Field Guide to Sprawl.*

47. Arlington actually fits into this area, while Alexandria's new section spills out into nonoriginal District of Columbia parts of Northern Virginia.

48. Douglas Porter, *Profiles in Growth Management* (Washington: Urban Land Institute, 1997).

49. See www.emporis.com (September 14, 2006).

50. James B. Kelleher, "OC Rising," *Orange County Register,* June 17, 2005, p. A1; Roger Vincent, "Orange County Getting Twin High-Rise Condo Towers," *Los Angeles Times,* June 15, 2006, p. B1.

51. Data from www.emporis.com (September 14, 2006).

52. Debbie L. Sklar, "The Next Capital of Cool," *Irvine World News,* February 20, 2003; Dana Parsons, "Our Cover Is Blown: TV Says We Are Hip," *Los Angeles Times,* April 11, 2004, p. A22; David Dean, vice president for strategic planning,

Irvine Corporation (a Spectrum developer), conversation with Robert Lang, October 30, 2002.

53. Andres Duany, Elizabeth Plater-Zyberk, and Jeff Speck, *Suburban Nation: The Rise of Sprawl and the Decline of the American Dream* (New York: North Point, 2000).

54. Jane Jacobs, *The Death and Life of Great American Cities* (New York: Vintage, 1961).

55. *Money Magazine* (http://money.cnn.com/best/bplive). *Money* took data on cities from OnBoard LLC, a real estate information company, and combined it with MOSAIC lifestyle segmentation data provided by Applied Geographic Solutions. *Money* started with a 271-city list and narrowed it by eliminating towns lacking the demographics typical of *Money* readers: college educated, working professional with well-above-average median income. In addition, the town had to be located no more than sixty miles from a major city, which *Money* estimated would ensure reasonable access to art and culture resources. Only cities with median incomes above $50,000 a year and unemployment rates below the national average were included in the analysis.

56. Plano's mayor was excited about this ranking and keeps a copy of the magazine on her coffee table. This information was conveyed to Robert Lang in a personal conversation on April 27, 2004.

57. Kate Ashford and others, "Best Places to Live," *Money Magazine,* August 1, 2006, pp. 94–108.

58. Superstition Vistas lies near the Superstition Mountains on state trust land in Pinal County, Arizona. The land is slated for development over the next several decades as an enormous master-planned community, which could be broken into several municipalities each exceeding 100,000 residents. Morrison Institute of Public Policy, *The Treasure of the Superstitions: Scenarios for the Future of Superstition Vistas* (Arizona State University, 2006).

59. William H. Frey and others, *Tracking Metropolitan America into the 21st Century: A Field Guide to the New Metropolitan and Micropolitan Definitions,* Living City Census Series (Brookings, 2004).

60. Lang, Blakely, and Gough, "Keys to the New Metropolis."

61. Ibid.

62. See also Lang and Gough, "Growth Counties."

63. Robert S. Lynd and Helen Merrill Lynd, *Middletown: A Study in Modern American Culture* (Harvest Books, 1931); Herbert Gans, *The Levittowners* (Columbia University Press, 1967); Elijah Anderson, *Streetwise: Race, Class, and Change in an Urban Community* (University of Chicago Press, 1992); Andrew Ross, *The Celebration Chronicles: Life, Liberty, and the Pursuit of Property Values in Disney's New Town* (New York: Ballantine, 1999).

64. See Stephanie Bothwell, Raymond Gindroz, and Robert Lang, "Restoring Community through Traditional Neighborood Design: A Case Study of Diggstown Public Housing," *Housing Policy Debate* 9, no. 1 (1998): 89–114; quotation on p. 89.

Chapter Two

1. San Bernardino, Riverside, and Orange (Santa Ana's home) Counties ring Los Angeles and have certainly boomed along with their county seat boomburbs. The

three now range from over 1.5 million (Riverside) to over 3 million (Orange), making them some of the largest urban counties in the United States. In fact, Robert Lang identifies all three (of twenty-three) as "MEGA Counties," or "Massively Enlarged, Growth, Accelerated Counties." Robert E. Lang and Megan Gough, "Growth Counties: Home to America's New Suburban Metropolis," in *Redefining Urban and Suburban America: Evidence from Census 2000,* vol. 3, edited by Alan Berube, Bruce Katz, and Robert E. Lang (Brookings, 2006), p. 62; also see Robert Fishman, *Bourgeois Utopias: The Rise and Fall of Suburbia* (New York: Basic Books, 1987); Robert E. Lang and Meghan Gough, *Metropolitan Growth Counties* (Brookings, 2004).

2. John W. Reps, *Cities of the American West: A History of Frontier Urban Planning* (Princeton University Press, 1979).

3. Ibid.

4. Ibid., p. 334. Mormons made their streets wide enough for a large wagon to make a U-turn without having to back up. These broad boulevards were easily adapted to later handle four or more lanes of automobile traffic and are now part of the urban landscape throughout much of the Intermountain West.

5. Ironically, Mesa now more than triples Salt Lake City in population—the city at the center of Mormon religion and culture. According to the Arizona WPA Guide (1939), Mesa's development remained in its original one-square-mile plan until 1931, when the town began to annex surrounding places.

6. Reps, *Cities of the American West*, p. 264.

7. Ibid., p. 376.

8. The WPA was a 1930s Franklin D. Roosevelt New Deal agency intended to provide government jobs to those who lost their jobs during the Great Depression. The Guides were a product of the Federal Writers' Project (a branch of the WPA). The American Guide Series is generally considered the apex of FWP publications. In his book *Travels with Charley: In Search of America* (1961), John Steinbeck raves about the Guides, even twenty years after their publication, writing that he wished he had room in his camper to lug them all.

9. "California: A State Guide Compiled by Workers of the Writers' Program of the Work Projects Administration in the State of California," in *California: A Guide to the Golden State* (New York: Hastings House, 1939), p. 378.

10. "Texas: A State Guide Compiled by Workers of the Writers' Program of the Work Projects Administration in the State of Texas," in *Texas: A Guide to the Lone Star State* (New York: Hastings House, 1940), p. 537.

11. "Arizona: A State Guide Compiled by Workers of the Writers' Program of the Work Projects Administration in the State of Arizona," in *The WPA Guide to 1930s Arizona* (University of Arizona Press, 1989), p. 351.

12. Wikipedia (www.wikipedia.org) is an open-source, web-based encyclopedia and as such it is subject to error. The information obtained from this site was cross-checked against other sources, including conversations with local officials.

13. Besides histories, many other interesting facts about boomburbs appear on their websites. For example, fourteen websites include detailed demographic profiles of the city.

14. See sunnyvale.ca.gov/local/ SVC%20CHRONOLOGY1.htm.

15. See www.auroragov.org/Visitors%20Guide/Pages/Our%20History.cfm; www.ci.westminster.co.us/city/history/default.htm.

16. See www.ci.oceanside.ca.us/community/history_print.asp.

17. See www.chulavistaca.gov/About/History.asp.

18. See www.mesalibrary.org/about_mesa/pdfs/MesaHistory-0703.pdf.

19. See www.wikipedia.org

20. See www.realestate-scottsdale.com/relocation/history.php.

21. See www.chandleraz.org/default.aspx?pageid=37.

22. See www.cityofhenderson.com/50/genhist.html.

23. See www.coralsprings.org/cityServices/CityHistory.pdf.

24. David Guterson, "No Place Like Home: On the Manicured Streets of a Master-Planned Community," *Harper's Magazine,* November 1992, pp. 55–64.

25. See www.santa-clarita.com/cityhall/history.asp.

26. Kenneth Jackson, *Crabgrass Frontiers: The Suburbanization of the United States* (Oxford University Press, 1985); Robert Fishman, *Bourgeois Utopias.* Dolores Hayden, *Building Suburbia: Green Fields and Urban Growth: 1820–2000* (New York: Pantheon, 2003).

27. Robert Lang was director of urban and metropolitan research at the Fannie Mae Foundation in 1999. He conceived and managed this project as part of a Fannie Mae conference that looked at the fiftieth anniversary of the 1949 housing act. See Robert Fishman, "The American Metropolis at Century's End: Past and Future Influences," *Housing Policy Debate* 11, no. 1 (2001): 199–213.

28. Historic population data for boomburbs are hard to obtain. Most of these places were unincorporated throughout their early stages of development and were therefore not tracked by the census. Some states kept tabs on population growth in unincorporated places, but the record is spotty. Localities also determined their own population, but these records are sometimes unreliable. Table 2-1 combines data from the WPA Guides (which used the 1930 census where it could), the census, state historical society websites, and boomburb websites. The data were cross-checked for accuracy where possible. No cases had conflicting data. However, these data remain less certain than the population figures from 1950 onward, which are all taken from the U.S. census.

29. See www.tsha.utexas.edu/handbook/online/articles/view/GG/hdg3.html.

30. "California: A State Guide," p. 233.

31. Docent at Taliesin West, conversation with Robert Lang, Scottsdale, January 30, 2001.

32. Ironically, as John Findlay notes, Disney's Tomorrowland section of the theme park, with its futuristic styles, began to immediately influence strip commercial architecture throughout the Western Sunbelt. According to Findlay, with the appearance of Disneyland, the futuristic vernacular architecture style termed "Googie" and "Space Age" swept across the Southern California strips with a vengeance. John M. Findlay, *Magic Lands: Western Cityscapes and American Culture after 1940* (University of California Press, 1992).

33. Kevin Phillips, *The Coming Republican Majority* (New Rochelle, N.Y.: Arlington House, 1969). Kirkpatrick Sale, *Power Shift: The Rise of the Southern Rim and its Challenge to the Eastern Establishment* (New York: Random House, 1975).

34. Michael Lind, "The New GOP: Hasta La Vista, Bubba," *Newsday,* August 8, 1999, p. A23.

35. Robert E. Lang and Patrick A. Simmons, *"Boomburbs": The Emergence of Large, Fast-Growing Suburban Cities in the United States*, Census Note 06 (Washington: Fannie Mae Foundation, 2001); Robert E. Lang and Patrick A. Simmons, "Boomburbs: The Emergence of Large, Fast-Growing Cities in the United States," in *Redefining Urban and Suburban America: Evidence from Census 2000*, edited by Bruce Katz and Robert E. Lang (Brookings, 2003).

36. William Fulton, *The Reluctant Metropolis: The Politics of Urban Growth in Los Angeles* (Berkeley, Calif.: Solano, 1997).

37. Dolores Hayden, *A Field Guide to Sprawl* (New York: W. W. Norton, 2004).

38. For example, Arthur C. Nelson and Casey J. Dawkins, *Urban Containment in the United States: History, Models, and Techniques for Regional and Metropolitan Growth Management* (Chicago: American Planning Association, 2004).

39. Carl Abbott, "The Portland Regions: Where City and Suburbs Talk to Each Other—And Mostly Agree," *Housing Policy Debate* 8, no. 1 (1997): 11–51.

40. The movie is based on an actual incident, and earned its first-time director and writer Steven Spielberg the screenplay prize at the Cannes Film Festival.

41. The *Washington Post* ran a story of Sugar Land that describes it as among the most reliably Republican in the nation and the converse of San Francisco, the most reliably liberal city. See David Finkel, "For a Conservative, Life Is Sweet in Sugar Land, Tex," *Washington Post,* April 26, 2004, p. A1.

42. William Fulton and others, "Who Sprawls Most? How Growth Patterns Differ across the U.S," policy paper (Brookings Center on Urban and Metropolitan Policy, 2001).

43. The U.S. census produces yearly estimates for population change at the sub-county level, based on the distributive housing unit method. This method uses building permits, mobile home shipments, and estimates of housing unit loss to update housing unit change since the last estimate. The census developed a household population estimate by applying the occupancy rate and the average person per household from the latest census to an estimate of the housing units. The estimates obtained from this method are controlled for by comparing to the final county population estimate. "U.S. Bureau of the Census' Estimates and Projections Area Documentation Subcounty Total Population Estimates," 2003 (eire.census.gov/popest/topics/methodology/citymeth.php).

44. Ibid. The tenth-ranked city was Joliet, Illinois, which nearly qualified as a boomburb but failed to sustain double-digit growth for all five decades since 1950.

45. Quoted in Lori Weisberg, "Chula Vista No 7 in the Nation in Galloping Growth," *San Diego Union Tribune,* July 10, 2003, p. A1.

46. According to a *New York Times* story, Gilbert "issues building permits only to developers who build within an [homeowners] association." Quoted in Motoko Rich, "Homeowner Boards Blur Line of Who Rules the Roost," *New York Times,* July 27, 2003, p. 14.

47. Office of Management and Budget, *Metropolitan Statistical Area Definitions,* June 6, 2003.

48. Lang and Simmons, "Boomburbs"; Lang and Simmons, *Boomburbs,* pp. 51–62.

49. Karen A. Danielsen, Robert E. Lang, and William Fulton, "Retracting Suburbia: Smart Growth and the Future of Housing," *Housing Policy Debate* 10, no. 3 (1999): 513–40.

50. Rick Hampson, "'New Brooklyns' Replace White Suburbs," *USA Today*, May 18, 2003, p. A1.

51. Patrick A. Simmons and Robert E. Lang, "The Urban Turnaround," in *Redefining Urban and Suburban America: Evidence from Census 2000*, edited by Bruce Katz and Robert E. Lang (Brookings, 2003), pp. 51–62.

52. U.S. Bureau of the Census, Table SUB-EST2002-03, "City and Town Population Estimates: April 1, 2000, to July 1, 2002," Population Division, July 10, 2003.

53. Shaun McKinnon, "Water: Growing Demand, Dwindling Supply," *Arizona Republic*, July 6, 2003, p. A1.

54. Edward L. Gleaser, "The New Economics of Urban and Regional Growth," in *The Oxford Handbook of Economic Geography*, edited by G. L. Clark, M. P. Feldman, and M. S. Gertler (Oxford University Press, 2000). Also see Richard Florida, "The Great Creative Class Debate: The Revenge of the Squelchers," *The Next American City* 5 (2004): 18–24.

55. Richard Florida, *The Rise of the Creative Class: And How It's Transforming Work, Leisure, Community, and Everyday Life* (New York: Perseus, 2002).

56. Jon Gertner, "Home Economics," *New York Times Magazine*, March 5, 2006, pp. 20–31.

Chapter Three

1. The 2000 census considered race and Hispanic origin to be distinct. This book uses the Office of Management and Budget definition of Asian, which is a person having origins in the Far East, Southeast Asia, or the Indian subcontinent. See also William H. Frey and Alan Berube, "City Families and Suburban Singles: An Emerging Household Story," in *Redefining Urban and Suburban America: Evidence from Census 2000*, edited by Bruce Katz and Robert E. Lang (Brookings, 2003).

2. Ibid.

3. William Frey, "Melting Pot Suburbs: A Study of Suburban Diversity," in *Redefining Urban and Suburban America: Evidence from Census 2000*, edited by Bruce Katz and Robert E. Lang (Brookings, 2003).

4. Robert E. Lang, *Edgeless Cities: Exploring the Elusive Metropolis* (Brookings, 2003).

5. Robert Suro and Audrey Singer, "Changing Patterns of Latino Growth in Metropolitan America," in *Redefining Urban and Suburban America: Evidence from Census 2000*, edited by Bruce Katz and Robert E. Lang (Brookings, 2003).

6. Ibid.

7. Race and ethnicity data are not reported similarly before 1980. Foreign-born data, however, are available from 1970 on.

8. The Brooklyn of today is experiencing a renaissance and is becoming home to cultural institutions and young, urbane, middle-class refugees from the Manhattan housing market. A *New York Times Magazine* article featured Brooklyn's emerging hipness and a bohemian culture that eclipses Manhattan's. James Traub, "The (Not

Easy) Building of (Not Exactly) Lincoln Center for (Not) Manhattan," *New York Times Magazine*, April 25, 2004, p. 28.

9. Patrick A. Simmons, *Patterns and Trends in Overcrowded Housing: Early Results from Census 2000*, Census Note 09 (Washington: Fannie Mae Foundation, 2002).

10. During the 2002 World Series, which featured the San Francisco Giants and the Anaheim Angels, a newspaper columnist wrote that San Francisco has everything but parking and that Anaheim has nothing but parking. Robert Morse, "San Francisco and Disney: It's a Small World (Series) after All," *San Francisco Chronicle*, October 16, 2002, p. B2.

11. Jim Hinch and Ronald Campbell, "Sunny Suburban and Dense," *OC Register*, April 8, 2001, p. B1.

12. William Fulton, *The Reluctant Metropolis: The Politic of Urban Growth in Los Angeles* (Berkeley, Calif.: Solano, 1997).

13. John Westcott, *Anaheim: City of Dreams* (Chatsworth, Calif.: Windsor, 1990).

14. Interestingly, when the Klan's proliferation in the 1920s caused neighboring towns to boycott Anaheim, the city formed a baseball team, which helped rehabilitate the city's image; see ibid. Today, Anaheim counts on tourism and sports teams (Angels and Ducks) to generate positive publicity.

15. Rick Hampson, "'New Brooklyns' Replace White Suburbs," *USA Today*, May 18, 2003, p. A1.

16. Ibid. For more information on income disparity and schools in Los Angles, see map by Metropolitan Research Corporation at www.metroresearch.org/projects/region_maps.asp.

17. Edward L. Glaeser and Jesse M. Shapiro, "City Growth: Which Places Grew and Why," in *Redefining Urban and Suburban America: Evidence from Census 2000*, edited by Bruce Katz and Robert E. Lang (Brookings, 2003).

18. Haya El Nasser, "Old Labels Just Don't Stick in the 21st Century," *USA Today*, December 17, 2003, p. 17A.

19. Suein Hwang, "The New White Flight," *Wall Street Journal*, November 19, 2005, p. A1.

20. Moser, known as "Mr. Naperville," built most of Naperville's subdivisions during the post–World War II boom, including Aero Estates, which has a private airplane runway and houses equipped with airplane hangars.

21. Robert Fishman, *Bourgeois Utopias: The Rise and Fall of Suburbia* (New York: Basic Books, 1987).

22. Mayor George Praedel stated that Naperville does not contain any public housing. Single-family housing made up 68 percent Naperville's housing stock in 2000, compared with 43 percent in Anaheim. George Praedel, interviewed by Jennifer LeFurgy, July 14, 2004.

23. Margaret Foster, "Time Running out for Four Chicago-Area Houses," *Preservation* (National Trust for Historic Preservation), March 29, 2006, p. 10.

24. Audrey Singer, *The Rise of the New Immigrant Gateways*, Living City Census Series (Brookings, 2004).

25. For updated figures for 2005, see the American Communities Survey at http://factfinder.census.gov/.

26. Clearwater also has a high average age of forty-one years. This combined with single households and women living alone could signify a high rate of widowed retirees.

27. William Frey, *Boomers and Seniors in the Suburbs: Aging Patterns in Census 2000*, Living City Census Series (Brookings, 2003).

28. Glaeser and Shapiro, "City Growth."

29. Peter Wallstein, "Bush Sees Fertile Soil in 'Exurbia,'" *Los Angeles Times*, June 28, 2004, p. A1.

30. Jennifer LeFurgy, *Boomburbs and the Vote: National Election Results in Counties Containing Large, Rapidly Growing Suburbs*, Special Report (Alexandria, Va.: Metropolitan Institute at Virginia Tech, 2005).

31. Carol Morello, "The Politics of Condo Dwellers," *Washington Post*, May 12, 2005, p. VA12.

32. Loretta Sanchez, interviewed by Jennifer LeFurgy, July 27, 2004.

Chapter Four

1. Timothy Egan, a *New York Times* reporter who often writes about growth issues, quotes the line in two stories. Timothy Egan, "Retail Darwinism Puts Old Malls in Jeopardy," *New York Times*, January 1, 2000, p. A14; Timothy Egan, "Dreams of Fields: The New Politics of Urban Sprawl," *New York Times*, November 14, 1998, p. A12.

2. The Dallas case analysis focuses on four boomburbs. Two, Plano and Irving, are dominated by office development and have a large white-collar economy. The others, Arlington and Garland, are more blue-collar towns, containing automobile and truck plants, warehousing, and diversified manufacturing. Arlington is also home to the original Six Flags theme park and the ballpark where the Texas Rangers play. Phoenix has two big boomburb job centers: Scottsdale and Tempe. There are also emerging and planned centers in Mesa and Chandler.

3. Gaithersburg is also home to Black's Guide, the commercial real estate data firm whose office data are used in this book.

4. This figure comes from averaging the unemployment rate for each of the fifty-four boomburbs from January 2003 to January 2004. The weighted average came to 5.15 percent.

5. Ebenezer Howard, *Garden Cities of To-Morrow* (London: Faber and Faber, 1902).

6. The quotation is from Gertrude Stein, *Everybody's Biography*. Ironically, Oakland has more "there there" than most boomburbs do.

7. Robert E. Lang, *Edgeless Cities: Exploring the Elusive Metropolis* (Brookings, 2003), pp. 61–62.

8. Mayor Day, conversation with Robert Lang, April 27, 2004.

9. The plan is to do extensive higher-density, mixed-use development around the ballpark so that people will stay after the game and spend money.

10. Bruce Katz, "Welcome to the 'Exit Ramp' Economy," *Boston Globe*, May 13, 2001, p. A19.

11. Christopher B. Leinberger, "Metropolitan Development Trends of the Late 1990s: Social and Environmental Implications," in *Land Use in America*, edited by Henry L. Diamond and Patrick F. Noonan (Cambridge, Mass.: Lincoln Institute of Land Policy, 1996); Christopher B. Leinberger, "The Changing Location of Development and Investment Opportunity," *Urban Land* 54, no. 5 (1995): 31–36.

12. Homer Hoyt, *The Structure and Growth of Residential Neighborhoods in American Cities* (Washington: Government Printing Office, 1939).

13. The Texas WPA Guide of 1939 describes both places as, even then, very desirable.

14. Favored quarters also exist in the Denver and Phoenix regions. However, the model does not work for greater Los Angeles (home to nineteen boomburbs), which exists more as a series of subregions, or what Vance calls "urban realms." Each of Los Angeles's urban realms has its own spatial logic and may contain its own favored section. For example, the urban realm of Orange County has a favored section, which is the southern part of the county. James E. Vance Jr., *This Scene of Man: Role and Structure of the City in the Geography of Western Civilization* (New York: Harper Press, 1977).

15. Wikipedia.com says of Orange, "Because of its classic "small town" look, many television shows and motion pictures have selected the Historic District (and other parts of Orange) as a backdrop, including *Lethal Weapon 4*, Tom Hanks's 1996 film *That Thing You Do!*, and the CBS television series *Ghost Whisperer*."

16. Peter Calthorpe, *The Next American Metropolis: Ecology, Community, and the American Dream* (New York: Princeton Architectural Press, 1993).

17. In Phoenix a transit plan was passed that will bring light rail to the downtowns of Tempe and Mesa. Around Dallas, Plano, Garland, and Irving have light rail to their downtowns. As of now, Arlington, does not have rail; its voters turned down bus service by the Dallas Area Rapid Transit, but the Arlington mayor believes the voters would vote in favor of rail.

18. For a comparison consider the Washington-Baltimore metropolitan area. The two cities are further apart than Dallas and Fort Worth, but they are part of the continuous northeast megalopolis. The federal Office of Management and Budget applied its standard formula of commuting patterns to "statistically" establish the region. The link between Washington and Baltimore is likewise tenuous. Instead of three big cities (one with over 300,000 people filling the gap between Baltimore and Washington, as in the Dallas Metroplex), the space is occupied by small, fragmented suburbs.

19. Love Field was made famous in the 1960s by the sad fact that it was where President Kennedy landed before he was assassinated in Dallas. Less well known is that Kennedy had actually flown into Love Field from Fort Worth's airport, illustrating perfectly what the FAA was arguing against.

20. Haya El Nasser and Paul Overberg, "A Comprehensive Look at Sprawl in America," *USA Today*, February 2, 2001, p. A1.

21. John D. Kasarda, "Aerotropolis: Airport-Driven Urban Development," in *ULI on the Future: Cities in the 21st Century* (Washington: Urban Land Institute, 2000). Interestingly, Atlanta's Hartsfield Airport is located south of the city and not in the region's favored quarter. Yet the airport is beginning to overcome its location disadvantage and stimulate nearby commercial development.

22. Peter J. Taylor and Robert E. Lang, *U.S. Cities in the "World City Network,"* Center on Urban and Metropolitan Policy (Brookings, 2005).

23. Firms from six key producer service sectors were investigated: accounting, advertising, banking-finance, insurance, law, and management consulting. Global service firms were identified as those with offices in fifteen or more cities, including at least one in North America, Western Europe, and Pacific Asia. In other words, these firms clearly have a global strategy for the service provisioning of their clients. One hundred such firms were identified: eighteen in accounting, fifteen in advertising, twenty-three in banking-finance, eleven in insurance, sixteen in law, and seventeen in management consulting. Offices of these firms were described across 315 metropolitan areas worldwide.

24. This office space is mostly located in Irvine and Costa Mesa.

25. Lang, *Edgeless Cities.*

26. *Black's Guide to Office Leasing: Dallas/Fort Worth Office Space Market* (Gaithersburg, Md.: Black's Guide, 2003).

27. The Atlanta and Houston figures come from *Black's Guide.* The Phoenix figure comes from Cushman and Wakefield, Global Real Estate Solutions, *The Phoenix Office Market, Spring 2004* (Phoenix: 2004).

28. Robert E. Lang, *Office Sprawl: The Evolving Geography of Business,* Center on Urban and Metropolitan Policy (Brookings, 2000).

29. Ibid. Houston gained an even larger share of its suburban office market through annexation. As a result, the central cities of both Dallas and Houston have a bigger share of their region's office market than do those of New York and Chicago, despite the fact that the latter two have enormous downtowns.

30. Lang, *Edgeless Cities.*

31. The mayor of Irving claims that Texas Stadium has no significant economic impact for the city. The Dallas Cowboys are now thinking of moving to Dallas in a new stadium at the county fair grounds. The stadium would replace the current Cotton Bowl. The land that Texas Stadium sits on could be redeveloped to generate even higher taxes than the current use.

32. Lang, *Edgeless Cities,* p. 1.

33. *Black's Guide;* Cushman and Wakefield, *Phoenix Office Market.*

34. Lang, *Edgeless Cities.*

35. Arthur C. Nelson and Casey J. Dawkins, *Urban Containment in the United States: History, Models, and Techniques for Regional and Metropolitan Growth Management* (Chicago: American Planning Association, 2004).

36. Lang, *Edgeless Cities.*

37. Because *Black's Guide* does not survey Phoenix, data from Cushman and Wakefield were used to analyze the region's office development patterns. According to this source, the Dallas office market had just over 159 million square feet of office space in 2004. The firm does not survey the Fort Worth market, so its numbers are a bit below *Black's Guide* figures for the region.

38. Data from Cushman and Wakefield, *Phoenix Office Market.*

39. Data from emporis.com. This is yet another aspect of Scottsdale that would not have made Frank Lloyd Wright happy. Under Wright's Broadacre proposal, cities would be decentralized but, at the major intersections, tall office towers would soar. Scottsdale has the decentralized part correct, but none of its

buildings soars. Frank Lloyd Wright Jr., *The Living City* (New York: Horizon Press, 1958).

40. See www.scottsdaleaz.gov/Airport/History.asp.

41. Mayor Hawker, conversation with Robert Lang, March 10, 2004.

42. Two of the runways are 10,400 feet; one is 9,300 feet. This means passenger jets such as an Airbus A320, a Boeing 737, and even a Boeing 757 can land at Williams.

43. Joel Garreau, *Edge City: Life on the New Frontier* (New York: Doubleday, 1991).

44. Chris Leinberger, "Urban Villages/Council Districts: The Future . . . or Frustration" (Phoenix: Fourth Phoenix Town Hall, 1984).

45. Christopher B. Leinberger and Charles Lockwood, "How Business Is Reshaping America," *Atlantic Monthly* 258, no. 10 (1986): 43–52.

46. Chris Leinberger, in conversation with Robert Lang, May 10, 2001, indicated that Joel Garreau was the first person to contact him after the *Atlantic Monthly* article appeared.

47. Data from emporis.com.

48. Cushman and Wakefield reports its office data by submarkets, which may or may not line up with a city, so it is hard to know how much of this space is in either of these two boomburbs.

49. The tallest building in downtown Phoenix is Bank One Center, at forty floors and 486 feet. See emporis.com.

50. Mayor Putnam, conversation with Robert Lang, April 28, 2004.

Chapter Five

1. These are all publicly listed companies on either the New York or NASDAQ exchanges.

2. The Lennar site was also searched, and it listed fourteen pages of projects in Phoenix alone, but it was hard to determine from its website in which cities these developments were located.

3. Many of the other projects are in the region's three CDP boomburbs, which are unincorporated census-designated places that contain over 100,000 residents. CDP boomburbs are explored more fully in the next chapter, on governance.

4. See www.census.gov/const/www/permitsindex.html.

5. Dowell Myers and Julie Park, *The Great California Housing Collapse* (Washington: Fannie Mae Foundation, 2002), p. 1.

6. Anthony Downs, review of draft of this book, July 2006.

7. Part of the controversy is who pays for these services. Myron Orfield finds that residents in older parts of metropolitan areas substantially subsidize the development of new places through a transfer of public funds. Myron Orfield, *Metro Politics: A Regional Agenda for Community and Stability* (Brookings, 1997).

8. A subsequent sampling of housing values at zillow.com shows that a price peak was often reached in the spring of 2006. In most boomburbs, values have dipped only slightly (often less than 5 percent as of September 2006); however, the prices in boomburbs around Las Vegas seem especially volatile. See Orfield, *Metro Politics*; Myron Orfield, *American Metro Politics* (Brookings, 2002).

9. Robert E. Lang, "Are the Boomburbs Still Booming?" in *Redefining Urban and Suburban America: Evidence from Census 2000*, vol. 3, edited by Alan Berube, Bruce Katz, and Robert E. Lang (Brookings, 2006).

10. Ibid.

11. Ibid.

12. The data on this site are managed by Patrick Simmons, who developed the hardship index as a way to better gauge the true impact of housing on less affluent family budgets. See www.dataplace.org.

13. Arthur C. Nelson and Robert E. Lang, "The Next 100 Million: Reshaping of America's Built Environment," *Planning* (January 2007): 4–6.

14. For a detailed analysis of these data, see Thomas W. Sanchez and Robert E. Lang, *Security versus Status: The Two Worlds of Gated Communities*, Census Note 02:02 (Alexandria, Va.: Metropolitan Institute at Virginia Tech, 2002). Also see Thomas W. Sanchez, Robert E. Lang, and Dawn Dhavale, "Security versus Status? A First Look at the Census's Gated Community Data," *Journal of Planning Education and Research* 24 (2005): 281–91.

15. Mike Davis, *City of Quartz: Excavating the Future in Los Angeles* (London: Verso, 1990); Joel Garreau, *Edge City: Life on the New Frontier* (New York: Doubleday, 1991); Edward J. Blakely and Mary Gail Snyder, *Fortress America: Gated Communities in the United States* (Brookings, 1997); Robert E. Lang and Karen A. Danielsen, "Gated Communities in America: Walling Out the World?" *Housing Policy Debate* 8, no. 4 (1997): 740–75; Andrew Stark, "America, the Gated?" *Wilson Quarterly* 22, no. 1 (1998): 58–79; Setha M. Low, *Behind the Gates: Life, Security, and the Pursuit of Happiness in Fortress America* (New York: Routledge, 2003).

16. David Guterson, "Home, Safe Home," *Utne Reader,* March–April 1993, pp. 31–43; David Guterson, "No Place Like Home: On the Manicured Streets of a Master-Planned Community," *Harper's Magazine,* November 1992, pp. 55–64.

17. Sanchez, Lang, and Dhavale, "Security versus Status?"

18. Ibid.

19. Karen A. Danielsen, "Hidden Enclaves: The Social, Market, and Policy Forces behind the Rise of Rental Gated Communities," Ph.D. dissertation, Virginia Polytechnic Institute and State University, forthcoming.

20. Karen A. Danielsen, "The Positive Functions of Gated Communities," paper prepared for the annual meeting of the American Sociological Association, Montreal, August 2006.

21. Lang and Danielsen, "Gated Communities in America."

22. Robert Lang toured the Aliante master-planned community in North Las Vegas in March 2004.

23. Robert Lang lived in Trillium at Rio Salado from January 1, 2006, to June 30, 2006, while in residence at Arizona State University as visiting faculty. The case analysis of this development is based on participant observation of life in this rental complex.

24. Guterson, "No Place Like Home," p. 59.

25. Ibid.

26. Ibid.

27. Mark Gottdiener, Claudia C. Collins, and David R. Dickens, *Las Vegas: The Social Production of an All-American City* (Malden, Mass.: Blackwell, 1997).

28. This case analysis is based on three visits to the development by Robert Lang, in March 2004, June 2005, and May 2006. "Gate-ready" refers to a development that is walled and ready to be fitted with gates.

29. Dolores Hayden, *Building Suburbia: Green Fields and Urban Growth, 1820–2000* (New York: Pantheon, 2003).

30. Urban Land Institute, *Great Planned Communities* (Washington, 2002).

31. This is now a fairly common design for master-planned community commercial structures in boomburbs.

32. "Aliante: An Exciting New Community," company sales literature, 2003. See www.aliantehomes.com.

33. "The name of the I-215/CC215 has been changed from the 'Las Vegas Beltway' to the Bruce Woodbury Beltway in March 2004. The [Clark County] Board approved a resolution recognizing Commissioner Woodbury for his many years and efforts in the future of transportation in this valley and of being worthy of having the Beltway renamed for him. Thanks to a tax measure voted on by the County residents, the beltway is expected to be fully completed by 2013, twice as fast as the original goal of 2025" (www.wikipedia.org [May 1, 2006]).

34. Robert E. Lang, Jennifer LeFurgy, and Steve Hornburg, *From Wall Street to Your Street: New Market and Design Solutions for Fixing Smart Growth Finance,* survey series (Miami: Funders Network for Smart Growth, 2005).

35. Town Lake is actually a dammed section of naturally dry Salt River, which is why Trillium is "at" Rio Salado (or Salt River). The city of Tempe dammed the river and filled it with water from the Salt River Project in order to create a "water feature" just north of its downtown. The idea was that it could turn a dry, barren river into an amenity and improve the value of land along its shore. The plan worked, and now projects are booming along the north and south shore of Town Lake, including Trillium at Rio Salado. The biggest project so far is Hayden Landing, an upscale, mixed-use development that will include housing, office space, retail, and a full-service boutique hotel. The high-rise condo units, or Bridgeview at Hayden Ferry Lakeside, start at $600,000, according to its website (as of April 2006).

36. Virginia McAlester and Lee McAlester, A *Field Guide to American Houses* (New York: Knopf, 1984).

37. Alice Ockleshaw, "The Evolution of the House," *Suburbanite,* January 2006, pp. 33–37.

38. President Richard M. Nixon was born and raised in a Craftsman mail-order home in Yorba Linda, California. His boyhood home is on display at his presidential library in Yorba Linda.

39. McAlester and McAlester, *A Field Guide to American Houses.*

40. Ibid., p. 479.

41. Jerry Ditto and Lanning Stern, *Eichler Homes* (San Francisco: Chronicle Books, 1995).

42. Interestingly, a revival in modern single-family home design has begun. Publications such as *Atomic Ranch* profile and promote midcentury design. Within these publications, homebuilders promote neomodern homes in several Southwest boomburbs. Also, new, attached single-family housing is quickly switching to more modern designs. This is especially true of infill and transit-oriented developments in

Southern California. Infill development specialists such as the Olsen Company, which builds homes in dozens of California boomburbs, are especially modern in their design.

43. Robert E. Lang and Karen Danielsen, "Monster Homes," *Planning* (May 2002): 20–25.

44. Dolores Hayden, *A Field Guide to Sprawl* (New York: W. W. Norton, 2004).

45. Lang and Danielsen, "Monster Homes."

46. U.S. Census Bureau, American Housing Survey 2001.

47. Ockleshaw, "The Evolution of the House."

48. Lang and Danielsen, "Monster Homes."

49. Paul Knox, "Vulgaria: The Re-Enchantment of Suburbia," *Opolis* 1, no. 2 (2005): 33–46; Thorstein Veblen, *The Theory of the Leisure Class. An Economic Study in the Evolution of Institutions* (New York: Macmillan, 1899).

50. Paul Shigley, "California Goes Verticle," *Planning* (April 2006): 44–47, quotation on p. 46.

51. Ibid.

52. Lang and Danielsen, "Monster Homes."

53. Barbara Thornburg, "You Call This a Loft?" *Los Angeles Times,* March 12, 2006, p. H1.

54. Robert Lang interviewed realtors in the spring of 2006 about homes in the northeast part of metropolitan Phoenix—or the so-called Favored Quarter. The impression he got from several agents was that Scottsdale, while desirable, also had grown citylike and that those who seek a small town "feel" are advised to consider the lesser known but much desired Paradise Valley and Fountain Hills.

Chapter Six

1. William Fischel, "An Economic History of Zoning and a Cure for its Exclusionary Effects," *Urban Studies* 41, no. 2 (2004): 317–40.

2. In fact, Knox and McCarthy point out that between the years 1984 and 2004 the share of U.S. municipalities governed by city manager systems jumped from 35 percent to 49 percent. Paul Knox and Linda McCarthy, *Urbanization* (Upper Saddle River, N.J.: Prentice-Hall, 2005).

3. For example, an article in the *San Diego Union Tribune* describes the debate in that city. Philip J. LaVelle, "Strong-Mayor Bid Criticized," *San Diego Union Tribune,* April 24, 2004, p. A1.

4. Knox and McCarthy, *Urbanization.*

5. The first such government was in Stanton, Virginia, in 1908.

6. Lawrence Southwick Jr., "Local Government Spending and At-Large versus District Representation; Do Wards Result in More 'Pork'?" *Economics and Politics* 9, no. 2 (1997): 173–201.

7. Mayor Boyd Dunn of Chandler, Arizona, is especially resentful of this political intrusion. In an interview with Robert Lang on March 10, 2004, at Chandler's city hall, Dunn noted that some of the most conservative elements in the Arizona state legislature are trying to curb local power. One Republican in the legislature has even gone as far as to call cities "terrorist organizations" for confiscating private property. Gilbert, Arizona's, mayor Steve Berman in a July 17, 2004, interview referred

to the ultraconservative leaders in the state legislature as the "mighty righties" and finds that they constantly seek to infuse nonpartisan local issues with hot button social wedges such as religion.

8. Because they technically do not run for office under a party label, it is difficult to get an exact number of how many boomburb mayors are Democrats and Republicans. To find out, one would have to call or visit with all of them, and even then there are instances in which a mayor would not reveal party affiliation.

9. Robert E. Lang and Meghan Gough, *New Metropolis Counties: Suburbs of Suburbs,* Census Note 03:03 (Alexandria, Va.: Metropolitan Institute at Virginia Tech, 2003); Robert E. Lang and Meghan Gough, "Growth Counties: Home to America's New Suburban Metropolis," in *Redefining Urban and Suburban America: Evidence from Census 2000,* vol. 3, edited by Alan Berube, Bruce Katz, and Robert E. Lang (Brookings, 2006).

10. Myron Orfield, *American Metro Politics* (Brookings, 2002).

11. Note that the "towns" of Herndon and Vienna, Virginia, are incorporated, giving them quasi-independence from Fairfax County. However, both of these places also pay substantial county taxes and are part of its school system.

12. Under Virginia incorporation law, cities are "independent" of counties. There are cities that can exist in counties, but they constitute unincorporated special taxing districts. An example of such an unincorporated "city" with Fairfax County is Herndon.

13. Orfield, *American Metro Politics.*

14. Lang and Gough, "Growth Counties." MEGA is short for massively enlarged, growth-accelerated counties. All of these twenty-three counties have experienced double-digit growth rates for the past five censuses and now have a population in excess of 800,000 residents. The MEGA counties that contain multiple boomburbs are Los Angeles, Orange, Riverside, and San Bernardino Counties in California; Maricopa County in Arizona; Clark County in Nevada; Dallas County in Texas; and Broward County in Florida. Many other MEGA counties have at least one boomburb. Lang and Gough, *New Metropolis Counties;* Lang and Gough, "Growth Counties."

15. Robert E. Lang and Dawn Dhavale, *Reluctant Cities: Exploring Big Unincorporated Census Designated Places,* Census Note 03:01 (Alexandria, Va.: Metropolitan Institute at Virginia Tech, 2003).

16. For example, a 2004 special issue of the journal *Urban Studies* covers the topic.

17. John Logan and Harvey Molotch, *Urban Fortunes: The Political Economy of Place* (University of California Press, 1987).

18. Joel Garreau, *Edge City: Life on the New Frontier* (New York: Doubleday, 1991).

19. William Fulton, *The Reluctant Metropolis: The Politics of Urban Growth in Los Angeles* (Berkeley, Calif.: Solano, 1997).

20. Robert Lang, having grown up in suburban New Jersey and now living in suburban Virginia, seeks to understand Sunbelt suburbs on their own terms and is not inclined to view them as an Easterner would. The German word for to understand, *verstehen,* has been taken to mean "sympathetic introspection" in translation by English-speaking social scientists and historians. This idea guides the boom-

burb research, which means the authors attempt to interpret the social worlds in these places through vicarious identification with local custom and culture.

21. William A. Fischel, *The Homevoter Hypothesis: How Home Values Influence Local Government Taxation, School Finance, and Land-Use Policies* (Harvard University Press, 2001).

22. For a review of home equity insurance programs, see Fischel, "An Economic History of Zoning"; C. Theodore Koebel, Robert E. Lang, and Karen A. Danielsen, *Community Acceptance of Affordable Housing* (Washington: National Association of Realtors, June 2004).

23. By contrast, in Western states, especially California, voters must use direct democracy to fight the growth machine. The chief mechanism for doing this is by voter requirements for new development, which, as Gerber and Phillips show, mostly fail to stop new development. Elizabeth R. Gerber and Justin H. Phillips, "Direct Democracy and Land Use Policy: Exchanging Public Goods for Development Rights," *Urban Studies* 41, no. 2 (2004): 463–79.

24. This was the basis of the lawsuits in the two Mount Laurel, New Jersey, cases. A poor minority family sued the town on the grounds that Mount Laurel was purposely excluding affordable housing. The plaintiffs won the case, and the state of New Jersey mandated that developing places provide for an allotted share of affordable housing. But most of Bergen County is built out, so the ruling does not impact its housing or land use conditions. Charles M. Haar, *Suburbs under Siege: Race, Space, and Audacious Judges* (Princeton University Press, 1996).

25. Haworth is a built-out suburb of almost exclusively single-family homes. Its businesses are retail shops in a small downtown (ironically, about the size of a small boomburb downtown) and two country clubs.

26. Pendall finds that New Jersey municipalities have the most exclusionary housing practices in the United States. Ralph Pendall, "Landscapes of Regulation," discussion paper (Brookings Center on Urban and Metropolitan Policy, 2006).

27. The name is inspired by James Buchanan's work on the economic theory of clubs. Places such as Haworth meet the criteria for being clubs. James Buchanan, "An Economic Theory of Clubs," *Economica* 32, no. 1 (1965): 1–14.

28. William Fischel, "The Rise of Private Neighborhood Associations: Revolution or Evolution," in *Property Tax, Land Use, and Land Use Regulation,* edited by Dick Netzer (Cambridge, Mass.: Lincoln Institute of Land Policy, 2004).

29. Ibid. Fischel notes a relationship between the increase in denser housing development and the number of homeowners associations. In regions such as Los Angeles, South Florida, Phoenix, and Las Vegas, where lot size generally runs small (averaging under 7,000 square feet), these associations help to manage relations between neighbors whose dwellings practically touch. By contrast, the Northeast and Midwest tend to have much larger lots, and this space provides residents a physical buffer in place of a regulatory one (that is, a homeowners association).

30. Evan McKenzie, *Privatopia: Homeowners Associations and the Rise of Residential Private Government* (Yale University Press, 1994).

31. Stephen E. Barton and Carol J. Silverman, eds., *Common Interest Communities: Private Governments and Public Interest* (University of California Press, 1994).

32. Oren Dorell, "Some New Cities Outsource City Hall," *USA Today*, September 15, 2006, p. A1.

33. Ibid.

34. Mayor Montandon, interview by Robert Lang, Las Vegas Technology Park, March 12, 2004. Several other mayors also mentioned being active in homeowners associations.

35. Mark Gottdiener, Claudia C. Collins, and David R. Dickens, *Las Vegas: The Social Production of an All-American City* (Malden, Mass.: Blackwell, 1997), p. 153.

36. See Fischel's "The Rise of Private Neighborhood Associations" on this point. Fischel also finds that homeowners associations even demand higher code enforcement standards in the areas near their community as a further hedge against neighborhood impacts on property values.

37. Mayor Hawker, interviewed by Robert Lang, Mesa, Arizona, March 10, 2004.

38. Fischel's "The Rise of Private Neighborhood Associations" makes this same point.

39. Mayor Berman, interviewed by Robert Lang, Gilbert, Arizona, July 17, 2004.

40. The state of Arizona will only allow homeowners associations if there is common property.

41. Robert Lang has served on the board of the Community Association Institute Foundation since 2005.

42. McKenzie, *Privatopia*.

43. Dolores Hayden, *Building Suburbia: Green Fields and Urban Growth: 1820–2000* (New York: Pantheon, 2003); Myron Orfield, *American Metro Politics* (Brookings, 2002); Myron Orfield, *Metro Politics: A Regional Agenda for Community and Stability* (Brookings, 1997).

44. Richard C. Feiock, "Politics, Institutions, and Local Land Use Regulation," *Urban Studies* 41, no. 2 (2004): 363–75.

45. Brent Herrington, interviewed by Robert Lang, Scottsdale, Arizona, March 10, 2004.

46. Ross noted this trend in Disney's new urbanist community, Celebration, in the late 1990s. Note that Herrington was Celebration's original town manager and set up the town's 501(c)(3) organization. Andrew Ross, *The Celebration Chronicles: Life, Liberty, and the Pursuit of Property Values in Disney's New Town* (New York: Ballantine, 1999).

47. Some master-planned community builders, such as the Del Webb Corporation, seek out unincorporated places because they will provide all of the elements of municipal government through the homeowners associations. Other developers will operate in boomburbs but negotiate planned unit development deals where they essentially run towns within towns.

48. Lang and Dhavale, *Reluctant Cities*. The 50,000 population mark was picked to match baby boomburbs. According to www.wikipedia.org, "A census-designated place (CDP) is an area identified by the United States Census Bureau for statistical reporting. CDPs are communities that lack separate municipal government, but which otherwise resemble incorporated places, such as cities or villages. CDPs are delineated to provide data for settled concentrations of population that are identifiable by name but are not legally incorporated under the laws of the state in which they are located. They are often informally called 'unincorporated towns.'"

49. Paul Overberg, personal communication with Robert Lang, September 22, 2004.

50. Robert E. Lang, *Metropolitan Growth Counties,* Census Note 01 (Washington: Fannie Mae Foundation, 2002).

51. See "U.S. Bureau of the Census 2000 Summary File One," 2001, at factfinder.census.gov/servlet/basicfactsservlet.

52. Land area and population density statistics are based on 1990 census data.

53. Ray Ring, "Taking Liberties," *High Country News*, July 21, 2006, p. 1.

54. According to Jacobs, the "wise-use" movement is a libertarian land reform movement that seeks to maximize both personal property rights and private use of public lands. Harvey M. Jacobs, *Who Owns America?* (University of Wisconsin Press, 1999).

55. A floor-to-area ratio of 1.0 would mean that a 5,000-square-foot house is allowed on a 5,000-square-foot lot. A 0.5 ratio would reduce the house to 2,500 square feet, or half the size of a lot.

56. For an article that describes the Oregon land reform movement behind Measure 37 and its precursor, Measure 7, see Carl Abbott, Sy Adler, and Deborah Howe, "A Quiet Counterrevolution in Land Use Reform: The Origin and Impact of Oregon's Measure 7," *Housing Policy Debate* 14, no. 3 (2003): 383–425.

57. George Homsy, "Sons of Measure 37: Lessons from Oregon's Property Rights Law," *Planning* (June 2006): 14–19.

58. Ring, "Taking Liberties."

Chapter Seven

1. Robert E. Lang, *Are the Boomburbs Still Booming?* Census Note 15 (Washington: Fannie Mae Foundation, 2004).

2. *Sprawl Hits the Wall: Confronting the Realities of Metropolitan Los Angeles,* Southern California Studies Center at USC and Brookings Center on Urban and Metropolitan Policy (Brookings, 2001).

3. David Rusk refers to these municipalities as elastic, in that they can expand their boundaries to capture new growth. David Rusk, *Cities without Suburbs* (Washington: Woodrow Wilson Center, 1993).

4. For information on the city of Chesapeake, see www.chesapeake.va.us.

5. Boomburbs figured in seventeen of the measures, and of these fourteen passed. See Haya El Nasser, "Red State or Blue, Americans Sick of Gridlock," *USA Today,* November 4, 2004, p. A3.

6. Kenneth C. Orski, "Transportation Referenda," *Innovation Briefs* 15, no. 8 (2004): pp. 1–2.

7. Lang, *Are the Boomburbs Still Booming?*

8. Steven Berman, interview by Robert Lang, Gilbert, Arizona, July 20, 2004.

9. In strip annexation, cities annex everything within a certain boundary and then pick up isolated unincorporated parcels within the area they have surrounded. It is a common practice in the West.

10. Boyd W. Dunn, interview by Robert Lang, Chandler, Arizona, March 10, 2004.

11. Lang, *Are the Boomburbs Still Booming?*

12. Michael Montandon, interview by Robert Lang, North Las Vegas, Nevada, March 12, 2004.

13. Lang, *Are the Boomburbs Still Booming?*

14. Clark County Conservation of Public Land and Natural Resources Act (or Public Law 107-282).

15. See www.usatoday.com/money/perfi/housing/2004-08-26-metroprices.htm.

16. Jennifer Shubinski, "BLM's Affordable Housing Program Still Unpopular with Municipalities," *Las Vegas Sun,* November 26, 2004, p. A1.

17. Ibid.

18. Douglas Porter, *Profiles in Growth Management* (Washington: Urban Land Institute, 1997).

19. Bob Day, interview by Robert Lang, Garland, Texas, April 27, 2004.

20. Pat Evans, interview by Robert Lang, Plano, Texas, April 27, 2004.

21. Haya El Nasser, "Suburban Office Parks Get an Urban Injection," *USA Today,* September 14, 2004, p. A15.

22. Steve Burkholder, interview by Robert Lang, Lakewood, Colorado, July 8, 2004.

23. Note that a first-ring suburb in a newer region such as Denver will be a different type of place than a comparable one in a Northeastern or Midwestern metropolis. Lakewood had its biggest burst of construction in the 1970s, which by Denver standards may make it an older community. By contrast, first-ring suburbs in the Northeast and Midwest often have a significant amount of housing stock that dates to the 1940s or even the 1920s.

24. Orski, "Transportation Referenda."

25. The West Corridor is a 12.1-mile light-rail transit project that will operate along the former Associated Railroad right of way (near 12th and 13th Avenues), from downtown Denver to the Lakewood Industrial Park to the Jefferson County government center in Golden.

26. Not everyone believes that FasTracks will bring only positive change. As Orski observes, "Smart growth proponents allege that the rail extensions, with their 57 suburban stations, will exacerbate sprawl. . . . Far from concentrating population in the city, as transit is supposed to do, they claim FasTracks will disperse population over a vast region along the Front Range, leading to more exurban sprawl and increased auto use" ("Transportation Referenda," p. 1).

27. Rusk, *Cities without Suburbs.*

28. Hugh Hallman, interview by Robert Lang, Tempe, Arizona, July 19, 2004.

29. Ronald Loveridge, interview by Robert Lang and Jennifer LeFurgy, Riverside, California, August 10, 2004.

30. Lang, *Are the Boomburbs Still Booming?*

31. Naomi Kresge, "Fontana Looking for a Way to Unify Three Sections," *San Bernardino Sun*, August 11, 2004, p. A1.

32. Hugo Martin, "Fontana Floors It and Feels Fancy," *Los Angeles Times*, September 10, 2004, p. B1.

33. Nico Calavita, Kenneth Grimes, and Alan Mallach, "Inclusionary Housing in California and New Jersey: A Comparative Analysis," *Housing Policy Debate* 8, no. 1 (1997): 109–42.

34. Kresge, "Fontana Looking for a Way to Unify Three Sections," p. 11.

Chapter Eight

1. The projections are from the Maricopa Association of Governments (for Phoenix), the North Texas Association of Governments (for Dallas), and the Southern California Association of Governments (for Los Angeles).

2. James E. Vance Jr., *Geography and Urban Evolution in the San Francisco Bay Area* (University of California, Berkeley, Institute of Governmental Studies, 1964); James E. Vance Jr., *This Scene of Man: Role and Structure of the City in the Geography of Western Civilization* (New York: Harper Press, 1977).

3. Vance, *Geography and Urban Evolution*, p. 78.

4. Homer Hoyt, *The Structure and Growth of Residential Neighborhoods in American Cities* (Government Printing Office, 1939).

5. Robert E. Lang and Paul Knox, "The New Metropolis: Rethinking Megalopolis," *Regional Studies* (forthcoming 2007).

6. Christopher Leinberger, "Where Bosses Live: Jobs and Development Follow," *Atlanta Journal Constitution*, June 8, 1997, p. A2.

7. Hoyt, *The Structure and Growth of Residential Neighborhoods*.

8. Robert E. Lang and John S. Hall, *The Sun Corridor: Planning Arizona's Emerging Megapolitan Area* (Tempe, Ariz.: Morrison Institute for Public Policy, forthcoming 2007).

9. Several more realms can be cut from this space, including a West Side realm of the LA Basin, a separate San Fernando Valley realm, and a San Gabriel Valley realm. Orange County can also be split into North County and South County realms. These finer divisions are not used here because it would make Los Angeles less comparable to Dallas and Phoenix in urban spatial terms.

10. Edward Soja, *Postmodern Geographies* (London: Verso, 1989).

11. Robert Fishman, *Bourgeois Utopias: The Rise and Fall of Suburbia* (New York: Basic Books, 1987), p. 211.

12. The system was developed by Henry Huntington, who also coined the name Southland for the vast expanse of Southern California that his trolleys served. The term remains in common use today.

13. Joan Didion, *Slouching towards Bethlehem* (New York: Noonday Press, 1990), p. 3.

14. Lang and Hall, *The Sun Corridor*.

15. Buckeye's "municipal planning area" contains over 500 square miles. Of this area, approximately 160 square miles are within the town. It is hoped that private landowners within the municipal planning area will agree to have their land annexed by the town.

16. The term was devised in 1971 by the North Texas Commission after a marketing study showed the Dallas region (other than the central cities of Dallas and Fort Worth) lacked a clear identity. The Metroplex refers to both these cities, plus all of the suburbs that surround and link them. For more details, see www.ntc-dfw.org/news/newsarchives/metroplex.html.

17. Note that there may be some discrepancy in growth projections between chapters 7 and 8, because of different sources and different projection dates. The buildout survey in chapter 7 used municipal data, some of which boomburbs and baby boomburbs generate on their own, based on land use and population estimates. Boomburbs

were surveyed about their growth patters to the year 2020. The data in chapter 8 come from regional councils of governments and cover the period 2000 to 2030. Regional-level data were used in chapter 8 so that there would be one consistent source for each metropolitan area. In chapter 7 the primary focus was on the buildout plans for individual boomburbs, which assumed distinct local data.

18. The question that often arises when discussing the future growth of Phoenix is where the water will come from for all these new residents. Few people realize that Phoenix, while certainly water constrained due to limited local rainfall, has perhaps the most capacity for growth based on water supply of any Western U.S. city (Lang and Hall, *The Sun Corridor*). Unlike Las Vegas, for example, Phoenix is not totally reliant on the Colorado River system for its water supply. Phoenix has in effect its own mini version of the Colorado system in the Salt River Project. In fact, the majority of water in the Valley of the Sun is from the Salt River system, which collects melted snowpack from the Colorado Plateau Rim, high above Phoenix.

19. Morrison Institute of Public Policy, *The Treasure of the Superstitions: Scenarios for the Future of Superstition Vistas* (Arizona State University, 2006).

20. Patricia Gober, *Metropolitan Phoenix: Place Making and Community Building in the Desert* (University of Pennsylvania Press, 2006).

21. Note that many of the peak oil predictions are somewhat overheated, especially the assessment offered by James Howard Kunstler, *The Long Emergency: Surviving the Converging Catastrophes of the Twenty-First Century* (Boston: Atlantic Monthly Press, 2005). In 2006 a major oil source was found in the deep waters of the Gulf of Mexico, which may signal a new era of exploration into similar offshore sites worldwide. Even more promising for the United States is a method to extract shale oil that infuses heat into the shale formation, turning it into high-grade crude oil, which can be pumped from the ground. This technique allows shale oil to be recovered in a much less environmentally damaging way than the old strip-mining method. The United States and Canada currently have over 4 trillion barrels in shale oil reserves, which is several times the current reserve estimate for Saudi Arabia.

22. Kenneth S. Deffeyes, *Beyond Oil: The View from Hubbert's Peak* (New York: Hill and Wang, 2005); Dowell Myers and Elizabeth Gearin, "Current Preferences and Future Demand for Denser Residential Environments," *Housing Policy Debate* 12, no. 4 (2001): 633–59; Arthur C. Nelson, "Toward a New Metropolis: The Opportunity to Rebuild America," discussion paper (Brookings Center on Urban and Metropolitan Policy, 2004).

23. Andres Duany, Elizabeth Plater-Zyberk, and Jeff Speck, *Suburban Nation: The Rise of Sprawl and the Decline of the American Dream* (New York: North Point, 2000).

24. James Howard Kunstler, *The Geography of Nowhere* (New York: Vintage, 1994); Kunstler, *The Long Emergency*.

25. Fishman, *Bourgeois Utopias;* Kenneth Jackson, *Crabgrass Frontiers: The Suburbanization of the United States* (Oxford University Press, 1985); Dolores Hayden, *Building Suburbia: Green Fields and Urban Growth: 1820–2000* (New York: Pantheon, 2003).

26. Jackson, *Crabgrass Frontiers*.

27. Another recent example of work along these lines is Robert Bruegmann, *Sprawl: A Compact History* (University of Chicago Press, 2006).

Index

FAA (Federal Aviation Administration), 83–84

Fairfax County, Virginia, 9, 17, 73, 124–25, 128

Family size: and cosmoburbs, 66; and New Brooklyns, 61–62

Fannie Mae Foundation, 4, 5, 99–100

Favored quarter model of development: Dallas Metroplex as, 81–82, 84; Phoenix as, 89–90; sector hypothesis, 81; and urban realms, 164

Federal Aviation Administration (FAA), 83–84

Federal Center, Lakewood, Colorado, 156–57

Federal Housing Administration (FHA), 32, 81

Federal Way, Washington, 76; business and commerce in, 76

FelCor Lodging headquarters, 77

Fermi, Enrico, 67

FHA. *See* Federal Housing Administration

Field Guide to American Architecture, 110, 111

Fischel, Bill, 126

Fishman, Robert, 12, 32, 68, 164–65, 173

Florida, 10, 71, 72. *See also specific cities*

Florida, Richard, 53

Flower Mound, Texas, 82, 89

Fontana, California: age of population in, 70; buildout plans in, 160–61; and future trends, 169; Hispanic population of, 56–57; as part of Southland region, 166; politics and policy in, 124

Foreign-born populations: and cosmoburbs, 66–67; demographic trends, 59–60; and New Brooklyns, 61–62, 61t

Fort Worth, Texas: office space development in, 85; as part of Metroplex region, 168. *See also* Metroplex region

Fountain Hills, Arizona, 120, 127, 166

Free-riders, 138–39

Fremont, California: Asian American population in, 57; business and commerce in, 77; education and income levels in, 69; foreign-born population in, 60

Frey, William, 55

Frisco, Texas, 93, 171

Frontage roads, 80–81

Fullerton City, California: Asian American population in, 57; business and commerce in, 77; and future trends, 169; as part of Southland region, 166

Fulton, William, 10, 48, 126

Gaithersburg, Maryland, 66, 71, 76, 78

Garden Grove, California, 44

Garland, Texas: buildout plans in, 154; business and commerce in, 81; and future trends, 171; growth in, 35; home prices in, 98; as part of Metroplex region, 11, 168; transportation and commuting in, 71, 81; WPA guide entry for, 25

Garreau, Joel, 12, 91, 126, 134

Gary, Indiana, 22

Gated and walled developments, 94, 101–09, 118–19, 132

General Motors plants, 77–78

Georgia, 72

Giant Industries, 85

Gilbert, Arizona: building permit data for, 96; buildout plans in, 150–51; county land within, 139; education and income levels in, 69; growth in, 49; homeowners associations in, 131–33; homeownership rates in, 100; housing stock, age of, 101; master-planned communities in, 95, 96; office space development in, 92; as part of Valley of the Sun region, 164, 167; politics and policy in, 129; and townhome developments, 116

Glaeser, Edward, 53–54